Those D...

A cri...

An autobiography by James C Brook

COPYRIGHT

Those Diana Moments

Copyright © 2021 by James C Brook

All rights reserved.

No part of this publication may be reproduced, stored in a retrieval system, or transmitted. In any form or by any means, electronic, mechanical, photocopying, recording or otherwise, without the prior permission of the copyright owner, except for the use of brief quotations in a book review.

Cover design by Josh Brook and Sally Berkeley

Table of Contents

FOREWORD	7
THE PRAM.	10
BEING BURNT.	12
THE ONE-LEGGED FOOTBALLER.	14
PHOTOGRAPHS: EARLY YEARS AND EAST MEON	17
THE BANANA.	23
THE BULLET.	26
DAD'S OLD SWORD.	30
CAUGHT SHORT.	32
THE HUSH-HUSH.	37
THE TREE.	39
MACARONI CHEESE	42
PHOTOGRAPHS: BOYHOOD	45
SHORTS.	49
'PERFECTLY ALL RIGHT.'	53
MR BROWN.	56

CAUGHT GOING EARLY.	60
THE CATCH.	64
SUNDAY ROAST.	68
THE FACTS OF LIFE.	76
THE BOY FROM THE PAST.	79
PARTY TIME! (NOT).	84
GETTING LOST.	87
THE CRUCIBLE.	94
GOD'S GIFT TO TEACHING.	102
LEAVING FOR COLLEGE.	106
CAUGHT IN FLAGRANTE	112
GOODBYE JANE.	116
BOOOOK.	124
THE DRIVING TEST.	127
GETTING ON A COACH.	135
MY FIRST CAR.	142
A WHITER SHADE OF PALE.	147
STOPPING GOLF.	152

HAVING A RANT.	158
POLITICS.	164
MY FIRST FLIGHT.	172
THE IDIOT WHO COULDN'T SWIM.	177
I GIVE UP TEACHING.	184
THICKO!	188
CRASH.	196
PHOTOGRAPHS: YOUNG MAN TO IT GUY	204
KEYS.	209
I PROPOSE.	213
I SELL MY FIRST PLAY.	220
GOODBYE DAD, GOODBYE MUM	224
THE MAN ON THE STAIRS.	231
I RECEIVE MY MANTRA.	240
OPENING THE WEDDING PRESENTS.	246
AND YET ANOTHER LESSON	250
GOODBYE JUDY.	255
THE HEINZ WOLFF LOOK-ALIKES.	262

FIRST CHILD: HANNAH.	268
TOM.	275
HELLO TWINS.	282
PHOTOGRAPHS: LIZZY, MARRIAGE AND THE FAMILY	292
GOODBYE PETER	298
THAT DIANA MOMENT.	306
MELVIN (THE BASTARD)	310
OUR FIRST GRANDCHILD.	318
HELLO GEORGE	324
PEOPLE BELIEVE ANYTHING.	332
BUYING MY CURRENT CAR	343
GOODBYE LIZZY	351
THE GRAND PLAN.	372
EPILOGUE.	379
PHOTOGRAPHS: CRINKLIES AND THE LAST TEN YEARS.	383
AFTERWORD.	392

Foreword

Where to start? When to start? How to start? Often, these are problems for any writer and/or teller of stories. But in this case, it's easy.

I'm starting at the end. I'm starting with now.

Here I am, sat at my desk, early September 2019. Rain has been forecast. To the side, my dog is dozing on his bed. I think I have a headache coming on, but usually – if I look for it – there's always a headache coming on. I am 74 years old and next February I will be 75.

On my dog walk this morning, while George was amiably zig-zagging from one interesting smell to the next, a small shaft of truth came to me.

There must be – out there in the great wide world – an appetite for a small, easy to read book called 'Those Diana Moments.'

A 'Diana Moment' I have decided, is a moment that is indelibly seared into the memory. An experience or image that is forever implanted in your brain and sits like a little fire in your interior landscape. We all have many such fires: personal, private, shared and public.

I remember exactly what I was doing and how I reacted when I heard Princess Diana had been involved in a car crash. It immediately took its place, a beacon of memory burning among the other fires: something I would never, ever, forget.

And as for where I was and what I was doing? Well, we'll come to that later. In truth, it's not that exciting.

This small book is essentially an autobiography signposted by memories I can't forget: the 'Diana Moments.' I am driving, if you like, from fire to fire, from indelible memory to indelible memory.

At first - as you must begin somehow – I tried to keep these events in chronological order. For my childhood, I mostly succeeded. Even as a teenager and at college, the timeline remained – more or less – intact.

But the more I have written, the more fractured has this timeline become. Because one Diana Moment, through mood, circumstance or necessity, often leads to another. And there could be years between them.

For this is not a relentlessly straight chronological daisy-chain through my history: it's more akin to a 3-D mosaic of my past.

So, to help you navigate through this maze, each Diana Moment has its own chapter. And each chapter starts with the same three items:

1. What
2. Where
3. My age at the time (as far as I remember)

Which brings me to a recurrent theme of this book: the unreliability of memory. Specifically, my memory. It is astonishing how I can remember incidents with vivid clarity but cannot always precisely give my age at the time. For memory is fragile and fluid, usually more reliant on feelings and emotions than on boring dates. And the process of examining them in detail and writing them down can be curiously destructive.

But you can only work with what you've got, and in many ways, memory – which starts from now – is all you have.

A small caveat here: this is not a book bravely containing absolutely all the Diana Moments of my life. I have omitted those that are too embarrassing, compromising or hurtful to set down. There are enough tell-all stories out there anyway. You could give this book to your aged granny to read aloud at a knitting circle. There is the occasional 'shit' to pep things up a bit and add verisimilitude, and the 'F-word' makes one (legitimate) appearance in reported speech in a moment of extreme stress, but otherwise, nothing untoward.

And, while we're about it, another disclaimer: for narrative purposes, sometimes I have shortened things down a bit, and/or omitted to mention non-relevant details, people or events.

Also, a note about photographs. There are no direct images embedded into this ebook. Instead I'm using links. Which is all fine and good, but if you're reading this when not connected to the web, then – sorry - they won't work. For various reasons, I have organised them into separate small chapters, arranged in a loosely chronological order.

So – having said all that - let us begin.

The pram.

What: I am in a pram, looking out.

Where: Outdoors.

My age: 1.

I must be very, very small. There is blue under my nose and above me an arching darkness ending in a horizontal line. There is a comforting sound and a feeling of freshness. So I think I'm in a pram snuggled down under a blue blanket. The black hood of the pram has been raised and is protectively sheltering my head. The noise I hear is probably my mother talking. And that's it, although for some reason I now think I'm outside a post office or a Boots the chemist.

I was born when Hitler was still alive. The Russians were invading Berlin and in a couple of months he'd be dead. Many, many years later my youngest daughter, then aged 8, would stand up in front of her whole school and proudly declare: 'When my dad was born, Hitler gave up.'

For completeness – the back story if you will - I must now add some details about my parents. But I must own up: I know little of their lives before I was born. For my father I have no more than a sketchy outline; for my mother even less.

And I have another confession: I don't really intend to find out. I do have a cousin who has an interest in such matters, and when I next bump into him at a family bash I might ask him to send me some sort of family tree, but that's probably it.

I know my dad was in the navy and my mother a Montessori teacher, who met my newly widowed dad somewhere along the line.

Newly widowed? Yep, my dad had been married before and had two daughters (Judith and Jane, my half-sisters) both teenagers, or thereabouts, when I came along. And I had a brother, Peter, eighteen months older than me.

I was born in a maternity home in Coulsdon, Surrey. For some reason my dad was abroad, or perhaps miles away in Dartmouth. My mother was going to going to call me John, but just in the nick of time a telegram arrived from Dad saying I should be named James.

And so the birth certificate was changed. I can still see it now, the paper yellowing, the entries written – not so elegantly – in faded fountain pen ink: 'John' with a single line diagonally slashed through it and – alongside - as if naming a usurper: 'James.'

The arrival of the telegram changing my name was very possibly the most dramatic incident of my first year. Which all goes to show how calm and placid my early months must have been. It did not last.

Being burnt.

What: I sit on an electric fire.

Where: Indoors.

My age: 18 months

I know this happened, as I still – over seventy years later – have the scars on my bum to prove it. And I think I remember it.

I was a toddler with a full nappy. My mother had gone to get a clean one, leaving me unattended for perhaps half a minute. On the floor was a portable one bar electric fire, the sort with a shiny parabolic reflector to guide the heat upwards at about forty-five degrees.

It must have seemed an ideal place to sit. A colourful little chair, right at ground level.

I do not know if it was fitted with any kind of safety bars or grid, but if so, it was not robust enough to withstand the sudden and forceful impact of a sturdy toddler plonking himself down.

If the nappy had been dry, I'd have probably caught fire. But it wasn't so I didn't. I sat on that single, red hot bar and began to smoulder. After a while - according to mum - I shrieked a shriek that could be heard on the moon.

She rushed in and so I was rescued, to spend the next month or so lying face down on a hospital bed, my scorched bottom swathed in bandages and cooled by mysterious tubes.

I am not sure, now, how much of this I actually remember and how much I am constructing from being told what happened. But it certainly sits there, in my mind, as a Diana Moment.

According to dad, for years afterwards I would regularly wake up the middle of the night shouting I was burning until one time he said to me 'stop it!' And I did.

The one-legged footballer.

What: A one-legged man kicks a football.

Where: On a muddy field.

My age: 6

At the time dad was the headmaster of a college near Alton (Hampshire) catering for disabled young people. My elder brother Peter and I were about 7 and 6 respectively and were playing football with some of dad's students. I have a clear impression of goals marked by discarded coats and of the weather being overcast. The ball – as was typical in those days – was constructed of robust but porous leather which soaked up moisture to such an extent that after five minutes of play on a muddy field it was sodden, layered with mud and weighed a ton.

No one ever, ever headed it on purpose and kicking it for more than a few yards required a monumental effort.

Peter and I were small and nippy. Dad's pupils were perhaps seventeen or eighteen and so appeared to us as grown-ups. Great big lumbering adults, playing with enthusiasm and no little skill. One had problems keeping upright, another wandered around in circles, and the star player had an arm missing.

But the man I remember the most vividly lacked a leg. Completely undaunted, he played using crutches and was amazingly adroit doing a sort of three-legged dribble. When he bore down on you, humping along with great heaves of his shoulders, the ball rolling heavily in front of him, it was both exciting and terrifying.

Sometimes he fell over and would resurrect himself like an unkillable monster from a horror film, clumsily lurching upright, his single leg, crutches and angular arms making him seem like a giant insect arising from the dead.

I am - of course – now retrospectively adding details I couldn't have known at the time. It was around 1950. I was six. We didn't have a television and I very much doubt I had ever been to the cinema, let alone seen a horror movie. In fact the first film I remember is *'The Court Jester,'* with Danny Kaye and that, the internet tells me, came out in 1955, when I was 10. But I am not writing for me then, but for me (and you) some seventy or so years later, when unkillable zombie monsters are commonplace.

Monster or not, he managed to bypass Peter and thumped his way towards me. I think I stood my ground, but more probably I remained where I was through fear and an underlying conviction I – the headmaster's son - would not get trampled on.

He swerved away – of course he did – and kicked the ball. Not just kicked: he planted his crutches down on either side and swung his whole body backwards until it was horizontal and then, with increasing velocity and force, forwards and down in a great arc.

That heavy, soggy, cannonball of a ball was kicked with such ferocity it soared joyously high into the air.

Open mouthed, I swivelled round to watch. Bits of mud came off, as if it was shedding the cares of the world.

There was a crump as the kicker, smiling broadly and laughing at his audacious challenge to a two-legged world, lost his balance and fell backwards.

Photographs: Early years and East Meon

Circa 1940. Mum and Dad off on honeymoon during the second world war.

I deduce 'honeymoon' as Dad looks smart! They went on a hiking holiday in Wales, but precisely where I do not know.

*Circa 1946. My brother Peter and I in the garden.
This is the earliest photo I have of us.*

*Circa 1947. The Brook family on the beach.
We're all here: (from the left) Jane, Dad, Peter, Judy and
Mum with me on her lap.*

*Circa 1950. Peter (on left) and I sailing the 'Water Rat'
off Hayling Island.*
Notice the careful adult hand on the tiller.

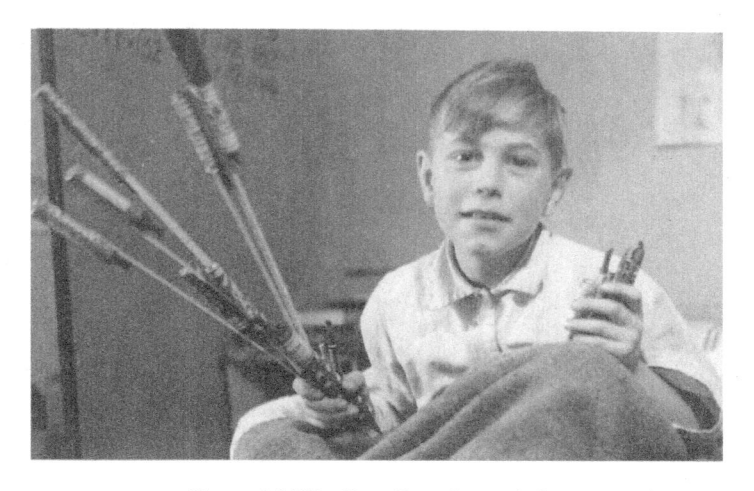

Circa 1953. Guy Fawkes night.
I had saved and saved to buy fireworks, but then I caught some kind of lurgy so had to stay in bed. My sister Judy kept my company and took this 'photo, telling me to 'look winsome'.

Circa 1954. Mum in the shop, wearing a long skirt for warmth.

This picture actually appeared in the local newspaper the 'Petersfield Post.'

Circa 1957. Judy in front of the Meon river.

I'm pretty sure this is from the mid 1950s or so, but it's difficult to tell: in photos she often had a timeless quality, so I could be out by 10 years.

Circa 1957. Jane.

A studio portrait taken around this time, probably before she went to Kenya as a nurse.

The banana.

What: I ask for a banana.

Where: In our East Meon shop

My age: 8

My dad gave up being a headmaster and we moved to a small Hampshire village (East Meon), where they'd bought a shop. Mum effortlessly turned herself into a shopkeeper while dad did the books and the rounds, going off every morning in a small three geared Ford van loaded with orders. Bread, baked beans, bags of sugar, cheese; you name it, we sold it (within reason). We even – sometimes - had bananas! Dad would try to save them for his selected, rich customers and kept them in a wooden box with a dull looking lid, hidden away behind the rest of the fruit. Sort of on display, but not on display, thereby satisfying both his egalitarian principals and his need to make rich customers feel special.

Needless to say, he always voted Liberal.

One day the shop was busy, with people queuing for packets of tea, bacon, dog food, anything else and - probably – cigarettes (everyone smoked). Mum was serving. Compared with shopping now, it was another world. You didn't wander round with a trolly, helping yourself before heading to a checkout. No. You gossiped while waiting your turn before going to the counter and requesting what you required. The shop person then scurried around collecting the order, placing the items one by one in front of the customer who - almost inevitably – would at the end add something else they'd previously forgotten.

Once all the items had been assembled, the server would quickly touch each one, moving them towards the customer, totting up the cost aloud as they went.

Totting up the cost? This was pre-decimal, so it was in pounds, shillings and pence, or 'LSD' as it was known, an insanely convoluted and non-logical currency that everyone thought was perfectly normal. Long after 'LSD' was consigned to the dustbin of ridiculous ideas, I remember attempting to explain it to one of my children. I gave up after '20 shillings to the pound' when I realised they thought I was joking.

As an aside, it's also about time they got rid of a measuring system based on the distance between King Henry I's nose and the end of his outstretched arm. Yes, I do mean yards. Not to mention other insane non-logical nonsenses like miles, feet and inches. I don't care if King Henry the eighth said with a smile 1760 yards in a mile. We ought to move fully to meters (and litres) and have done with it.

Anyway, there were four customers in the shop, waiting their turn, comfortably muttering acid comments about the latest scandal or the cost of school shoes.

Standing by the fruit, I shouted 'can I have a banana Mum?'

Instantly, all talking stopped. Four faces turned towards me. Behind them I could see Mum wishing she were somewhere else.

Then, bananas were rare. It was only eight years after the war and meat was still rationed. Cargo ships, I am sure, had better things to ferry about than yellow fruit with a short shelf life.

A hatchet-faced woman was the first to respond. I remember her distinctly as I was suddenly very frightened. She marched over towards me as if I were a worm and she a hungry bird.

"Bananas? You have bananas?" She was half asking me, half asking my mum and at the same time making a statement to our other customers.

Mum appeared at her side. "They've just come in, the first we've seen. They're still green." This was a lie. They had been with us a week and were now perfect. I'd eaten one that morning. Mum was lying. My mouth dropped open but before I could say anything she looked at me and said "you'll have to wait a day at least." She waved towards the other customers, indicating there was work to be done and I'd be the one to do it. I was already scooting away when she added "Now, are you going to help out?"

And everyone started tut-tutting about how lazy boys were.

Later, dad said he was very pleased this had happened, because his moral dilemma over bananas had been resolved. My wonderful mum was more pragmatic. She told him to hide the best in a better place next time.

The bullet.

What: I hit a live bullet with a hammer.

Where: In our back yard.

My age: 8

This is a memory I have never – until now - shared. Why I have kept quiet about it for so long I'm not quite sure. Certainly, to my peers it might have seemed wondrously dangerous and given me kudos.

But very probably I was too scared and didn't wish to have to prove it by doing it again in front of witnesses.

I was a secretive, somewhat morose and lonely child, given to tantrums and sulks, always hiding away with a handful of stolen sweets and a book.

One of my favourite haunts was the attic. Gloomy and dark, full of boxes, pregnant with evidence of unimaginable past lives.

There was an old stereoscope and a set of unconvincing 3D sepia images of the first world war. Guns being fired, troops clambering up ladders, fuzzy figures running through a smoke-filled dystopian landscape, cheerful faces having a cigarette or drinking out of battered tin mugs. I was very taken with one showing the use of a corpse instead of a sandbag: the dead leg sticking out as if to poke you in the eye.

How many were 'real' and how many posed or constructed for propaganda purposes I do not know.

My dad, born in 1903, was just too young for WW1 and just too old for active service in WW2, when he was in the naval reserve at Dartmouth and – as far as I could make out – spent his time teaching elementary seamanship. If he was ever asked if he saw any action, he'd tell his one war story. He was out in a rowing boat with half a dozen or so cadets when a plane zoomed down towards them. It could have been German. It could have been attacking; coming straight at them with the sun behind, it was difficult to tell.

Twelve or so pairs of frightened eyes looked at my dad, waiting for instructions.

He shouted, 'Under the thwarts!' (Or some such) and they all – dad included – scrambled to get under the seats. Within seconds all that could be seen was two rows of bottoms sticking up.

The plane banked away, clearly showing the roundels of the RAF, the pilot most likely laughing at the panic caused.

It was in the attic I found a small tin box containing three or four bullets.

We'd got in a TV for the coronation, and it seemed wonderous to be able to sit in our living room and watch events taking place in London.

But to me, for most of the time, it was like a magic goblin in the corner, showing clean cut cowboys in simple tales of good besting bad. A fantasy world of horses that never needed grooming, pristine shirts, a lot of shooting but no blood.

The Lone Ranger. Oh boy, was he impressive. Riding his horse at full gallop, he'd fire his pistol (bang!) and – in the far distance – a bad guy – also riding at speed – would have his own pistol shot out of his hand (ping!). And so disarmed, they would surrender.

He was my hero of heroes. And his bullets were specially cast in a secret silver mine. (It never occurred to me to ask why).

So when I found the little tin box, I knew what it contained. Bullets.

Excited and enthralled, I took them downstairs and out into the yard, put them on a slab of concrete, sat on an old Mazawattee tea advertising board, spread my legs on either side and proceeded to hit at them with my dad's large hammer.

Even though I was only eight, it was undoubtedly the dumbest – and most dangerous – thing I ever did in my entire life.

I cannot justify it by pretending the Lone Ranger's bloodless adventures gave me the impression bullets were harmless. I knew they were deadly, but somehow didn't connect this deadliness with any danger to myself. Bizarrely, it made it even more essential to hit them with something really solid. Like a hammer.

I used two hands, bashing away, the bullets skittering about and the concrete crumbling.

God, I was so, so lucky. I hit one square and it fired. (Bang!) Through sheer chance it was pointing towards the narrow gap between my feet. Or perhaps it had been bent and was angled upwards so when it went off it cleared my legs.

Our yard was surrounded by outhouses and I remember to this day the bullet ricocheting (ping!) from one wall to another.

I had ringing ears but was otherwise completely unharmed. So was the shed where we kept large tanks of highly combustible paraffin, which we sold by the gallon for use in heaters.

A brick was chipped, but no windows broken.

I don't remember what I did with the remaining bullets, but I do remember an overwhelming feeling I had to hide the evidence.

I probably dug a hole and buried them. They could still be there, unfired.

As I am still here, unharmed.

Dad's old sword.

What: I bend dad's sword until it breaks.

Where: In the attic.

My age: 8

I asked my dad about the sword in the attic, and he explained it was from his navy days: lieutenants had swords and sometimes wore them. I probably asked him if he'd ever killed anyone with it and he would have shaken his head, amused at the idea.

He then went on to say the mark of a good sword was that it could be bent in a circle, with the tip touching the hilt.

I very much doubt mum was within hearing range, or she would have added something along the lines of 'James! Don't you dare try!'

But she wasn't, so she didn't and I did.

The sword had a gold tassel on the pommel and was resolutely inflexible.

Trying to bend it by wiggling the tip into a joist and pushing at the handle just resulted in splinters of wood shearing off. Wedging it between rafters and standing on the handle was more successful, but all I'd done was construct an inefficient trampoline for one.

In the end I had to stand on the point with one foot, place the other foot a little way along the blade and with both hands haul the handle towards me.

The tip and the pommel didn't meet; in fact they barely got to within shouting distance. I think I was possibly a third of the way there before it broke, casting me down with a great big thump.

I told my dad I had broken his sword and he just nodded his head sadly and said it didn't matter. My Mum cast her eyes upwards and continued to knit.

Remembering it now, I rather think dad knew what he was doing. I'd been manipulated into breaking his sword, but for what reason I do not know.

I feel strangely vindicated.

Caught short.

What: I am caught short.

Where: Bell Hill, Petersfield.

My age: 8

Being 'caught short' has several uses, from a general lack of something to needing cash for a purchase right through to not managing to get to a toilet in time.

It is this last meaning that is relevant here.

We bought the shop in East Meon in 1952, the year before the coronation. I was 7, Peter 8. We started attending Dunhurst, the preparatory school for Bedales public school. Run on progressive and liberal principles, Dunhurst had teachers you called by their first names, small classes and the inspiring motto 'work of each for weal of all.'

Sensibly, it placed more emphasis on personal development than learning facts. I wish all schools everywhere had the same ethos.

Dunhurst was near Steep, a small village a short distance from Petersfield, which in turn was some 5 miles from our shop in East Meon. Each school morning Peter and I walked to the bus stop outside the church, caught the Hants and Dorset bus to the outskirts of Petersfield and then walked for about half a mile up Bell hill to the school. The whole journey took maybe forty-five minutes. Going home was the same but in reverse.

One day we were coming back, hurrying along because we were a bit late and if we missed the bus there'd be a twenty-minute wait for the next one. I needed the loo. A number 2. Number 1s were easy and known as a slash. But number 2s took longer: for starters you had to find a concealed place near broad, bum-wiping dock leaves.

We were already late, but I was desperate: something had to give. So we hatched a plan. To us, at the time, it seemed perfectly simple, sensible and fool proof.

While I vanished into the bushes to do what I needed to do, Peter would continue and catch the bus. On getting home he'd tell Mum, who would ring a customer on dad's round. The customer would tell dad when he called in and he'd collect me and drive us both home, delivering any remaining orders as we went.

What could go wrong? All I had to do was sit tight and wait for dad's little Ford van to come tootling along the road.

The plan worked very well. Up to a point.

Peter caught the bus (which was on time) and on getting off ran home and told Mum, who – to be on the safe side – rang more than one customer and managed to talk to dad, who then drove like fury to collect me.

I wasn't there.

The plan failed because I had no watch or way of telling the time. And when you're young and active with nothing to do, time passes very, very slowly.

I probably gave it 10 or 15 minutes – if that – before deciding Peter had missed the bus or got home but hadn't told mum.

'Hadn't told mum?' That was totally unfair. My brother was responsible, conscientious and kind, far more so than myself. Of course he would tell mum he'd left his little brother doing whoopsies in a bush five miles away. He'd probably already begun to doubt the effectiveness of the scheme before even catching the bus. And when it all went wrong, he never blamed me: as the older brother, he had been in charge, so he dutifully shouldered the responsibility. God, he must have got the rollicking to end all rollickings, but of this I knew nothing.

So after a short while waiting at the roadside I felt abandoned. The thought was quite thrilling and needed action.

So I decided to walk home. It was only 5 miles or so after all.

Off I went, striding down Bell Hill, already picturing in my mind a lonely – but ultimately triumphant - trudge through the half-light. This image was so powerful I was pleased my brother had all the money and return tickets: however faint hearted my future self might become, catching the bus would not be an option. I was so taken with the romance of the adventure I rather hoped it would start raining, to make my heroic trek even more imposing.

At the bottom of Bell Hill I heard the whine of a small engine being pushed hard and dad whizzed past, going back the way I had come, our little van bouncing and complaining at being expected to go over 40 mph.

His eyes were fixed ahead, and he didn't notice me. I hurried on, glancing over my shoulder in case he came back, determined to hide if he did.

He didn't. As I learned later, on not finding me where he expected, he knocked on some doors and soon a search had been organised. Then he went on to the school, thinking I might have returned there. The hunt expanded, the more so when teatime was over.

Meantime I was plodding along the A272. It was getting satisfyingly dark but remained disappointingly dry. A bus approached from behind, cheerfully lit up and full of passengers. I ducked behind a bush until it had safely passed.

I made it to Langrish – about halfway – and was beginning to get fed up with the whole thing (romance quickly fades if confronted by tired legs and an empty stomach) when a couple of boys on bikes appeared and let out a great shout of 'Found him!' I vaguely knew them and – tempted by the prospect of food – followed them home.

Fortuitously, their mum was one of the customers my mum had rung when trying to contact dad. When I turned up, she immediately started dialling.

Fifteen minutes later I had eaten a jam sandwich and drunk a mug of tea. Then mum arrived and my adventure was over.

To be brutally honest, I don't think I really appreciated what all the fuss was about until my first child was born some 30 years later: becoming a parent forces us to understand our own.

The Hush-Hush.

What: I am mentioned in the end of term show.

Where: Dunhurst School.

My age: 9

I'm really surprised I remember this with such clarity: it is a tiny thing that had little or no effect on my life as far as I could tell, both then and in retrospect.

But the – sometimes wayward - logic of this autobiography demands for it to be included, so here it is, in all its manifest insignificance.

At Dunhurst, at the end of each school year – or it might have been the day before the Christmas holidays - the older kids, with the help of the teachers, put on an entertainment called the 'Hush-Hush,' so named because it was meant to be secret, or 'hush hush.'

It was a sketch show with a heavy emphasis on in jokes and references that could only be understood by other members of the school. A lot of dressing up was involved, it didn't last long and – being the last event on the last day of term – was powered along by the general atmosphere of anarchy.

There was always a theme, and for the Hush-Hush in question it was the four countries that made up the UK. Sounds dull, but I doubt it was. At one point four actors, one for each country, went up to a table and laid down the national flowers, while a fifth actor gave a running commentary.

England of course was a rose and the narrator said something funny about roses and Englishness. Following on, Wales had its moment with a daffodil.

And then, out of the blue, the narrator said 'James Brook, who liked prickly things, bought a thistle.' And a boy wearing an unlikely kilt marched on with an object resembling the Scottish national emblem. I was so dumbstruck on hearing my name I cannot remember if it was a real plant or just something made of cardboard.

I was too agog to even notice Ireland.

I have absolutely no idea why they chose me. Most likely, it was nothing personal and they just drew my name out of a hat. Or – maybe, just maybe – they thought of prickly schoolboys and settled on me. Who knows, and from this distance, I don't really care.

But somehow the astonishing thought I had been recognised by the powers that be has stayed with me, bright, fresh and still astounding, to this day.

The tree.

What: I hide up a tree.

Where: Dunhurst school woods.

My age: 9

To a small boy, the first glimpse of Dunhurst was impressive. You turned off Bell Hill and went up a tree-lined drive and - to the left, on top of a small slope - the building loomed into view like a battleship. It was probably an old manor house, for I remember mullioned windows, weathered brick and tall chimneys.

The grand façade looked down on some playing fields where cricket was practiced and beyond them – still in the school grounds – was a small area of woodland.

Pretty imposing, but round the back were newish brick-built classrooms where most of the lessons took place.

Sometimes, when the weather was clement and/or a teacher had run out of ideas, the whole class would troop off to the woods and play games. Lots of healthy running about and shouting. And after a while we'd return to the classroom and do something supposedly more educational.

One of the games we played was hide-and-seek. Usually you just hid in a thicket, or behind a tree or maybe in a ditch. But one time I decided to go higher.

I picked a big oak, climbed up and up, and finally sat astride a convenient branch and waited to be spotted.

Down below were shouts and screams and the usual tumult. But – up in my eerie - I was so still and silent a bird came and perched for a while on a nearby twig.

The noises from below tapered off, then stopped. They'd be getting ready for another game. Soon they would realise I had not been found and the whole class would begin looking. Such things had happened before.

So I remained motionless, not making a sound.

And d'you know what? They didn't notice I was missing. Not a single one of them! Not my so-called friends or the teacher. No one. Through a gap in the leaves I saw them wandering back over the playing fields towards the main school building.

They'd just buggered off and left me, like a discarded hermit, sitting high up in my tree.

A pleasant thrill of self-pity stole over me. I'd been forgotten and abandoned!

I decided to stay in my tree – for perhaps a day, maybe two - until I was so faint with hunger I'd slide off and fall lifeless to the ground. Even if I wasn't dead already, the impact when I hit bottom would undoubtedly kill me. That would teach them! I pictured my funeral. Such a sad occasion. The whole school would be there, utterly distraught, standing around a big hole and sniffing while a bell tolled mournfully in the distance.

After ages and ages (maybe 10 minutes, probably less) I got down from my tree and went to join my classmates.

And no-one had noticed I wasn't there.

Macaroni Cheese

What: I refuse to eat macaroni cheese.

Where: Dunhurst school.

My age: 10

I have never been a fussy eater. On the contrary: give me a plate of nosh and – generally speaking – I'll hoover it up like a demented vacuum cleaner. When we had the Sunday roast, with dad carving the meat, he always left me to last: but often I'd be finished before he'd served himself and loaded up his plate with his full entitlement of roast spuds and gravy.

At Dunhurst we ate at tables of perhaps 6. There was a big argument once about who won the second world war, with one boy stating, 'without the Americans, Hitler would have won.' An idea so radical it brought down an avalanche of scorn and was never mentioned again.

At school – as at home - I'd eat everything.

Except macaroni cheese. There was something about the textured alien sliminess of it and the way the tubes seemed to look at you. And as for the taste, overheated grated cheddar cheese smelt like – and to my senses tasted like – dog pee.

For the record, I now find macaroni cheese delicious. Its place in the pantheon of foods I hate has been taken by avocado, bulgur wheat, cous-cous and all things spicy, which are truly foods of the devil.

But as a schoolboy I found macaroni cheese vile and disgusting and I'd leave it alone. Eventually it'd go to the pigbin and be turned into delicious bacon.

School mealtimes, I recall, were not particularly well stewarded, with the teachers taking a commendably relaxed attitude towards faddy eaters, bad table manners, raised voices and the occasional argument about Hitler.

But (isn't there always a but?) in my last year, things changed. I don't know if there was a new head, or a new policy or just a different teacher, but indubitably, a small chill seemed to have been introduced at mealtimes: teachers, instead of just standing around and dreaming or chatting about golf, began striding purposefully between the tables.

And when the dreaded macaroni cheese arrived and I just shoved it around before leaving it, there was a looming presence at my shoulder.

I was asked what was wrong with the food on my plate.

I shook my head and mumbled something in reply.

I was told to eat it. Starving children in India were mentioned. The teacher strode off with a warning he'd be back.

The disgusting muck remained untouched.

All the other diners had long since finished, so I was the red-faced centre of attention. When he returned, things became somewhat Dickensian. I – plus my plate of now cold, congealing but still untouched macaroni cheese – was whisked away to a room I had never seen before, with dark wood panelling on the walls and a table of solid and intimidating size.

I was sat in a chair, the plate placed in front of me and a fork introduced into my hand.

I was left on my own with instructions to eat.

I did not. I scraped the foul stuff from the plate into my handkerchief, tied a knot or two and shoved it into my pocket.

The teacher returned, inspected my plate and – using some species of insane logic - congratulated me on behalf of starving children everywhere.

Going home I threw my handkerchief – plus contents – into a ditch.

I felt very guilty about the handkerchief.

Photographs: Boyhood

Circa 1957. I'm outside the back of our house in East Meon.

Every time I look at this, I change my mind as to how old I am. Early teenager I think: what we now call a tweenager.

Circa 1960. Me and my hairstyle.

I caught the train to Portsmouth and got a crew cut. When that grew out, I experimented for a while with gelled-up rocker style complete with a D.A. at the back. Not my finest hour.

Circa 1960. Me as a dark and soulful teenager. Everyone but me hates this photo. So here it is.

Circa 1961. At 16 or so I became a sub-prefect and house captain. Undoubtedly because I was the least-worst option.

Circa 1961. Peter at 18 or so looking smart in his first ever suit.

Soon after he went to New Zealand and worked on our uncle's stock farm. He returned as a radio disc-jockey and soon got a job with the BBC as a continuity announcer, which gave him time to develop his property business.

Shorts.

What: I am the only boy in the school wearing shorts.

Where: Petersfield Secondary Modern School.

My age: 11

One way or another, private schooling became too expensive, so - at the age of eleven - first Peter, then me, were sent to Petersfield Secondary Modern School (PSM) which – in those days – was in a cluster of buildings and Nissan huts close to the main square.

Oh boy, was it different from my previous school, Dunhurst: no-one said 'Actually'; you caught a dedicated school bus to get there; the custard was spectacular and nobody, absolutely nobody, wore shorts. Except me. For two days.

Turning up in my shorts was like being a nudist queuing to see a football match. Not recommended, even on a warm September day.

The girls - and this has been true for large sections of my life – ignored me, while the boys – all with legs decently clad - formed a non-appreciative circle. Comments were passed. I tried to remain indifferent.

I'd had a conversation with dad the evening before. He'd said something along the lines of "All ready for tomorrow, James?" And I'd said "Yeah" or some-such non-helpful phrase.

This kind of half grunting response was then usual with me. I was not a bright and sunny child.

Unusually, he persisted "Got everything you need?"

"Yeah." There must have been something in my tone which indicated uncertainty, as he tried for an unprecedented third time.

"Nothing worrying you, is there?"

"Nah." This was a lie. I felt distinctly uneasy. I'd caught glimpses of boys and girls waiting for their school bus. They looked rowdy and a bit unkempt: totally different from my previous classmates, who might be unkempt, but were always civilised.

Peter, with his energy and good cheer, had seamlessly fitted in, but I felt like an ill-prepared explorer, armed only with a cleft stick, embarking in a leaky canoe to go into the wild and untamed Amazonian Forest.

Mum, quietly knitting, piped up. "If anyone says anything, just ignore them."

And dad, grateful for the intercession, returned to the crossword.

I managed to ignore the hostile taunts until one boy who – I quickly learnt – was the class bully, whacked my bare shins with a ruler and the others started pushing me around.

That evening I demanded long trousers. Mum said my shorts were new. I said I'd wear them at home but not at school. Mum said that way I'd grow out of them before they were worn out. I said I didn't care.

I believe dad got dragged into what was turning into something ferocious. True to his instincts, he'd have said something placatory and wandered off, closing the door on my voice yelling through my tears that I was never, ever going back to school until my knees were covered.

Mum was sensible, practical and had a fine grasp of when to push and when to give way.

She said: "let me see what I can do."

Immediately, I became quiet. Mum had taken over and – as she always did – would come up with an answer. It didn't take her long and - like most good solutions – it was a compromise: If I agreed to go to school the next day, she would undertake to provide me with long trousers for the day after.

She made it seem so simple: even today I remember the relief I felt as I said yes.

To get them, she needed to go into Petersfield. That meant leaving the shop, which was awkward as next day both our shop girls were off. But mum picked up the phone, and an ex-shop girl – now married with a baby – organised. In fact I heard she parked her pram – complete with occupant - by the dried dog food. Customers were delighted: something to cuddle and something to chat about.

And the following day, when I took my bare knees to school for the second and last time, it rained and during break time we stayed indoors, so I was happily able to hide my legs under a desk.

That evening my new trousers were altered for length and on my third day at PSM, worn. And as I found my place in that feral, heaving mass of teenagers, where bullying, aggression, kindness and friendship were all readily available, I ceased being different and the attention of the crowd moved elsewhere.

I often wish my mum was still with us. And running the country.

'Perfectly all right.'

What: My sister Judy refuses to serve rotten cat food for supper.

Where: The shop at East Meon.

My age: 13

When we had the shop, one of the family duties was to finish up food that was for some reason unsellable. Usually this meant it smelt off but not too off, or bruised but not too bruised, squashed but not too …. you get the idea. If it was edible but not suitable for the great buying public of East Meon, the family would eat it.

Dad always categorised whatever it was and however battered and horrid it looked as 'perfectly all right,' which became a family catchphrase.

Once, while I helped him stocktake, we found - tucked away at the murky back of one of the upper shelves – a rusty tin of cat food that had 'blown.' The contents had somehow gone rotten, producing a gas that eventually caused the tin to swell up into a vaguely spherical shape, larger than a fist but smaller than a football. The brightly coloured label had clung on, clearly stating the contents were for cats.

I had an idea. "I'll give it," I told dad, "To Judy and tell her you said we'd have it for supper."

I can't remember why Judy was on kitchen fatigues that day: Mum must have gone off to one of her WI meetings.

Judy was a very kindly soul who took her duties in the kitchen extremely seriously.

She was also the most gullible person I have ever met.

I found her in the kitchen industriously doing the washing up. I held out the distorted tin of cat food and said, "Dad says to cook this for supper."

She looked at it and me with an expression I now recognise as complete incredulity. I can't fully remember the conversation, but I'm pretty sure she said words of extreme protest. I like to think I said something along the lines of 'Dad said it'll be fine with potatoes.'

She stormed off to talk to him. I trailed behind.

Dad was up a step ladder with his head thrust between some shelves.

Judy, holding the can as if it were a bomb, remonstrated.

Dad withdrew his head. 'It's perfectly all right' he said and waved a vague hand in her direction before sticking his head away again.

Judy returned to the kitchen. She was in obvious distress at the prospect of poisoning the family with rancid cat food. After randomly stacking some plates (a displacement activity if ever I saw one) she stomped – muttering 'I can't, I really can't' - back into the shop.

I suspect this time dad 'fessed up, as Judy served up sausages.

But by this time I was feeling somewhat guilty, so did what I often did when things got sticky: I went to my room, closed the door and pretended to myself it was nothing to do with me.

Something I frequently did, one way or another.

Mr Brown.

What: A new teacher begins.

Where: Petersfield Secondary Modern School (PSM).

My age: 13

For the first couple of years at PSM I did not do well. I was confused, lonely and thoroughly bored. I discovered a sour enjoyment in creeping up behind someone less robust than me and executing a manoeuvre of my own invention (knee into the back of their knee, hands on shoulders pushing down) that invariably resulted in a confused yelp of alarm as they descended to the ground.

Then I'd stick my hands in my pockets and stroll off, experiencing a curious mixture of accomplishment and guilt, as if I'd successfully cheated in an easy exam.

After doing this a few times someone did it to me and I like to think this stopped my activities, but I have a remorseful feeling it only made me more circumspect.

Academically, I was poor. At home I still read voraciously and could beat dad at chess, but in the classroom, I affected to believe everything was intellectually beneath me.

I had started PSM in class 1A, a ranking probably derived more from an assessment of my articulate parents and the evident charm of my brother than from any written test.

But after a year in the middle of 1A and another year at the bottom of 2A I was informed I would start the next year in

3B. I expect some teacher had said 'that'll teach the little turd!'

I'm sure my parents were quietly despairing. I spent most of those summer holidays in a permanent sulk and communicated in grunts. So much so dad once left me a letter, propped up against my breakfast bowl (whenever possible, I ate alone). The opening sentence went something along the lines of 'James, I'm writing this letter as it seems the only way of talking to you.' I don't remember anything more. I'm pretty sure I just skimmed through the remainder and went on behaving badly.

Now, sixty years or so later, with all the wisdom of hindsight and the experience of decades of adult life, I look back on me then and conclude I was basically a little shit.

So I began my third year at PSM a resentful, irritable member of 3B, slumming it – or so I thought – among the nearly thickos.

To my jaundiced and disrespectful eye, all the teachers I encountered appeared tired and lacklustre, lacking the energy to command my respect. In truth, I suspect they'd just given up: it's hard enough being a teacher anyway, let alone being bright and buoyant for a sulky teenager.

And then fate decreed that Mr Brown should arrive in town and teach maths to class 3B.

He was short(ish) and entirely bald. A decade or so on I heard, by chance, that the pupils at that time referred to him privately as 'Kojak' after the shaven headed TV detective. And if you work the dates, it means Mr Brown must have stayed on at PSM for a good many years after I left.

So he taught 3B maths and – to cut a short story even shorter - I flourished.

Five years later, when I was at college studying for my brief and hated non-career as a useless teacher, I realised Mr Brown did not follow the fundamentals of teaching as laid immutably down by the lecturers at Nottingham College of Education. To wit, proceed from the known to the unknown, as if education was a train journey from your local station gradually advancing to undiscovered destinations.

At its most basic, it means asking primary school pupils: 'if Jonny has 10 smarties and 5 friends, how many smarties does he give each friend to make it fair?'

Mr Brown, a forceful personality in front of a class, couldn't be arsed with all that. He would have scowled and said: 'divide 10 by 5 and anyone who gets it wrong will be shot.'

Only once do I remember Mr Brown relating maths to what might be considered a real-life experience. We were doing something with volumes and flow rates when he said, 'Of course there's always the idiot who sits in a bath, turns on both taps and pulls out the plug.' And the whole class, astonished and delighted, laughed.

I spent one term in 3B and after Christmas I was promoted to 3A. And at the end of that year I was rated number 3 in the class. They even gave me a prize for climbing the most places in one scholastic year.

I've often wondered about this episode in my life. And now I am writing it down it is starting to resemble one of those memoirs entitled 'my inspirational teacher.'

But 'inspirational' implies a lifting of spirits and a heightening of expectation, as if you were a butterfly escaping from a chrysalis. So I'm unconvinced it is the right word to describe Mr Brown's energetic, robust, no-shit teaching methods.

I think 'kick up the arse' is a better way of looking at it.

Caught going early.

What: I get caught trying to sneak off early.

Where: Petersfield Secondary Modern School (PSM).

My age: 14

A word about the PSM school buses, which – disconcertingly - were always coaches resembling those that took your grannie to the seaside. They pottered along circuitous routes from village to village, eventually reaching PSM in time for assembly.

It would be easy and perhaps entertaining to write about cantankerous drivers and pupils getting slung off and having to walk home, but I was involved with only one such incident. The driver – egged on by some fourteen-year-old girls saying he looked like Elvis (he didn't) - began driving fast along the country lanes and swerving from side to side.

At that time (late 1950s), seat belts were only used by fighter pilots, show-offs in open-topped sports cars and Donald Campbell breaking speed records. The idea that seat belts should be compulsory was generally viewed as a gross violation of individual liberty. So what if drivers, passengers and small children were regularly thrown through windscreens: it was probably their own fault.

So when the bus was flung this way and that it caused tremendous hilarity, as we were suddenly thrown around like dried peas in a tin can. Amid the delight one girl claimed to have vomited, a boy gashed his head and started bleeding while a girl with black hair almost sat in my lap. My testosterone levels were probably about average for a boy of 14, which means – of course – I remember to this day her rucked skirt and tantalising nearness.

I learnt later the driver had been moved and no longer drove school buses. Or he might have been sacked. I expect some spoilsport complained.

I can't remember why, but during this time I began to ride my bike to school. After all, it was only 5 miles with a couple of hills and gave me the illusion of independence, so why not.

On one such day during the last double period before home time I was in an English class and the teacher – complete with leather patches on his elbows and chalk dust in his hair - was filling his pipe ready to light up the moment the lesson ended. He usually did this with about half an hour to go: an enjoyable five minutes sitting at his desk, hoicking out dottle, fussing with pipe cleaners and refilling from his leather pouch. A boy came in with a message, and it was announced the school buses would be leaving early. There was a muted cheer and about half the pupils filed out of the door. I joined them.

Considering I had come by bike, my logic was somewhat dubious, but the rationale impeccable: I thought I could get away with it.

While everyone else stampeded towards the gates, I peeled off to the boy's toilets and hid in a smelly cubicle. And when I could hear nothing, I cautiously emerged.

It was scarily odd, being outside during lesson time. It was quiet. The buildings seemed to loom over me. My confidence waned, but my options were now limited. I could somehow hide out to the end of the school day or find my stuff in the cloakroom, make my way to the bike sheds and go home.

Both seemed equally perilous. I tossed a mental coin and – unsurprisingly – going home won.

I made it to the cloakrooms without being spotted, put on my coat and fastened bicycle clips around my ankles. All was still quiet. I made my way to the door: the bike sheds were perhaps fifteen yards away, across a stretch of tarmac. If all went well, in 2 minutes – less – I'd be out of the gates and free.

Off I set, crouching low and hugging a brick wall. Ferrets have probably looked less furtive.

A voice that could cut glass: "YOU! Boy! What are you doing?"

Miss Murray, the deputy-head, was not a woman to be messed with. She had that indefinable air of absolute authority, the trip-trotting stride of command and the justifiable conviction she was always, always, right in everything she did.

I stopped short, like a butterfly ruthlessly pinned on a specimen board.

I mumbled something. She strode over, heels clicking on the tarmac. (OK, so tarmac is fairly soft and therefore heels don't click, but I'll swear to God hers did. It was as if even the ground she walked on changed to conform to her will.)

I was marched to the headmaster's office and deposited in front of his desk.

"I caught this boy," said Miss Murray, "sneaking out of the school."

And then – thank God – she left.

I can't remember what the headmaster said. I do recall his eyes looked very very tired, and his voice was weary, as if he was completely fed up with having to deal with Miss Murray's endless parade of miscreants and criminals.

I don't think I was punished, just told off and sent back to the classroom. Passing the bike shed I had a sudden urge to escape but didn't act on it.

The English teacher, now with a freshly filled and expectant pipe ready for the end of the lesson, just nodded when I came in, before continuing to drone on about precis (or something.)

The catch.

What: I catch a ball at a village cricket match.

Where: East Meon Cricket pitch.

My age: 16

My brother Peter at 17 or so was one of the star batsmen for the East Meon village cricket team. I think he batted at 3 or 4. I was a make-weight who was never asked to bowl, usually batted at 11 and fielded out near the boundary where I couldn't do much harm.

But, but, but: every dog has his day.

I can't remember what league we played in if indeed league there was: it could have been no more than friendly matches between villages and was as much a social event as a sporting one.

The highlight was the enormous tea between innings when everyone sat down and got stuck into sausage rolls, pies, pasties, sandwiches, chicken drumsticks, frankfurters, cake and anything else the wives and girlfriends could dream up. It really was stuff-your-face time.

I don't know how it was managed, but one Sunday the visiting team was clearly (in their view) slumming it. The captain was tall, wore a cravat and possessed a large disdainful roman nose. He even had his own pads, a bat smelling of linseed oil and starched white trousers.

We batted first and scored well, mainly due to Ted 'coming off.' Ted was a gigantic farm hand with muscles the size of hams. Used to slinging bales of hay around with a pitchfork and possessing a good eye, he was a batsman with a big bat and the capacity to brutally savage any bowling …… if he 'came off.' Most times he didn't and – like me – was bowled by the first straight ball. But sometimes, maybe once every 3 or 4 games, Ted would survive an over or two and start connecting. And when he did, oh boy oh boy, was it thrilling to watch. The bowler would bowl, Ted would swing his great heavy bat and – BIFF! - the ball would be dispatched over boundaries and fences, often never to be seen again. There would be a great cheer, the umpire would lift both arms to signify a six (as if the scorers needed telling), a boy would be dispatched to find the ball and – as a backup – a replacement ball would be fetched.

And in this game, Ted got his eye in and the score rattled along like an express train. But Ted only dealt in fours and sixes, so the batsmen tended not to swap ends and the bowlers had the chance to get the rest of the side out. Which they duly did.

And so it came down to me, batting as usual at 11. If Ted could stay in for 3 or 4 more overs, our score would - for us – be massive. The captain walked part way to the crease with me. He said 'try and score a one, don't get out, give the bowling to Ted, I mean a one at the start of an over, for balls 5 or 6 just block them away, forward defensive, even if there is a run, don't do it unless it's a 2 of course. Or a 4, but don't try to score, just stay in, that's the main thing, you'll need to use your own judgement for ball 4 of an over, but there y'go.'

He left and – somewhat bewildered – I stood at the stumps and took my guard: middle and leg. We always asked for 'middle and leg.' I didn't even know what it meant. I stood upright, twiddling my bat and looking around the field as if spotting gaps for the precise placement of my exquisite stroke play. Then I placed the end of the bat near my toes and waited for the first ball.

The bowler bowled, I swung my bat, missed by a yard or two and my stumps got flattened.

Few people spoke to me during tea. I ate my sandwiches, pies, pasties, chicken drumsticks and cake in silence.

When we fielded, I was placed near the cowpats on the boundary. And the game resumed.

They batted, we bowled, they scored runs and we got wickets. It got intensely close: I can't remember the exact figures, but it was something like 15 runs needed, 2 wickets remaining.

And their top batsman was still in with maybe 50 runs, carefully scoring ones at the end of the overs to keep the strike.

And then it happened. Our bowler bowled, the star batsman swivelled a bit and helped it round the corner.

Towards me on the boundary.

It was in the air, plummeting down, maybe 10 or 15 yards away.

I ran towards it. I can get up a fair bit of speed, so maybe 'hurtled' is the word to use. I stuck out my hand and flung myself forwards.

I was still in mid-air when it landed – miraculously - plumb into my hand and stayed there.

I thumped down and rolled a bit, my hand – clutching that ball as if it was the crown jewels – held aloft, triumphantly declaring it had never touched the ground.

'Joy' is not the first word to associate with a cricket match. 'Tedium' is more usual.

But in that moment, in those few seconds of elation as my yelling teammates ran towards me, 'joy' is only just adequate.

We did win the match and afterwards the opposing captain, complete with his small entourage of followers, sought me out and said it was the best catch he had ever seen.

To which I replied: 'I know.'

There was collective intake of breath and he turned away, obviously thinking I was an arrogant little sod.

I didn't understand his reaction: for on that day, at that moment, I knew it was the best catch in history and for all time. So of course I said, 'I know.'

And I like to think I'd say it again, but I doubt the chance will occur and if it did, I wouldn't.

Sunday roast.

What: A paraffin heater catches fire.

Where: East Meon.

My age: 14.

I never knew either of my grandfathers.

According to a half-remembered conversation with dad, his dad lived the life of a country gentleman. He never did a stroke of work in his life and when short of cash just sold another field or – if pushed – an orchard. I believe he died from lung cancer: quite appropriate as he spent every evening in a dedicated smoking room puffing away.

Mum's dad was a Portuguese diplomat. I have a photograph somewhere of a dapper man dressed in a neat suit, spats, polished shoes and a homburg hat. I do not know what happened to him: by the time I began taking a soggy interest in such things, he seems to have faded out of the picture. I expect the family archives (by which I mean old stuff in dubious boxes in dusty attics) would yield more, but I am disinclined to look.

For if truth be told I am not that curious: they were both dead before I came along, and my parents seldom spoke of them; so their direct impact on my life was minimal.

However, their widows became, in time, 'London Granny' (mum's mum) and 'Brighton Granny' (dad's mum.)

Brighton Granny lived – as you would expect - in Brighton. She occupied a flat on the second or perhaps third floor of a tall apartment block a short distance from the sea. Wearing a small black hat, she would take a daily constitutional to the pier and back. To Peter and I the proximity of the sea was of course exciting, but whenever we went there it seemed to be raining.

Brighton Granny came and lived with us at East Meon for a while; she'd sit in the garden and paint, occasionally making forays to the loo and/or the kitchen.

Considering she had a very privileged background (through her I am related to a lord of the realm: we visited them once, for a family bash: I remember a big house with peacocks on the lawn) she herself was modest and unassuming, only betraying her upbringing with a cut-glass accent, a dislike of teabags and an insouciant indifference to illness.

By contrast London Granny (who – surprise! - lived in London) seemed rather grand. She was familiarly known as 'M.A.' which was short for 'Maria Augusta.' Her hair was elaborately permed into concrete swirls, and I cannot remember seeing her without at least one string of pearls round her neck. She and her sister Jo had a flat on Putney hill. Jo worked in an office and was much prized for her ability to speedily add up a column of figures. It was said she was even faster and more accurate than my dad, who had a unique sixpenny bit method. But – disappointingly – they never had a race.

I can't remember why, but when I was about 11 I stayed with them for a few days. M.A. gamely took me around London, visiting the zoo and so forth by taxi. My most vivid memory however was going to see the film 'Forbidden Planet' with Robby the Robot, great special effects and an invisible monster that gave me nightmares for weeks afterwards. I have been a science fiction fan ever since.

Once every month or so, on a Sunday, M.A. and Jo would journey down by train, arriving at Petersfield station sometime before noon. My father would be waiting, the family Hillman Minx all polished and tidy for the occasion.

Twenty or so minutes later they would arrive in state at East Meon, to have a small glass of sherry followed by the Sunday roast and an afternoon nap. At 4:30 my mother would wheel in a trolley loaded with sandwiches, cake, biscuits and our best china tea service.

Peter and I were told to eat at least two sandwiches before launching into the cake. Peter once tried making what he called a sandwich sandwich, which consisted of three sandwiches piled on top of one another. By nearly dislocating his jaw he managed to heroically bite his way through the six slices of bread and various fillings, but his mouth was so full mastication took an age. Meantime I had scoffed my minimum sandwich requirement and had already consumed my first slice of cake. I remember this incident as I had intensely mixed feelings afterwards: envy (the sandwich sandwich was a brilliant idea) and pride (getting to the cake first). The joys, triumphs and disasters of childhood are strange indeed.

One Sunday dad had departed about 35 or so minutes previously to fetch M.A. and Jo from the station. Mum, Judy and myself were in the house. I don't remember Peter being there, but then he was often out.

As an aside, Peter had the extremely useful ability of being invisible until food was served, when - as if by magic - he'd miraculously appear. I'm not sure how he did it. Or maybe he did this once, by accident and - memory being so fickle - over the years I have taken this as the norm.

Anyway, all was peaceful: mum was in the kitchen; I was trying to avoid being asked to lay the table and Judy would have been in her default mode of fussing over something.

And then – as if we were characters at the beginning of a drama – there was a tremendous knocking on our front door.

In those days the only shops open on a Sunday sold newspapers and other necessities like cigarettes and sweets. Groceries could not be found. If someone was desperate, they came along to us anyway. So my first thought was someone had run out of milk.

Mum opened the door. A large chap called Tiny stopped hammering and barged his way in, shouting (and here I paraphrase) "You're on fire! Fire!"

I dashed upstairs.

In one of the little used bedrooms above the shop, a paraffin heater had caught fire. A column of flame and smoke reached from floor to ceiling. The top of the sash window was slightly open, and smoke was pouring out.

I should add: to modern eyes, the paraffin heaters of those days were insanely unsafe. There was a tank of highly combustible paraffin just a few inches below a naked flame. I believe the flame was meant to go out if the heater was tilted, but only the demented (or suicidal) would put it to the test.

It had been the smoke Tiny had seen from the pub over the road and had spurred him into action. A crowd of interested spectators was assembling, most carrying pints.

I stood by the bedroom door: I hadn't a clue what to do.

Judy arrived: she'd had the presence of mind to get our one and only fire extinguisher. A conical device, with a nozzle at the top and a plunger at the bottom. To activate, you hit the plunger.

"Mind out!" she yelled and began bashing neat puncture holes in the floor with the nozzle.

I shouted "Other end! Other end!" But she was so hyped up all she did was redouble her efforts.

While Judy and I were occupied in destroying pitch-pine flooring, mum and Tiny - in attendance as an auxiliary fire-fighter - had come in and were doing sensible things. He opened the window and Mum began pulling up the carpet. Then, together and seemingly without fuss, they wrapped the carpet around the heater and threw the whole smoking bundle out of the room and into the street below.

I would like to say it exploded like a bomb, but I'm sure it didn't. In fact it was probably running out of paraffin anyway.

But what certainly happened was dad – at that precise moment – came round the corner in our polished-up Hillman minx bearing London Granny and great aunt Jo. They were passing the war memorial and saw the crowd ahead and something descending from an upstairs window.

A couple of seconds later he stopped and was soon inspecting the damage. London Granny – who always liked knowing what was going on – also clambered out. From my viewpoint (I was by now leaning precariously out of the window) all I could see of her was a large hat, complete with flowers. One would have thought she was at Ascot races.

Mum joined them. M.A. – enjoying herself enormously - stood magisterially, as if pronouncing judgement, while Jo waved from the back seat of the car. She wasn't impersonating the queen: the Hillman only had two doors, so she was trapped and wanted to get out. No one paid her any notice.

The carpet and its contents smouldered for a while and the crowd began to disperse, drifting back towards the pub. But the entertainment wasn't over. In the distance came the distinctive, insistent get-out-of-my-way totally thrilling sound of a fire engine in full emergency response mode. It came hurtling into the village and skidded to a stop, completely dwarfing the by now rather pathetic little heap of smoking hessian and twisted metal.

The pub landlord had made a phone call, dialling '999' for the only time in his life. He said afterwards his hand was shaking so much he nearly hadn't managed it.

The crowd reassembled, ready for act two. And the firemen didn't disappoint. My goodness they were efficient, shouting commands, unrolling hoses and readying all sorts of different fire extinguishers. It was like watching a particularly muscular ballet.

The man in charge – with a helmet more resplendent than the others - had a short chat with dad and a longer one with mum, before coming in to see the room where it had started. He shook his head at the holes in the floor and – with considerable alarm – inspected our conical fire extinguisher. "Wrong type," he said dolefully: "it would have made matters worse." We all looked at Judy, who looked at the floor.

Then, having made us realise what a lucky escape we'd had and how fortunate we were that he was amongst us, he - with considerable ostentation - unfastened a small box from his belt, put it on the floor, pulled up a telescopic aerial, unclipped a microphone and pressed a few buttons.

He glanced at us, held the mike to his mouth and said "Chief here. Over!"

There was a burp, followed by a stream of static intermingled with what might have been words spoken in Martian.

More button pressing. "Chief here! Over!" Yet more static. The fire chief said. "New kit! Piece of Junk!" He walked to the window and leant out, bellowing instructions to the men below.

And by the time he had refused a cup of tea, given dad a pamphlet about fire extinguishers, said hello to the cat and smiled at Judy, (who blushed) the carpet and heater had been comprehensively put out and dragged to the side, all the hoses and other kit had vanished and the men were aboard with the engine running.

The fire engine executed a stately three-point turn and drove sedately away. The spectators gossiped their way back into the pub and it was all over.

Like all good stories, over the years this tale has only increased with the telling. But this skeleton of events is true: the paraffin heater did catch fire; Judy did punch holes into the floor; mum was instrumental (as always) in saving the day; dad – with M.A. and Jo – drove up just as the saga was reaching a climax; the fire engine arrived; the spectators from the pub had a fine time and the Sunday roast was indeed a bit late that day.

The facts of life.

What: dad does 'the talk.'

Where: In the dining room at East Meon.

My age: 15

As was usual in many families, Sundays in our house were structured differently from the other days of the week. Dad always gave mum breakfast in bed, and she seldom made an appearance much before 10 or so.

When she did come down, fully dressed and ready for action, she'd get stuck into cooking the family lunchtime roast. This varied in a loosely regular pattern: beef, pork, lamb, chicken: all served with roast potato, gravy and greens: usually cabbage, sometimes sprouts or beans, depending on what was going off in the shop or growing in the garden. Occasionally there would be fish: a great big slab of cod, with white sauce, boiled potatoes and the usual veg.

One Sunday morning, while Peter and I were munching away at breakfast, dad came in somewhat furtively and sat down.

This was odd: usually by the time my brother and I were up on a Sunday, he would have already fed himself and Mum and be out in the garden or in his office, doing accounts.

Our jaws stopped. Dad just sat there, in his high-backed Windsor dining chair. His face was red and he avoided looking straight at us. The lazy Sunday atmosphere became filled with tension.

Sunlight was angling through the window and little dust motes hovered over my cornflakes.

I had the feeling someone had died.

Dad went an even deeper shade of crimson and said 'erm ….,' coughed to clear his throat and fell silent again. I had never seen him looking so miserable.

After a while, I stood, ready to go. Or Peter stood. Maybe we both did.

This seemed to break the logjam. Abruptly dad looked at the fireplace and said 'I need to talk to you about the facts of life.'

We both sat down: now we were all thoroughly embarrassed.

Peter said 'Oh, we know all about that.'

I nodded and lied enthusiastically. 'Yes. All about it.'

Dad was mightily relieved, but he had one more go. 'D'you know,' he asked, this time looking at the cat: 'the difference between …' he took a running jump at the next couple of words: 'masturbation and mensuration?'

Peter said 'Yes.'

I nodded and lied again. 'Yes.'

The cat said nothing.

Dad stood and headed for the door. 'Well, that's a relief.'

He went and Peter and I gloomily resumed breakfast.

And that was all the sex instruction I had except – maybe a year later – in school we were told there was to be a special class, one for boys, one for girls.

So the girls trouped off and a middle-aged, balding man with glasses and a paunch stood in front of us. He fiddled with a flip chart and said an indistinct opening sentence. He was embarrassed. We were embarrassed. If there had been a class goldfish, it too would have been embarrassed.

The man in front of us mumbled swiftly on, speeding through the flip chart, giving us glimpses of unknown internal organs, tadpoles and – thrillingly – what might have been a willy. After less than fifteen minutes he asked if there were any questions and ran for the door before anyone could say anything.

And that was it. In matters of sex I was now regarded as fully educated.

But I wasn't, and the 1960s, with all its much-publicised free love, drugs and sexual liberation was just about to begin.

And completely pass me by.

The Boy from the past.

What: I meet a boy I used to know.

Where: On a cold and windy Hampshire sports field.

My age: 15

This Diana moment has a long tail, stretching back to when I was around 9 or 10, attending my first remembered school: Dunhurst.

A football game is taking place. A teacher is refereeing, so this would have been an officially sanction activity, not a rowdy kick-about. I remember the surface being muddy and the air cold. There were perhaps 10 of us, all boys.

At some stage – I don't know why or how – we split into unequal teams: myself and two others against all the rest, making it perhaps 3 vs 7.

And we won. An astonishing, glittering achievement. We chased harder, kicked the ball further and might even have passed it once or twice. I'm pretty sure I scored at least once.

The three of us walked back, arms around each other, chanting 'We beat the rest! We beat the rest!'

The boy in the middle was our star player. He was fairly new, so I didn't really know him, but he had his left arm around my shoulders, we had accomplished a remarkable feat and the whole world was splendid.

He started praising himself, and we nodded along with it. He said he was the best footballer in the school, and we nodded a little less. He said he could have won it on his own. After a pause we murmured something about it being a team effort.

He stopped, and so did we. He swivelled away from me and stood over the other boy, the smallest of the three of us. I remember their two faces inches apart. The star player had a large, kinked nose and his squinty eyes were too close together.

He became insistent, demanding agreement. The other boy said nothing, his moonlike face tilted upwards.

I can't remember precisely how it ended: I expect a teacher loomed into view or we became caught in the general flux of pupils returning from the playing fields. But my exultant mood had evaporated and for the next hour or so I felt sour and unsettled.

But the next day was the next day, and the incident was tucked away in the past and forgotten for some 5 or 6 years, as I progressed from Dunhurst to Petersfield Secondary Modern (PSM).

In 1960 or thereabouts, the school leaving age was 15, and PSM was in its second or third year of gearing up for pupils who wished to stay on and take further exams. I was one such child, driven to further study through no sense of academic curiosity, more a case of sticking to what I knew.

For I am not, nor ever have been, a person who relishes change. It is only with the extreme creaking of reluctant gears and the resolute yanking of rusty tillers I can switch from one path to another.

At aged 15 I was at school, faced with the choice of continuing there or entering the unknown, scary universe of adulthood.

It was absolutely no contest. I stayed on, vaguely thinking I might go on to university. After all, I was taking six 'O' levels, which appeared an awful lot and involved a great deal of study. As a footnote, the 'O' in 'O level' stood for 'Ordinary.' This was obviously too aspirational, as some years later they were renamed as 'GCSE' or 'General Certificate of Education.'

At that time, in Hampshire, there must have been a dearth of fifteen-year-olds able to chuck things as – somehow - I ended up in a bleak field waiting to throw the javelin in the East Hampshire Junior trials.

There must have been five or six of us, standing around, waiting for an official – any official – to come and set things in motion. The wind was bitter: a couple of us were smugly wearing track suits, ostentatiously jogging up and down and doing stretching exercises.

I was wearing my raincoat on top of my usual school sports kit of shorts, polo shirt, black socks and plimsoles. The wind, relentlessly buffeting my shins, turned my feet into distant peninsulas of numbness.

One of the track suited boys came jogging up and, about a yard away, stopped and stretched, flexing his shoulders, before arching his back and spreading his arms, turning his face up towards what little sun could be seen.

He was in profile, and I had a flash of recognition. A large, kinked nose and squinty eyes glaring down and a soft, moonlike face looking up.

I found myself saying "Were you at Dunhurst?"

He turned towards me. It was the smaller boy, grown into muscular solidity. His face was robust and square, the placid dough-like curves now flattened and baked by adolescence into hardness.

It was very clear he had absolutely no idea who I was, but we went through the social motions, both pretending to resume a friendship that had never existed.

He'd moved seamlessly from Dunhurst to Beadales public school and - hearing I was now attending the local secondary modern - a subtle change crept into the conversation. His stance became straighter: the minimal height difference between us elongated and his voice took on the cadence of superiority.

I became distinctly aware of my rather grubby raincoat.

Wishing to show I was not just another thicko, I asked about 'O' levels, anticipating being able to insert "I'm taking six y'know." with devastating effect.

I should have known better: even at PSM, six was not that exceptional but – thankfully - he didn't grant me the space to parade my academic non-achievements. He'd already mapped out his future and gave me a spiel probably honed over numerous teas with elderly aunts.

First, University ('Actually, one only thinks of Oxford or Cambridge, doesn't one') followed by a stellar career in one of the professions ('probably law, maybe medicine: I'll decide later'). And as for exams? He'd already got four 'O' levels under his belt and next year was going to take an early 'A' level plus another cluster of 'O's ('Actually, the thing that matters is not what they are but how many you get: ten 'O's and four 'A's is absolutely a minimum.')

He then proceeded to launch the javelin twice as far as I did.

In truth, I expect he was nothing more than a full-on bullshitter who happened to be good at chucking a spear. But at the time I believed him and felt diminished. That evening I found my vague university aspiration had evaporated.

But staying on as a student beyond PSM became increasingly attractive and in time morphed into a decision to become a teacher.

I even managed to convince myself it was what I wanted to do.

Party time! (not).

What: I do not go to my brother's 18th birthday party.

Where: a hay barn.

My age: 17

Going back for a moment to my bonfire analogue, the fires in my internal landscape are many and varied. And when I visit them, to extract these narratives, they flare and become intense and real, begging to be heard and set down.

Or at least, most of them do. Some memories however seem to dislike attention and scrutiny. And when you peer into them, they are dark in the centre, an absence signifying there is more forgotten than remembered.

This memory, of not going to my brother's 18th birthday party, is one such.

Very possibly I am suffering here from selective amnesia. I am sure I have completely forgotten details because they reflect badly on me. Truly, I do not know if this is a good or bad thing. Forgetting an important bit of your past could be called a mini suicide, for if we are not the sum of our memories we are as nothing.

But why remember that which makes you ashamed of being you? Particularly from when you were a teenager struggling to swim in a violent current of incoherent, raging hormones and overwhelming shyness.

Enough said: I am not a particularly deep or reflective person. I like to think I am not writing this book as therapy for a largely uneventful and perhaps wasted life. No: I am doing this in the hope it will make money. Make of it what you will, but I would like enough money to build my own house.

Sometimes, while I'm sat here, stabbing down these words on this electronic paper, my mind slips sideways and begins to think of my house. It will not be excessively large and certainly not luxurious but needs to have enough space and bedrooms for my whole family to stay over and will be efficient, with a heat exchanger, thick insulation, loads of glass and a view including trees. Not to mention an adjacent play park for grandchildren plus dog walks, a cinema and a small supermarket.

In other words, I daydream the impossible dream for a while before returning to the here and now. To this page in fact, where I am struggling to tell you how and why I did not go to my brother's 18th birthday party.

And why this has loomed, sour, untouched and festering quietly, for nearly 60 years.

On the face of it, it's perfectly simple: I did not go because I was not invited. At least, that is what my memory tells me, before seamlessly sashaying into a recollection of sitting alone in my room, listening to the rest of the family cheerfully donning coats and shoes before departing noisily and happily for my brother's 18th birthday party. In a haybarn. And later, much later, of lying in bed and hearing them return, and the following day listening to them talking about how Mrs Cook (why was she invited and not me?) had two glasses of cider and went so blotto she danced the can-can, fell over and had to be taken home.

But this internal narrative, nurtured for many of the following months, cannot be other than false.

For I am certain that, during the summer of 1960 I was once more at odds with the world and spent my time on the surly lookout for insults and offences, sulking both when I found them and when I didn't.

I did not receive an invite. Of course I didn't: no-one in my family did; it was just assumed we were all coming. Family is family, after all. And – obviously - Mrs Cook had an invite, otherwise she would not have been there. But me? By what twisted logic did I require a written invitation to my own brother's 18th birthday party, in a haybarn?

Almost certainly what happened was I let it be known I wasn't going to go and when no-one objected, I retreated into a mega-sulk. Which – of course - made everyone glad I wasn't going.

In other words I comprehensively cut off my nose to spite my face, a thing I did with some regularity.

And that's really it: no more to be said. One memory duly put in its place as just another example of my stubborn teenage stupidity.

Getting lost.

What: I get lost on my first trip on my first motorbike.

Where: between Reigate and East Meon.

My age: 16.

Here, *'Getting lost'* - however apt - is not intended as an ironic metaphor for my life up to this point. I physically got lost pop-popping along the leafy A roads of Surry, Sussex, Hampshire and probably Kent.

Pop-popping? I was riding an elderly two stroke BSA Bantam, acquired from my cousin Simon. And, to complete the little I know of the provenance of this machine, Simon had inherited it from his elder brother Robin a year before.

It had all been organised by – of course – the mothers: mum and Aunt Rosemary (my dad's sister). We'd all meet up for Christmas, alternating between East Meon and Reigate, with various grannies, other aunts and the occasional cousin sometimes joining us for the occasion.

So on the Christmas before my sixteenth birthday in February, it was all arranged. I'm not sure if I had much of a hand in it: the driving forces were most probably Aunt Rosemary's desire to have one less oil dripping machine hogging her drive, and mum's acute need to get a gloomy and moody teenager out of the house.

Accordingly, in early March, I got on the morning train and headed to Reigate. The plan was to learn to ride the Bantam that afternoon and bring it home the following day. Dad had donated an off-white pre-war cork helmet and a pair of thick gardening gloves, my brother loaned me a pair of his football socks for warmth, mum checked I had all the necessary documentation and my sister Judy said 'Oh, do be careful!'

I got there in time for lunch and in the afternoon Simon and I rode off to a nearby gravel pit for practice. I rode pillion and after fifty yards he stopped. 'Listen,' he said: 'when we go round a corner don't sit upright: lean with me.' He revved the engine a bit and added ominously 'Or we'll crash, as sure as eggs are eggs.'

It seemed curiously inappropriate to put my arms around him, so I compromised by gripping his shoulders and – when he leaned - I leaned.

The gravel pit had tracks, so was obviously used by bikers, but very fortunately none of them were there, which meant I could make a fool of myself with only Simon as a witness. He gave me a brief lesson covering the many essentials: petrol; ignition; kick-start; clutch; gear change; accelerator; front brake; back brake and what to do if the chain fell off which – apparently – it frequently did. To give him his due, that evening Simon tightened some nuts and the chain remained stoutly in place for the next few weeks.

I put on the cork helmet and dad's gardening gloves and sat astride the beast. As instructed, I held the clutch in and moved the gear lever with my foot until there was a clunk. On twisting the throttle the little engine pop-popped energetically and a tremor of powerful anticipation made the petrol tank vibrate.

I felt fully in command, so when Simon yelled 'gently let out the clutch!' I released it all at once.

I would like to report something spectacular happened, with the bike cartwheeling away while I flew off to land in a puddle, but the truth – as it usually is - was far more mundane. There was an anti-climactic jolt and the engine stopped.

My cousin sighed. 'Gently, gently catchee monkey ….. Now, let's try again.'

It was getting dark by the time we called it a day. Simon showed me how the lights worked and home we went.

That evening it was decided I needed more practice, so the following morning Simon gave me a master class in navigating traffic, using hand signals for slowing down and left and right turns. It was all very similar to being on a pushbike except – as he pointed out more than once – on a motorbike you went much faster.

I practiced on some of the quieter roads and after lunch put on my brother's socks, tied my overnight bag on the back, buckled the cork helmet under my chin, donned the gardening gloves and set off.

Somehow, in all the flurry of leaving, no one – myself included – asked if I knew the way home. It was just assumed that sitting in the back of our Hillman Minx once every two years while we drove from East Meon to Reigate (and then back again in the dark) would somehow magically imbue me with the knowledge to navigate the same route on my own.

After all, during the war, dad had driven overnight through London in the blackout and got to Portsmouth before dawn. He did get lost but stopped near Nelson's column and used a sextant to head in the right direction.

So for me, in daylight, Reigate to East Meon should be a doddle.

I pootled off, reached a junction and turned left, as that was easier than turning right. I followed this left turn strategy and – inevitably – passed my cousin's house again. Luckily no-one noticed, so when again at the junction I turned right. It was curiously liberating.

It took me three loops around the town centre before I managed to get out of Reigate and along a country road. By then I had formulated a plan: I would go around pretty much at random, checking road signs for towns I recognised. London didn't count as I knew that was in the wrong direction. Logic suggested that eventually I would get close enough to home to know where I was.

I fancied I was like a bee, buzzing along from flower to flower, waiting for a cross scent to tell me where the hive was.

As strategies go, it was not entirely stupid and paid off when I saw a sign for Dorking. I was sure we went through there on our biannual trips to Reigate and indeed, one glance at a map will confirm this.

So, about thirty minutes after leaving my cousin's house, I felt confident I was on my way home.

Unfortunately, between that signpost and the next, Dorking vanished. I was confronted by various other destinations, none of which I recognised. Undaunted, I picked one that pointed away from London, revved the engine and started off again.

I'm not certain how I managed to end up in East Grinstead. I'm sure it is perfectly nice town, but should emphatically not feature on any route from Reigate to East Meon.

Nor – I hasten to add - should Brighton, but I managed to get there an hour or so later.

I sat astride the Bantam and saw the sea stretching out beyond the pier. And had an inspiration. All I needed to do now was keep the sea on my left and I'd eventually end up in Portsmouth. And from there I would be able to navigate my way home as I'd gone there once to get a haircut.

Feeling proud of my reasoning, I set off.

But – like practically every other destination that afternoon – the sea mysteriously dematerialised, and once more I found myself heading inland.

If you trace my route on a map, it is evident I was meandering around the South of England like a lost drunk after the pubs closed.

I flashed past a badly position road sign and caught a glimpse of a destination starting with 'P,' thought 'Portsmouth!' and headed in that direction.

When I reached Petworth it was getting properly dark and the fuel gauge was trembling over the zero mark. I started to panic. I had a strange feeling I might have been killed in a crash, and I would be forever wandering through a parallel universe of evaporating towns and ghostly people.

This feeling was so real it wiped out my natural inclination for self-indulgence and forced me into doing something sane. I found a call box and rang home.

Dad answered.

'Oh' he said 'we were expecting you ages ago. Where are you?'

I told him 'Petworth' and his voice became cheerful. 'Oh, that's not far.'

I went on to say I had no funds and little fuel.

And dad – just like that - had the solution. "Petworth? Our accountant lives there. You can borrow some money off him. I'll ring him now. Just say who you are."

He gave me a name and an address, which I clung onto, desperately repeating it under my breath. He rang off and – muttering furiously - I returned to the Bantam. Only to realise I still had absolutely no idea which way to go. But somehow, having a precise address made it legitimate to ask for directions.

And fate – as if to prove a point – decreed the first person I asked gave me precise instructions. Five minutes later I rang a doorbell and dad's accountant – who was waiting for me - handed me a five-pound note, pointed in a vague Westerly direction and said "good luck!"

And I was back home almost in time for supper.

There is a schoolboy joke which at the time I thought funny: *'what is red and throbs between your legs?'* the answer of course is *'a post office motorbike.'*

I do not find it funny now, but then I'm not a teenager anymore.

The Crucible.

What: I act in a play about the Salem witch trials.

Where: Petersfield.

My age: 17

I'm not sure what attracted me to amateur dramatics. A year or so before, the dreaded Miss Murray (She who could make the very earth bend to her will) had walked my whole class down to St. Peter's Church in the town square. It was late November and it transpired she was auditioning potential readers for the annual Christmas service.

We knew nothing of this as we dutifully filed into the pews. Miss Murray positioned herself midway towards the back.

She spoke, her voice as clear as a bell in that great cavernous space. "Brook!" I jerked into sitting straight. "Go up into the pew and read what's in front of you."

I walked like a robot up the curving steps and found myself looking down at my classmates, all of whom were staring up at me.

"Brook!" Miss Murray's voice was imperious. "Read!"

I did so: the words were familiar: I had heard them once a year for my entire school life. *'AND there were in the same country shepherds abiding in the field, keeping watch over their flock by night. And, lo, the angel of the Lord came upon them, and they were sore afraid. And the angel said unto them, Fear not: for, behold, I bring -'*

Miss Murray had been growing increasing impatient. Her voice entered like an arrow into my ears. "Out loud, you stupid child!"

The class laughed. I went red and gripped the sides of the pulpit, fingers going white under the pressure.

I mumbled "Sorry Miss." She stared at me. I corrected myself "Sorry Miss Murray."

Somewhat mollified, she said "Brook, you have a nice voice: use it."

There was an involuntary 'Ooooo!' from the class. A compliment from Miss Murray! I felt my vocal cords tying themselves into knots. I swallowed and swallowed again.

"When you're quite ready."

My voice came out high pitched, somewhere between a squeak and the cry of a bat. "And there were in the same country-"

"Thank you Brook! You can come down now."

Her next victim gave me a smirk as we awkwardly crossed on the steps.

Unsurprisingly, I was not invited to be one of the readers at the Christmas carol service. Not then, or ever. But her remark about having a nice voice stuck with me and a year or so later, once my motorbike made me more mobile, I joined the Winton Players, an 'amdram' group based in Petersfield. They are it seems, even now, still going strong.

They were casting for 'The Crucible' by Arthur Miller and I landed the smallest role of Herrick, the town marshal.

To tell true, I got the part rather in the same way I got to play in the village cricket team: there was no-one else remotely suitable. Herrick was middle aged and turning to alcohol; I was seventeen with a nice voice and had never been drunk in my life.

Over the rehearsals my part was whittled down, loosing words and sentences at such a steady rate I was in danger of being rendered mute, or even vanishing altogether. But I survived, unlike the character of Ezekiel Cheever, who was ruthlessly dismembered before the first reading, his lines and actions either omitted altogether or cunningly smuggled across to others.

Now-a-days, I know 'The Crucible' is a complex, powerful dramatic allegory, written at the time of - and in response to - the McCarthy hearings in the USA.

In the play characters are condemned to death on 'evidence' that – to modern eyes – appears completely insane. Events start eating themselves, and any voice of reason is relentlessly squashed. Some of the Winton players were bewildered by this: after the first read through they were asking 'what is wrong with these people? Are they stupid or crazy?'

However, I did not think that. I can't say I ever reflected deeply on the meaning of what was being depicted. The inherent madness of the Salem witch trials largely passed me by. To a child – and I was hardly out of childhood – the adult world had long seemed ruled by laws that didn't make sense, circular logic and my own insignificance. So the tight, insular community of 'The Crucible,' with grown-ups following a logic alien to reason, was in some ways almost comprehensible.

So I got on with learning my dwindling supply of lines, practicing them out loud as I pop-popped between East Meon and Petersfield. I now wore a new helmet but kept the cork one neatly tied to the back in a futile attempt to convince onlookers there was a girl somewhere who regularly rode my pillion.

For me, the main draw of amateur dramatics – both then and later - was not the chance to grandstand on the stage, using my nice voice to wow the watching punters. No, it was being part of a team and being useful: I made tea; I read the parts of absent actors; I painted scenery and helped others learn their lines.

In short, belonging to a group focused on one objective (presenting 'The Crucible' over four set days at set times) meant I could bypass social awkwardness. Projects - of practically any stamp – mitigates shyness.

So - perhaps for the first time since becoming a teenager - I was fully involved in something other than myself. I would like to think my behaviour at home improved, but I have no recollection of it. But nor can I recall any blazing rows or melt-downs, so perhaps it did.

Rehearsals went on for ever but – suddenly – it was the week of the performance. We decamped to Petersfield Town Hall and mysterious people I had glimpsed but fleetingly until then surfaced like large fish from the depths of the sea. They walked purposefully around with lighting equipment, costumes and carpenter's tools.

A nice lady gave me a costume. Wearing it, I looked somewhat piratical. She surveyed me with her head on one side. The director came over, and they both stared at me. He said 'Ummm.. Not convincing as a Puritan, is he?' But she was more confident. 'All it needs is a collar.' From a pocket somewhere she produced a white circular segment of cotton, which she tied around my neck. And I was instantly transformed from a cutthroat villain into a Puritan jailor.

The power of clothing never ceases to amaze.

And so I was all set to give the good citizens of Petersfield, Hampshire my deathless interpretation of Herrick (much reduced), the Marshal in Arthur Miller's classic tragedy 'The Crucible.'

And we come to the 'Diana Moment' of this particular recollection.

It is the first performance. I am waiting - with another cast member - in the wings. The first act is over. It went well and behind the curtain is a buzz from the (not that numerous) audience. Without a doubt they are echoing many of the actors after the first read thru, asking 'what is wrong with these people? Are they stupid or crazy?'

The second act is underway, gaining momentum, with harder voices and greater emotional flux and flow. From rehearsal after rehearsal, I know exactly what is happening, and precisely how long it will be before I will have walk on stage, make a gesture and say one of my few lines.

Everything is hyper-real. The lights on the stage are bright and seem to give out a yellow halo. Even though I can't see them from this angle, the audience is undoubtedly there, a palpable, inescapable presence, like half real ghosts, neither in nor out of this world. Beside me, my fellow actor tensed.

Just as our cue came, he turned to me, whispered 'Christ, I hate all this!' and took four steps out onto the stage. All I had to do was follow behind as Marshall Herrick, the jobsworth jailer doing a job, however distasteful it might be.

And this is what I remember, the Diana Moment: it went fine. I walked on, waited, said my line, did my gesture and walked off.

No trips, no stumbles, no dries, no glance at the audience: it went exactly as rehearsed.

After days of worry about make-up, my motorcycle breaking down, forgetting my lines, other actors forgetting their lines, nudging scenery so it fell down, needing a pee at a critical moment ... (this list could go tediously on and on) it was all good and went without a hitch.

So I am remembering the relief of discovering I could do this unnatural thing: walk out in front of hundreds of people and not let the side down.

Since then I have belonged to many amdram groups and taken part in many plays. And – if I am honest – as an actor

I have never proved to be anything other than a spear carrier who only occasionally dropped his spear.

However – as in many dramas - there is an interesting coda.

After the final performance of The Crucible, amid all the backslapping camaraderie, it was somehow arranged I would take home – on my pillion – the girl who played Abigail Williams, the antagonist of the drama. Undoubtedly, she was one of the stars of the company. I can't now remember her name, but she was another teenager, slender with striking features. On stage she played her large part (so many lines!) with convincing, ferocious intensity.

On her, the cork helmet looked particularly fetching. She perched herself up behind me; her arms encircled my waist; her long, interlaced fingers gratifyingly tight on my stomach.

To extend the experience, I should have driven slowly and carefully, but of course I didn't. I revved the engine and - pop-popping furiously - we departed with a satisfying spray of gravel.

It was raining. For five minutes we were OK, skimming along the black wet roads. She shouted in my ear 'This is fun!' We took a bend: the bike slid out of control and we both ended on the ground. Her finger was slightly hurt, my arm was slightly bruised, the bike looked ill.

A car stopped: another cast member offering help.

I righted the bike and it started, so I said I was fine. Abigail asked if I was sure, and I replied I was. She got into the car and was driven off.

I rode home slowly, my front light wrenched askew, throwing a beam into the sky.

At the next meeting of the Winton players, she came over and said she had been worried about leaving me on the roadside in the rain, and was I alright?

I said I was and asked if she was alright.

And she said she was.

And that was it. I don't think I ever saw her again.

Film plots have been constructed from flimsier material, but - unfortunately - I am not living, and never have lived, in a romantic comedy.

God's gift to teaching.

What: I am interviewed by the principal of Nottingham College of Education.

Where: A dusty office somewhere on the South Coast.

My age: 18

After passing my 6 'O' levels (Certainly Maths, further maths, English and English literature. And then memory fails, so pick any two from History, Geography, Technical Drawing and Woodwork) I still required an 'A' level to go to a Teacher's Training college or – as they were somewhat tautologically labelled - a College of Education.

Accordingly, I began attending Churcher's College, Petersfield, the local grammar school, with the aim of taking (and passing) 'A' level maths.

At Churcher's I found myself something of an anomaly. There, my six 'O' levels hardly registered on the achievement seismograph and only doing one 'A' level considerably reduced my timetable. About a quarter of my lessons – maybe even more - were labelled 'Private Study' (or some such). While other pupils were reluctantly heading into the science labs or waiting for the biology teacher to make an appearance, I'd repair to the sixth form reading room and pretend to myself I was studying maths. In reality, I did nothing much very, very slowly.

I struggled. The jump from Secondary Modern 'O' level maths to grammar school 'A' level seemed immense. Everything was different, even the language! Words I had never met before were used with casual familiarity. I was confronted with the constant dilemma of not knowing what was being taught yet not wishing to fully reveal the plummeting depth of my ignorance.

So I sat there near the back of the class wondering what 'statics' and 'dynamics' were, with diagrams of forces and inclined planes and matrices as a way of solving equations. I felt like a soldier holding a bow and arrow facing a whole platoon armed with bazookas.

And yet, and yet: slowly things improved. Some osmotic learning process took place and in tests my scores slowly climbed from zero. I think I got as high as twenty-five percent. Once.

So it is something of a mystery how I passed 'A' level maths (just). I can only think there was a tsunami of mathematical ignorance among all the other students in the country and – to keep the pass rate respectable – they lowered the standard.

So thank you, all 'A' level maths students who – that year - were even worse than me.

To find a suitable college, I got out a map and a pair of compasses: I didn't want to be too close to home or too far away. I decided a hundred miles was probably about right and began measuring distances and consulting lists of colleges.

How I fixed on Nottingham I'm not sure, but I applied and a little while later got invited to an interview down near Havant somewhere.

The principal of Nottingham College of Education sat behind an old, dark wooden desk. In front of him was a single application form, a note pad, a ball point pen and a wristwatch.

He had springy tufts of greying hair and looked like everyone's third favourite uncle. He glanced up briefly and waved towards the chair in front of the desk. I sat down. There was a silence as he finished reading the application. Even upside down, I recognised my uneven, awkward script. My mother had the most wonderful copperplate handwriting. I did not.

He looked up. His eyes were kind and his voice courteous. "Mr Brook," he said. "You have fifteen minutes to convince me you are God's gift to teaching. Now please stand behind that chair and tell me why you are."

A couple of days before, I had asked mum and dad about being interviewed. Mum was characteristically pragmatic: 'They probably won't listen to what you say, more how you say it. So don't mumble or grunt.' Dad – going somewhat red in the telling - launched into a story about being interviewed for a teaching post. As they'd finished, dad had extended his hand for the customary handshake, but the interviewer had walked away to a window and stared out. Without looking round he'd said "Before coming to see me, Mr Brook, did it not occur to you to clean your fingernails?"

Dad said he had never felt more humiliated in his life. He didn't get the job.

So, I had scrubbed my nails and was now prepared. I placed my immaculate hands on the back of the chair, forgot mum's instructions and mumbled something about changing the world through education.

The principal leant back. "Pretend," he said, "that I'm a class of 30 bored and hungry thirteen-year-olds waiting for lunch."

The word 'pretend' fired me into action. This was all just a pretence! A stage with an audience of one. I drew on my inner actor and said the same guff about changing the world through education, but - remembering mum at last - without a single mumble or grunt.

When I had finished, he said "run out of words?" I nodded. He smiled. "Then sit down and we'll have a short chat."

A month or so later I had a letter through the post: I had been accepted as a student at Nottingham College of Education and would start in September.

I am in deep and absolute debt to my parents for many, many, many things: a vast ocean of unconditional love and support that I – to my shame – barely noticed at the time. And tucked in there, a small yet vital cog, was the sound advice to always scrub your nails before an interview and – when there – don't mumble or grunt. Thanks mum. Thanks dad.

But as it turned out, I probably would have been better off if it had all gone wrong. For I was a miserably useless teacher and didn't last long.

However, as failures often say: it's all grist to the mill.

Leaving for college.

What: I get on a train to Nottingham.

Where: St Pancras railway station, London.

My age: 18

I have always found change somewhat scary. In many ways, it's even more frightening when you've been the sole person to set it all in motion, as then there is absolutely no-one else to blame.

And so it was with my decision to go to Nottingham College of Education and become a teacher: mine and mine alone, no scapegoating allowed.

During the summer, various letters and packages arrived from Nottingham. The postman would come into the shop and put them - with a deadening thump - on the counter. They were for the most part dull reading lists or cheerful tips and advice for new students. But with each delivery, my sense of dread increased.

For they meant this life-changing change was actually, really and certainly going to happen. Every item of post forcefully reminded me – as if I needed reminding – that a severe upheaval to my life was galloping ferociously towards me, gaining solidity and reality with each passing day.

And I was scared. I wanted to leave home, I needed to leave home, but becoming a student a hundred miles away seemed ridiculously drastic.

And – as was my wont – I started making things worse by telling myself a series of half lies and semi-truths, polishing them up to make them seem more formidable than they really were: shyness became crippling shyness; a difficulty in making friends turned into a future of perpetual loneliness; my struggles with maths doomed me to being classed as a thicko for ever. It became obvious I'd be totally miserable at college for a year or so before being thrown out as a waste of time, eventually ending up as a solitary, uninteresting tramp, dying a lonely death in a ditch somewhere.

Scratching this self-indulgent itch of self-pity became my main occupation for that miserable summer. I'd go to a wood or climb a hill and mope for half an hour before feeling hungry and going home.

But all bad times must come to an end and as September approached, I found myself busy with preparations.

I appropriated a large trunk from the attic. Made of canvas, bentwood and some species of cardboard, it had a rusty lock and smelt of mildew. Dad fixed the lock with oil and mum the mildew with bleach. When opened right out it took up a large area of my bedroom floor. That trunk stayed with me for many years, transporting my belongings from bedsit to small flat to bedsit, often serving also as a wardrobe or coffee table. I would like to say I have it still, but – somewhere along the line - it got abandoned.

Towards the end of August neat piles of washed, ironed and sorted clothes, many new, appeared on my bed. Mum – but of course – had read the helpful 'hints and tips for new students,' and her youngest boy was not going to go to Nottingham College of Education without the requisite number of underpants.

The trunk was filled and my brother sat on it so I could click the lock.

He said, 'You'll be OK, Jamie." It was a statement, not a question. I grunted agreement and he raced off to coax the family Hillman Minx to go more than sixty miles an hour towards his girlfriend.

A week before I was due to start, the trunk – carefully labelled with my name, college address and room number - was collected by two men in an enormous lorry with 'British Road Services' proudly printed on the side. It parked on the bridge, blocking the pub from view.

The trunk was wheeled over on a trolley and flung into the dark interior, abruptly vanishing from sight. The tailgate was swung up, closed with a clank and secured with small iron pegs. The engine started, the vibrations making the windows rattle. With the grinding of gears, a three-point turn was clumsily executed. Finally, they were off, transporting the trunk out of sight but into my future.

Watching it depart I knew I was now committed. A week later, I followed.

Dad and I went to London on the train. Having never been to London on my own, they said they were worried I might get lost on the underground. But now, I think that – given the chance - they would both have come with me all the way to college, inspected my room and helped me unpack.

But – as ever with my parents – practicalities and common sense ruled, so a compromise was agreed. East Meon was in the South. London was in the South. So going to London was legitimate. Going further North – to Nottingham - would not be.

Trains to Nottingham departed from St Pancras Railway Station, a name so exotic and distant it wasn't even on our monopoly board. We arrived at Waterloo and immediately descended to take the tube.

For people – like myself – who are seldom in London, travelling on the underground is always a surreal experience. It's the map that does it, with its equally spaced stations on straight lines. A work of genius that disregards the train lurching around corners, having the occasional pause and taking longer to reach some stations than others. And – like all works of genius – it leaves you disorientated, depositing you precisely where you want to be but with no idea of where you are or how you got there.

St Pancras seemed comfortingly small compared with Waterloo. Dad was wearing his usual old mac and flat cap. He was fiddling with his pipe and a pair of bicycle clips. We went over to the departure board, and there it was: 'NOTTINGHAM' in big fat shouty capital letters.

There was maybe half an hour to wait. We stood in front of the departure board and staggered our pee visits to make sure 'NOTTINGHAM' stayed where it was. Dad lit his pipe and suggested we went and sat on a vacant bench about twenty yards away. This seemed a little distant to me, but we went there anyway. Dad got comfortable, pulling a crumpled newspaper from his pocket and cleaning his glasses with a less than pristine handkerchief.

I sat for a couple of minutes and went over to the gate. A man went through, waving a small square of paper at the surly guard.

I went back to Dad. "Have you got my ticket?"

He looked up. "I thought you got one through the post?" Seeing my appalled expression he lumbered to his feet. "Oh, there's plenty of time." He went and joined the queue for the ticket window.

I hovered between the gate and the queue. More and more people were going through to the train. A man in uniform appeared and started walking very slowly toward the front. I was sure he was the driver. Regardless of the time (there was still over five minutes to go) I was convinced that when he got there, the train would crank into action and depart. Without me.

Dad was now second in line but the woman in front of him was leaning on the counter and chatting away as if gossiping over her back fence to a neighbour. She was wearing thick beige stockings and worn-down shoes.

Never had I hated anyone so much in my life. I glanced at the clock and when I looked back a miracle had happened: she was walking slowly away, and dad was asking about tickets. He'd pulled out his purse and held it ready, the leather top flapping down. He turned to me. "Do you qualify," he asked, "as an adult?"

I found a compartment with a window seat. Dad – outside - was clutching his platform ticket. The glass separating us was streaked but not too dirty. At the top was a gap between chrome mounted sliding windows.

I stuck my hand through. He reached up and held it. His fingers were large, comforting and calloused. Familiar.

There was the blowing of whistles and a shout or two. He let go. I let go. We both let go. He stood back and the train moved. I pushed my cheek against the window and had a last glimpse of dad standing on the platform. He was waving with one hand while the other was already clutching his pipe.

At the end of the platform the man I had thought was the driver was stacking boxes. He paid no attention as my train accelerated past.

Caught In flagrante

What: I surprise a couple.

Where: Nottingham College of Education.

My age: 18

At college, for the first few weeks, there must have been – for me – a succession of important 'firsts': first arrival at Nottingham, first glimpse of the college, of my room, of fellow students; the first freshers ball, first meal in the canteen, first lecture, first this, first that.

None of which I can remember. I do have a vague recollection of feeling homesick, but I also recall a conviction I felt homesick because I thought I should feel homesick. But nothing has that glowing intensity that identifies a Diana Moment.

But, indubitably, things had changed. I was – nominally - no longer a child, living in my parent's house. I was now over one hundred miles away but - more importantly - I no longer met anyone who knew me before. No-one, absolutely no-one, had any expectations of how I should look or behave, with the possible exception of the college principal, who had interviewed me for a brief 15 minutes several months before. I don't think that counts.

The golden opportunity was there to reinvent myself, but I know I didn't take it. I remained just the same uncertain, shy, moody teenager as before. I suspect the people who have the confidence to reinvent themselves are probably not the sort who feel the need to do so.

The first Diana Moment at college was several weeks in and occurred during a football match.

Then, the football pitches were close to the halls of residence, which were divided into self-contained accommodation blocks for ten students. It was all very neat and functional. There was even a cleaner who came round a couple times a week to vacuum the floors, wipe down the surfaces and ignore the washing up.

In my block there were three second year students and one of them — who's name escapes me, so we'll call him Ron — had a pal, an ex-student who occasionally slept on his floor on a Lilo otherwise hidden away. They said it was all OK, and they'd got permission. I believed them, which illustrates the trusting soul I was.

His pal's girlfriend was a third-year student at the college. Her blond hair was always in a bun.

I was playing football: an assessment game, to see who'd be good enough to play for the college. As an aside here, I did manage (just) to squeeze into the lower ranks, where I lumbered around ineffectually hoofing the ball forward. We lost most games: the worst one was against a scratch team from a Catholic seminary, who came already changed on a coach with a purple logo on the side. My word, they were fit! They beat us something like ten nil, scorned our changing rooms and vanished back into the coach with hardly a spot of mud on them. Their goalkeeper spent most of the game reading the bible. Or perhaps I'm just imagining that.

At half time a chap who I'd briefly met came limping over. "James" he said: "do me a favour. Ron's room is empty, and I've hurt my ankle. Do me a favour and run as fast as you can to his room: go straight in and you'll find a support bandage by the sink. He said I could have it, but I forgot. Straight over, straight in. There's no one there."

Now, from the wisdom of my years, I'd say he was talking too much. Suspiciously too much.

But now is now and then was then. I went charging off.

Our block was only about fifty yards distant: it didn't take long. I belted up the stairs, studs clattering, opened Ron's door and went in.

Ron's pal was there, of course. With his girlfriend, of course. On the bed, of course. Her hair had escaped the bun, her knees were raised and her clothes rucked up.

Ron's mate propped himself up on his elbow. "Oh," he said. "Erm …. what are you after?"

She turned her head towards me. Her eyes were bleak. Her voice could command mountains. "Get out."

I got.

Back at the football I wasn't sure what to do, but the chap with the limp had stopped limping and didn't come over, so I ignored him.

A couple of days later I was sitting alone in the main common room. A large open space with coffee tables and Scandinavian chairs.

"Hello." She sat down. Her hair was immaculate, the bun tight against her head. Before I could say anything, she said "All OK?" in the same tone you use to address any casual friend you haven't seen for a few days.

My intonation was – I hope – equally off hand and unconcerned. "Yeah, fine thanks."

"Good." A brief, warm smile and she'd gone. Obviously, she had heard of the trick played on me, sought me out alone and - in a conversation of no more than five or six words – made it OK.

A very kind and gracious lady. I hope she is still alive and trust she is happy.

Goodbye Jane.

What: I hear my sister Jane had died.

Where: Nottingham college of education.

My age: 20

I am now 75, so inevitably, people I know will have died. Of my close family, Jane was the first. Jane, my sister: a good person, who died at the age of thirty-three, in 1965, from a cancerous tumour in the brain.

Dad and Mum still had the shop, Peter was in New Zealand, I was at college and Judy - based in London – was illustrating children's books.

We all knew she was extremely ill of course. Except – and this might seem bizarre – Jane herself.

Well, no. She had been a nurse, so she must have known.

To take a step back: a reminder.

My sister Jane was the younger of two girls, daughters of dad and his first wife, Evelyn. His other daughter – my sister Judy - crops up frequently in this memoir. Evelyn died of lung cancer before the war, leaving Dad with two teenage children. He married mum and Peter and I came along.

So – strictly speaking – Judith and Jane were my half-sisters, but I have never thought of them as such.

Of my siblings, I knew Jane the least: by the time I started noticing things, she was training to be a nurse. She was slender and energetic, with a serious and moral turn of mind. She got engaged to a naval officer and they began converting some empty rooms above the shop. I remember the smell of paint and Jane – in cut-down blue dungarees - singing quietly as she hung wallpaper.

And then it all fell apart. Abruptly, Jane returned the ring, and the officer was never seen again. Sometimes, of an evening, I could hear her crying: mum would put down her knitting and quietly leave. The door to Jane's room – which led on to the half decorated flat above the shop – would open and close and soon the crying would dissolve into sobs and – after a little while - all would be quiet.

I would have been eleven or twelve. For some reason, she confided in me. I think all the other members of the family were out and the cat couldn't be found.

I remember her hands twisting together as she said "he told me. He told me he'd been to a brothel. In Hong Kong. A brothel."

Her eyes were intense and unblinking. I was not sure what a brothel was, so I just looked at the floor.

"And I," she continued "had always kept myself clean for him."

She ran off.

Years later, after Jane died, I told Judy of this conversation and she shook her head and said "poor, poor Jane."

She never confided in me again. But then – as a family – we did not talk much about personal matters. My mother in particular believed in getting on with things and 'least said, soonest mended.'

A little while later (I am unsure of the dates) Jane went to Africa and sent us photos of Kenyan hospitals and postcards of Mt. Kilimanjaro, the picture annotated with biro: an arrow pointing to the summit and the words: 'I got here!'

In Africa – as dad once put it - 'she caught religion.' He said this in the same indifferent manner he might have said 'she caught a cold.' But – soon after she died - I caught an inadvertent glimpse of a sheet of paper on his desk. I could read the top line. His handwriting was instantly recognisable: 'Prayer of an Atheist.'

After a year or two she returned from Africa and enrolled to train as a missionary. By then I was at college, so know little of the details. She lived at home and at regular intervals, clean looking people, in smart, well-ironed clothes, would turn up; Jane would sweep them into the front room for bible study.

I have always been uncertain about religion: I admire it for the comfort it brings, but rather despise it for the faith it demands. I suspected then – as I now believe – that all religions are essentially bogus.

I once asked Jane, as she stood in front of the hall mirror carefully primping herself before going to church, why she bothered with how she looked. Surely, if God was God, he couldn't care less about her appearance.

She carefully checked her lipstick before saying (and here I paraphrase): 'if you're going to meet your maker, you want to look your best.' Then she went, stepping lightly along in the morning sunlight, down to the war memorial, turning right over the bridge, past the alms houses, through the lychgate and so into the church.

She never finished her course, never became a missionary, never married or had children: the list of things she wanted to do was far, far longer than the list of things she actually did.

During the summer she often felt sick and tired: she spent many hours in bed with headaches. She went into hospital and came back with her head swathed in bandages after a biopsy. All her movements were careful and considerate towards herself, as if she were made of fragile glass.

Her friends came often, sitting with her for hours, reading the bible and praying.

The biopsy results were not good.

I went home for Christmas. Once, Jane managed to get dressed and made it to the living room, declaring she would watch TV with us. Mum and Judy began to fuss with cushions, making a little nest on the sofa. I was dispatched to find a pillow.

Jane burst into tears. "Stop treating me," she said, "as if I was ill!"

Dad told me later he and mum had been in a quandary: should they tell Jane how bad it was, that the prognosis was only a few months?

Her friends said yes, that she needed time to prepare to meet God.

The doctor said no, that he was sure Jane – who, remember, had been a nurse – must already know. She hadn't asked about the biopsy because she didn't want to face the reality, and it would be unkind to force her to do so.

So dad and mum decided to keep quiet.

Whatever else I might say about religion, I am forever grateful to her kind friends in those last few weeks. They understood the logic and disagreed with the conclusion, but kept their thoughts to themselves. As Jane got worse and the morphine dose increased, they quietly withdrew.

I was back at college when Dad rang. His voice, over the phone, was hollow. The news was as expected. That morning, at home, in her room, my sister Jane had peacefully ceased to be. Mum had been holding her left hand, dad her right: Judy didn't make it back in time from London.

I put the phone down and felt nothing. I told no-one. My ears had heard, my brain had listened, but my sluggish emotions had yet to catch up.

The Diana Moment came nearly a day later. I was a member of the college dramatic society and we were sat in a circle on the floor playing one of those games so beloved of such groups: a ball of scrunched up paper held together with Sellotape was thrown at random from one member to another, the thrower calling out the name of the target along with a theatrical question. The ball would be caught, the question answered and so on.

It was all very jolly.

(The ball is thrown by TOM at JENNY.)

TOM: 'Jenny: name a Shakespeare character.'

JENNY: *(catches)* 'Romeo!' *(She throws the ball at PAUL.)* 'Paul: who wrote about daffodils?'

PAUL: *(catches)* 'Ha! Easy! Wordsworth!' *(He throws the ball at ROGER.)* 'Roger: name me the play, Charley's something or other.'

ROGER: *(catches)* 'What?'

PAUL: 'Charley's something or other.'

HANNAH: *(Helpfully)* 'Your Dad's sister.'

ROGER: 'What?'

JOHN: 'Charley's Dad's sister!'

(General laughter, other hints and tips)

ROGER: *(Confused)* 'What? Oh, shit, I'm giving up.' *(He throws the ball at JAMES.)* 'Name a Shakespeare character!'

(slight uproar as he didn't give the name of the target and you can't have the same thing twice intermingled with calls of 'idiot! Charley's Aunt.')

ROGER:*(Defiantly)* Charley's what? Never heard of it!

(At first, they do not notice that JAMES failed to catch the ball. He has hunched up, arms hugging his folded legs

against his chest. A tear runs down his cheek. Suddenly he pushes himself backwards, stands and departs. A silence falls as they watch him go, but then the ball is retrieved and the game continues.

JAMES finds he needs to be alone. He walks outside and wanders around the carpark, attempting to memorise five car number plates.

He recognises this as a pointless exercise, but continues anyway.

Eventually he manages to get to his room without talking to anyone.

And the next day he is morose, but then he is often morose, so no-one remarks on it.

Slowly, his world returns to normal.)

I was very surprised at my reaction. After all, the news had been anticipated and I did not think of Jane and I as being particularly close. I expected to feel a bit sad for a while before continuing as before.

But the application of arrogant logic to understand and govern raw emotion, is – almost by definition – wasted effort, and the feelings released by grief are primal.

I did not understand this, and it is unlikely I would have listened had I been told. But this Diana Moment, coming out of the blue and forcing me to respond to feelings of a depth I had never before encountered, gave me much pause.

Some Diana Moments are more significant than others, and this was undoubtedly the most significant of my life so far.

But I find it almost impossible to coherently assemble the words to explain exactly why. Death redraws the map, and for a while you are lost.

Booook.

What: I am exposed to a wider world.

Where: In a classroom in Nottingham.

My age: 18

This is an odd Diana Moment. In some ways it exposes a few aspects of my life rather neatly, but in others it is so trifling and small it's astonishing it has survived for nearly sixty years. It must have outlasted many other, more vivid (at the time), memories which – by definition – I don't remember.

So, what is it, this Diana Moment? It's a fellow student from college, standing in front of a class of primary school children. He is saying '..so, get your books out please.'

He had, I remember, glasses and sparse hair. I was standing at the back with three or four other students. It was during my first term at college. We'd learnt some educational theory and now, we were being exposed to real children in a real classroom. It was quite unnerving. I felt like a laboratory rat being shoved into a real maze without the promise of a treat if I got to the centre.

The children – almost certainly handpicked for docility and schooled in asking polite, easy-to-answer questions – sat at their small desks; the classroom walls were colourfully arrayed with pictures and a map of the world with a big 'YOU ARE HERE!!!' pointing to the small Islands of the UK.

The student – and I had absolutely no idea who he was or where he came from – didn't say ' … so, get your books out please' No. He said '..so, get your booooks out please.'

And this, with amazing, pinpoint accuracy, skewered everything I knew about how people should talk. For he wasn't trying to be funny or different; it was no more an affectation than an ingrowing toenail.

Quite simply, 'Booook' is how he pronounced 'book,' with a long extended 'boooo' finishing with semi-tone drop on the 'k.' He might booook a table at a restaurant or read a booook on a bus and his local library would be full of booooks.

I realised there must be – out there in the great wide world – whole towns and even cities full of real people pronouncing the English language differently from myself. Real people. Not just actors in Z-Cars putting their vowels through a mangle whenever they spoke. Real people, like the man right there in front of me: a pleasant, likeable chap, interacting well with the children, pointing at things in their booooks.

For, in 1963, I was not well travelled. In fact, I'd hardly travelled at all: just as far North as South London, East to Brighton and West to Cornwall, where we stayed for a week in a caravan. It rained.

Therefore most of the UK was unknown to me. Sure, I'd heard of places, but they meant very little. Even exotic cities like Liverpool or Manchester only existed on the Saturday afternoon Grandstand football teleprinter.

I'd been told they existed, and I believed it, but did not know, not for certain sure. For I'd had no direct proof.

Until, in a small classroom in Nottingham, I heard a strange pronunciation of a hitherto familiar word. The person saying it was, without doubt, right there in front of me, standing a few yards away. I had seen him drink tea and eat a digestive biscuit, so there was no denying his reality. But saying 'booook' demonstrated he did not come from my own familiar, parochial world. It was a small version of seeing an alien land and everyone saying 'Oh! So, there is life on other planets!'

He was the proof: I now knew there was a wider world out there. Accordingly the map on the wall gained significance. All those places were really there! It was as if both the UK and 'Abroad' lost the fuzziness of a mere concept and gained a harder, more defined edge.

We've all seen dramas where someone – usually a man – is trying to persuade someone else – usually a girl – to come away with him; to dust off the provincial confines of her hometown and come to the bright lights of a large city. He will undoubtedly say a passionate variation of 'but Celia! Believe me! Believe me! There's a whole world out there!'

Sometimes she goes with him, sometimes not.

Had I been her - after hearing 'booook' - I would have replied: "Believe you? That's irrelevant: I <u>know</u> there is a world out there."

The driving test.

What: I fail my driving test.

Where: Chichester.

My age: 17

On turning seventeen I acquired a provisional driving licence, booked a driving test in a few weeks' time, put new string on the 'L' plates and asked my reluctant Dad to teach me in our old Hillman Minx convertible.

After all, he'd taught Peter, and Peter had passed first time. Moreover I'd been pop-popping around on my BSA Bantam for a year – and even passed my test (at the second attempt) - so: how hard could it be?

Dad had sighed, shrugged and gamely said he supposed we could give it a go.

He was a busy man, and the car was not always available, but two or three times a week we got out there, driving along quiet 'A' roads and even quieter 'B' roads, where unexpectedly meeting a cow or tractor were the main dangers.

As an instructor, Dad admirably believed in simplicity. Before we started any lesson, he'd say 'remember: MSM and keep your distance.'

'MSM' stood for 'Mirror, Signal, Manoeuvre' while 'Keep your distance' equated to driving like a cautious old lady.

I was often desperate for someone else to come out with me so I could practice.

Mum always claimed it was all far too difficult for her. Rubbish of course, but when she wished she could be as imperious as the emperor of Japan. Judy couldn't drive while Jane – who could - was in Kenya, a tad too distant for a half hour drive around rural Hampshire.

Which left Peter, who was usually good naturedly up for a laugh. Well, I think we went out together just once. He spent the whole time alternating between: 'Go on Jamie, give it some welly!' And: 'Jesus Jamie, slow down!'

The test day was in early April. It was sunny and warm. I drove to the test centre and backed in, parking at a jaunty angle between two sparkly clean driving school cars. Dad and I climbed out and stood back. The Minx looked old, careworn and rusty. The fabric of the hood was frayed and the front bumper had a dent.

"Maybe," dad said, "we should put the top down. It'd give you better sightlines." He glanced at his watch, which was always four minutes slow, on some dubious double logic of his own invention. "Plenty of time. These people are always late." He began putting the top down. I went into an office labelled 'Driving test, reception.'

Of course – as luck would have it – the examiner was ready and waiting. He was about 30, carried a ferocious clipboard and smelt of French cigarettes.

We went outside. Dad was hitting the half-folded top of the Minx with a mallet he kept for the purpose.

The examiner pointed at a car about twenty or so yards away. "Please read that number plate."

I complied. The sound of hammering ceased. The examiner looked at the three cars, lined up as if ready for a race: two greyhounds flanking an old mongrel who'd wandered in for a pee. Dad had reversed the mallet and was now using the handle to tuck bits of the folded hood into place.

The examiner said "So. Which car?"

My voice was scarcely above a mutter "The Hillman."

He lifted an eyebrow. ".. Right."

As if on cue, dad paused for a moment and gave us a friendly wave before resuming his wrestling match with the hood. He poked in the last reluctant fold, tossed the mallet onto the back seat and walked round to the front. "All ready now!" he called.

We watched him disappear into the reception area, which doubled as a waiting room.

As we walked over the examiner asked – in the sort of tone that expects a negative reply - "You have the keys, I trust?"

It gave me great joy to take them from my pocket and jangle them. "Yes."

"So you drove here?"

"Yes."

"And *you* parked?"

"Yes."

".. Right."

We got in and settled ourselves. He carefully positioned his immaculate shoes, avoiding the damp patch on the floor. My brother once claimed mushrooms grew there, but I've never believed that.

My examiner clutched the front of his clipboard. "OK, when you're ready Mr Brook, please drive out and turn right."

I had never driven the car with the hood down. Dad was certainly correct: I could see more. Except for directly behind, where the folded hood - being old, cranky and down too early in the year - had decided not to lie nice and flat, but to block out everything from half a lamp post down. If a very tall person walked behind us, I'd be able to see the top of their head. Probably.

Undaunted, I started the engine, got into first gear without too much noise and – with a surprising smoothness – my first driving test began.

It seemed to go OK for 5 or so minutes. I didn't stall the engine and – with both roof and window down – making hand signals was a doddle. The examiner contented himself with giving instructions of the 'take the next left turn' variety. His biro didn't seem overly busy and with the sun shining and a spring freshness in the air, all seemed to be good.

And then he said: "there is a roundabout coming up. Please take the third exit."

A roundabout! Roundabouts were unknown in the roads around East Meon. It was always something Dad I intended to practice, but never did.

I started to fret. The roundabout loomed into view, with arrows, road markings and signs like ancient hieroglyphics. My heart sank and my hands grew sweaty.

I got my gears muddled, my steering muddled, my feet muddled and my signalling muddled. I don't think I even slowed down. I remember brakes screeching and a fair bit of beeping and certainly shouting, which could have been me or the examiner or other drivers. Most probably it was all three.

But on the plus side it was all over in seconds, no-one was injured, no cars were dented and we did take the third exit onto a quiet suburban street. With an effort my examiner released his fingers, one by one, from his clipboard.

He managed to keep his voice relatively urbane. "... Right." A pause. And then, with the certain recklessness of surviving a near-death experience: "OK. Let's try a three-point turn, shall we?"

Now a three-point turn is something I'd practiced and knew how to do. It was also a matter of family contention. So, without thinking I said "Ah! The three-point turn. Dad and me, sorry, that should be Dad and I, argue about this, and Peter doesn't know. Why is it called a three-point turn when - if you draw a diagram - there are only two points?'

Rather niftily, while talking, I'd pulled over and waited for a car to pass.

The examiner eventually said "What?"

The car went by. I cranked the wheel around and we moved, straddling the middle of the road.

"Why is it called a three-point turn when there are only two points in it?" The car stalled. I added helpfully: "If you draw a diagram, there's only two points."

A Humber appeared from seemingly nowhere and politely settled down to wait.

The engine started first time. I forgot I was meant to be going forward and found reverse. The car lurched back. Looking over my shoulder I realised I couldn't see where we were going and - afraid of bashing into something – I jammed on the brake. The Minx stalled again and stopped.

Growing increasingly frantic, I started the engine with the car still in gear. We took a lurching bunny-hop backwards and stalled. Again.

Meantime a Ford and a motor cycle had arrived. I was getting quite an audience.

By now I was resenting my continued ability to stay alive. It seemed imperative to apologise so I grasped the top of the windscreen and heaved myself up, calling "sorry, sorry, sorry."

A third car arrived and then a fourth. The motor cyclist revved his engine.

Flopping back down I took a deep breath and let it out slowly. The steering wheel and the gear stick, not to mention the pedals, now seemed to exist on a malevolent, more distant, planet.

The examiners voice was calm. "Neutral. Put the car into neutral."

I pressed down on the clutch and moved the gearstick to neutral.

"Now start the engine." I did so. It was so nice having someone telling me what to do.

"Right. Now, clutch down and into first gear." I obeyed. "Good. And go to the side of the road and park."

His voice was so soothing it eliminated all problems. I drove the car the few yards to the side and parked perfectly.

I heard a long breath escape from my companion. "Now, handbrake on, engine off."

We sat there in silence as the Humber, the Ford, the motor cycle and the other cars went on their way. The sun had vanished, but I hardly noticed: my mood had descended so far South of happy it had reached Antarctica.

The examiner said ".. Right. Out you get. I'll drive."

Back at the test centre he parked at the same jaunty angle as I had. I think it was to do with the wing mirrors.

The Diana moment, from which this spate of memories stem, came as he climbed out of the car. He closed the door before leaning back in. And for a moment – and this is what I remember - the persona of the driving test examiner dropped away, like a cloak slipping to the floor. He suddenly seemed younger, likeable and good humoured. "Well," he said: "that was different. I don't think I need to tell you you've failed." He dropped a sheet on paper on the driver's seat. "There y'go. Good luck next time."

And he was gone.

On the paper was written: 'TAKE PROPER LESSONS' in big bold capital letters.

I showed dad, who immediately said, "good idea. I'll pay."

And, to finish this off, I took lessons with a man who liked to be called 'The Major' and drove a Triumph Herald with large 'L' plates riveted to the roof. After a month or so I retook the test and this time got all the way round before being failed. Again.

The Major said 'Ummmm …... A few more lessons I think.'

The stupid thing was, when – at the next try - I finally passed and later that day went out on my own in the Minx, I had nowhere I wanted to go and no-one to go and see. I drove around for about twenty minutes, stopped for a while (because I could) and then drove home, feeling utterly depressed and deflated.

Getting on a coach.

What: While hitching I get on a coach.

Where: In a layby on the way to Nottingham.

My age: 19

As a Diana Moment, this exists more in retrospect than it did at the time.

Let me explain: I remember the incident quite clearly, but it didn't become a 'Diana Moment' for a couple of years, because by then I'd gathered more experience and realised – in retrospect – what had been going on, even though – at the time – all I'd felt was a deadening unease.

Anyway, here's what happened, and how – later – I remember it.

During my first year at college, in an uncharacteristic bout of adventurous optimism, I decided to hitch back to Nottingham after the Easter Break.

I'd heard tales of hitchhikers being given sandwiches and there was an urban myth going around of a friend of a friend of a friend having a vivid experience in the hands of a curvaceous young woman driving a Ford on the A42 five miles North of Tamworth. And Tamworth was sufficiently close to Nottingham to somehow make this credible.

The day before leaving, during lunch, I announced my intention to hitch. Judy immediately said "Oh, do be careful!"

Mum frowned and I was expecting her to say something about Y fronts in the wash, but instead she asked where I intended starting.

Apart from establishing the location of Tamworth, I was unsure of the geography. All I knew was I needed to head North.

Mum – ever astute – followed up with: "have you got a map?"

I looked down at my slice of ham and some boiled potatoes left over from the previous evening. I mumbled that I did not. I was sort of vaguely intending to follow the same strategy as when I'd got lost on my Bantam: head in the general direction and hope to see useful signposts to places I knew. Eventually I'd meet a driver who knew where Nottingham was, and they might even take me there.

Mum said "We have one. I'll get it for you." She looked at me. "Make sure you use it."

The debate moved on to where I should start and how I should get there. It was one of those interminable family discussions of the no-one knows but everyone has an opinion variety.

In the end mum settled matters, as she so often did. She would take me – plus map and clean underpants – to the nearest point of the A272 and deposit me at a convenient spot.

Dad suggested I started early. I said 10 o'clock. He said 7. Mum said 8. We left at 8, on the dot. Dad and Judy watched us go. Dad gave a wave and Judy called out "take care!"

I was driving. It was nice having Mum with me. The Hillman rattled along, heading up the hill past farms, tithe cottages and private drives to rambling manor houses belonging to the horsey landed gentry.

She produced an envelope and slid it into my duffle bag. "Some money: just in case you get stuck."

I said: "Thanks Mum."

She patted my knee, I patted her hand, and the sun came out.

At a layby on the A272 we got out. She gave me a hug and a kiss, got into the driver's seat, waved, executed a neat U-turn and drove off. I stood, my duffle bag resting on the ground by my feet. The Minx reached the signpost for East Meon and mum's arm extended to indicate a turn. For a moment the car was broadside on, then it had gone.

So there I was, standing on my own at a layby on the A272 between Privett and Bordean, looking up and down an empty road.

I decided to have a quick pee. A car appeared. I waved my thumb. It didn't stop, the driver looking straight ahead as though I didn't exist. I nipped behind a tree, undid my fly and – of course – three cars passed before I could get back.

Later, I understood this to be an immutable law: it doesn't matter where you are: if you have a pee while hitching you miss a lift.

I can't remember the first driver that stopped, or where he dropped me off. Nor did any other the others make an impression except for one man in a red Ford Zephyr: he cruised to a halt about twenty yards past where I was standing. When I opened the door and said 'thank you for stopping' he looked wildly alarmed and spilt some coffee from a thermos into his lap. He hadn't even noticed me and had only stopped for a bit of packed lunch.

He was very good about it: just grinned and said he'd have to change his trousers and that gave him an excuse to finish early. But he drove off without offering a lift.

However I did make steady progress North, altering course according to the dictates of my invaluable map. As ever, Mum was right: without it I could have been sucked into Birmingham for half a day.

Sometime in the mid-afternoon I was once again standing at a layby. I was, I think, roughly midway between Leicester and Nottingham. The cars were going past, I was waving my thumb and thinking soon it'd be all over. The initial excitement had gone and now it'd turned into a bit of a slog. I was looking forward to a cup of tea and putting my feet up.

A large coach appeared, pulled in and stopped some distance on. The door hissed open. I paid it scant attention and continued to throw my thumb at likely looking cars.

"Did you want a lift?" Her voice was soft.

I jumped and turned. And there it was: the Diana Moment although - at the time – I didn't recognise it.

She was wearing a green sleeveless dress with a flower motif. It hugged her body from knee to shoulder, swelling beguilingly over her breast. Her bare arms were tanned. Her legs – what I could see of them – were smooth. She had a tentative, somewhat lopsided, shy smile.

I was instantly smitten.

And here, in cruel retrospect, when I examined her image a year or so later, is what I then saw: crow's feet; mascara; tan from a bottle; thin arms with scrawny joints; a slightly tipsy slurring of the words and chipped nail varnish. And I can also see her age: only slightly less than that of my mother.

Her smile became broader, her eyes larger, one eyebrow tilting invitingly. "I said, did you want a lift?"

I said "Er, yes. Thank you." and followed her to the coach.

I watched her ankles going up the steps; she was wearing white leather strapless sandals with a heel.

I stood by the driver. The door hissed shut. There were some thirty or forty passengers, ranging in age from ancient to maybe twenty. Grandmothers, Mums, Daughters. An all-female outing from God knows where for God knows what.

Most of them appeared to regard me as an embarrassing intruder, while some were more openly hostile. From the back seats my lady gave me a wave.

"Back here!" she cried. "Come and join us!"

Two other heads appeared: the back seat had obviously been populated by the rowdier elements of the outing.

"Yes, come on!" said one, and laughed.

"Back here, with us!" trilled the other. And laughed.

Without moving I said. "I'm not going very far."

They all laughed from the back seat. "That's what you think!"

Increasingly, I was wishing I were somewhere else.

I turned to the driver and asked. "Where are you going?"

He was already pulling out of the layby. He was wearing driving gloves with a weave of string over his knuckles.

"Nottingham" was his reply.

"Oh!" I said. I glanced round. My lady – with a determined look on her face - was coming up the aisle. The coach lurched from one lane to the next and she clutched the corner of a seat.

I addressed the driver. "Can you drop me at the next roundabout?"

He grinned: "What's it worth?" I couldn't think of a reply, but almost immediately he began slowing down.

My lady had finally reached us. She put her hand on my arm. She said "We don't bite. Just a bit of fun. Come on!"

Over her shoulder I could see lines of unfriendly eyes, except for two pairs at the back, watching like predators.

The coach pulled to a stop. The door hissed open. There was no layby: the driver had just pulled in slightly and parked. I could see dusty grass, some pebbles, a cart track and a broken signpost.

I said "Sorry." Clutching the duffle bag to my chest, I descended and got off. As the coach departed the tyres pinged out a couple of small stones.

I had to walk a short distance before finding a suitable place for hitching. I was back at college in about an hour.

Essentially, this most fleeting of Diana Moments was just a woman in a green dress, asking if I needed a lift. And me saying 'yes.'

But beneath that I must have sensed something wasn't right, or as I thought it should be. And – once on the coach – I'd had immediately felt increasingly uneasy and so left as soon as I could.

It wasn't just the hostile eyes or the evident amusement from the driver. There was, I believe now, something more fundamental, which I didn't realise until later, turning this mundane incident into a Diana Moment.

Yep, OK, to cut to the chase: I sensed she was both needy and phoney: old, used, dried up desperate mutton dressed, oiled, primped and primed to appear as lamb.

My first car.

What: I buy my first car.

Where: Nottingham.

My age: 20

I bought my first ever car while I was at Nottingham college. In an idle moment I had entered a newspaper competition. And won first prize: a car!

Well, not quite. The cheapskate newspaper had more than one winner, but the budget was for only one car. So we each got a share: just over £87. I stared at the cheque. To a student in 1964, it was riches indeed. I might not have a shiny bright brand-new car, but I had been given the means to buy a reasonable second hand one.

I got hold of a chap living in the same block. We'll call him Ted. Ted's uncle in New Zealand was a car mechanic, so – by a process of osmosis unknown to science – Ted must know a lot about cars. Even if he didn't, it didn't stop him.

I told him I had a £50 budget and we scanned the small ads in the local paper. Ted stabbed his finger down. His hair was auburn and his skin pink. If he stood in front of red curtains and blushed, his head vanished. "That's a good car! Get that one!"

It was for a Jag, £200. A car, Ted told me, to die for.

I shook my head and pointed at a *'Good little runner'* for £30. "What about...?"

Ted was scornful. "They're rubbish! My uncle could tell you: their engines fall out after 30 thousand miles, guaranteed!"

In the end, we agreed a Simca Aronde (*'Good clean car, no rust, runs well'*) at £50 would do. I rang the man and that very evening – just as the light was failing - it was there, gleaming seductively under the lamps of the college car park.

The seller wore a coat with a fur collar, had Brylcreemed hair and a 5'oclock shadow. He told us he was selling it for a little old lady who used it once a week to go to church, but – sadly – her eyesight was failing, so she'd stopped driving. She'd had the car for years and only wanted it to go to a good home, so that's why it was so cheap. And, by the way, others were interested and 'cash is king.'

Ted revved the engine, and declared it ran OK.

We drove around the car park and checked the lights. The gearstick was on the steering column which – I told myself – was why first gear was difficult to find.

The seller nodded approvingly at our thoroughness and said – to Ted - "I see you know a lot about cars."

Ted puffed himself up and drew me to one side. "I'd snap it up," he said: "too good to miss."

So I snapped it up. I rang home and told dad. He spoke from a long experience of keeping old cars on the road and stressed the importance of oil. "If you run out of petrol, you just stop. No real harm done. If you run out of oil, you don't stop, but your engine might never go again." I said I'd keep a can of oil in the boot. But I didn't.

And – shortly after becoming a car owner - I acquired my first college girlfriend. Sometimes I pretended they were not linked, but looking back I'm pretty sure they were.

Kate was willowy, came from North London and had long hair. I think the relationship was a bit of an experiment for both of us and – as shall be seen – didn't last: one way or another, the car lasted longer in my life than she did.

At the end of term we set off down the newly constructed M1 motorway. I would drop her off at home and continue on to East Meon.

I had never driven on a motorway and I'm pretty sure the car hadn't either. It seemed to take rather a long time to crank our speed up to 70 MPH. But we got there and cruised along. After about an hour Kate pointed at the dashboard: "What's that mean?"

I peered through the steering wheel. A red light shone back. I'd been resolutely ignoring it for 10 minutes, but now a nasty, sickening knot formed in my stomach. So I said I wasn't sure, but we'd stop when we could. The car seemed to be more sluggish, so I put my foot down. Pretty soon I couldn't get our speed above 60. A faint knocking could be heard, like a distant ogre trying to break into a castle.

We passed a sign informing us the next service station was in 10 miles.

Another red light came on and our speed dropped to 50. The knocking became louder, more persistent. As did the knot in my stomach. I continued trying to disregard both and we soldiered on.

I must hand it to that Simca Aronde. Despite being driven by an idiot, making painful noises, slowing down and successively turning on every warning light it possessed, it still kept going, finally expiring in a cloud of steam on the slip road to the services. I opened the bonnet and was greeted by further steam, oil everywhere and the certainty the engine was totally buggered.

I sat down in the driving seat and stared vacantly ahead. Kate said something but it barely registered. The car rocked as she got out, slammed the door and marched off.

I felt nothing so intensely it was memorable. A Diana Moment of total numbness and disconnection with the world and myself.

I should have listened to dad, about the oil.

How could I be so dumb?

I just want to die!

Then Kate came back, noisily opened the door and said her brother was on his way, to rescue us.

I surfaced back into the real world. My car - instead of being a complex machine capable of movement and going round corners – was now just a heap of useless metal and – if the expression on her face was anything to go by – Kate was rapidly becoming an ex-girlfriend.

Much to my surprise, I eventually managed to get the car repaired, but my relationship with Kate was doomed: it limped on for another term and died in the summer holidays. Yep, OK: 'died in the summer holidays' is just another way of saying 'I was dumped.'

And, looking back: I really can't blame her.

And as for the car? I cannot remember exactly what happened. I do know that – even after being fixed - it was never quite right: the windscreen wipers would mysteriously fail to function and starting became so erratic I had to park it – facing down – on a slope.

I expect the next time I hauled it along for repair the mechanic offered me ten quid and I said yes.

A whiter shade of pale.

What: I hear Procol Harum on the radio while in my car.

Where: Driving towards a hill just South of East Meon.

My age: 22

Describing actual music – the notes and suchlike - with words is way above my skillset as a writer. Simply, I don't know enough: my knowledge of how music is constructed is very much at the level of 'Doh, a deer, a female deer, ray, a drop of golden sun..'

In other words, I know zilch.

But I'm going to have a go at describing how music can affect me. Specifically, how one bit of music made me sit up and take notice and – in so doing – created a Diana Moment.

A 'Whiter shade of pale' by Procol Harum didn't change my life or alter my character in any significant way: far from it. But it hit me in right in the gut.

The summer of 1967 came to be known as 'the summer of Love,' but all that flower power, festivals, flares and pot largely passed me by. I was far more interested in bridge, eating, feeling lonely and being resentful. And as for 'pop' music, I might watch 'Top of the Pops' or 'Juke Box Jury' if they were on, but I recall little pleasure from them.

I had been a teacher for one year. I'd hated every minute. Teaching is a near impossible job requiring a wide range of difficult skills ranging from people management to enthusing over unrequired and useless facts. A range of skills I just do not possess.

I once met a teacher – a bitter man, worn down by the pram in the hall, the lack of money and his own ineptitude. He declared universal education was a stupid waste of time, for there was little point in trying to teach the thick and the uninterested. They would of necessity pick up the skills needed for their grotty lives by living that grotty life, and if they didn't well, life is tough.

So he advocated big lockable gates at school entrances, letting in only pupils who wished to learn and those who wished to teach.

He sprayed spittle and smoke, dropped cigarette ash on the floor and everyone tried to avoid him.

But after a year of teaching I found myself often thinking he could be right. And whenever I did, I despised myself.

So during that summer I was facing the future with a growing sense of doom, dread and defeat.

Was this it? Chalk and talk and fret and stress for the rest of my life? Years of pretending I'd get better at it and things would get easier, but at the same time knowing this was not true. Teaching had relentlessly exposed me to me as what I was, and what I was, was an unhappy, useless teacher.

Having made few friends where I worked, I had gone home for the holiday. Mum and Dad had now retired to a bungalow at the top of their garden and built a small annex where M.A. and Jo – my maternal grandmother and her sister – were now living. Every Sunday they would make a stately procession to our living room, to sit and sip sherry while Mum popped in and out from basting the roast and Dad sat there thinking about the weeds in his vegetable patch.

I filled the long days driving aimlessly around, parking, reading and worrying about the future. One evening, after supper, I headed South, thinking to go over the hill and down to Clanfield, where I'd turn left onto the A3 and dawdle up to Petersfield, to drive past my old school before completing the loop back to East Meon.

A mile or so from the village, just as I was starting to ascend, a strange and instantly beguiling music, unlike anything I had ever heard before, bleed out from the radio and infiltrated the car.

I was transfixed.

Prior to that moment, my musical tastes had been a mixture of things I listened to because everyone else did (Elvis, the Beatles, Bob Dylan) things I enjoyed (The Beach Boys, Joan Baez, Beethoven) and things I was trying to appreciate but didn't really like in the least (string quartets).

In other words the usual mixture of good stuff, goodish stuff, mediocracy, pretentious tomfoolery and dross.

'Good Vibrations' by the Beach Boys had given me pause, but 'A Whiter Shade of Pale' made the hair on the back of my neck stand up. Really. Absolutely. Literally.

I pulled over and stopped. I didn't dare kill the engine as this made the radio hiccup.

The words, shaped like a ghost and sung like a wraith, made little sense, but I understood them.

Sometimes – very, very occasionally - when writing, I put down a sentence that cannot be improved. It sits there, five or six, maybe ten or fifteen, words in English where every single one works hard to justify its existence on the page.

And when that happens it is a joy. And further, when read, it bestows that joy on the reader, for they are beholding something perfect.

For me, the opening lyrics of 'A Whiter Shade of Pale,' complete with those stately descending chords, burrowed straight into my soul.

Yep, OK: maybe I'm over cooking this. 'Soul' might seem bit strong and I should put in some caveats about time, place and mood, etc etc. For surely, if the listener is not receptive, the beauty is lost.

Whatever: that is a debate for deeper minds than mine.

While it was playing, I sat unmoving in the car. And when it had finished, I remained where I was, trying and failing to remember precisely what I had heard.

Eventually I went on my way, uninspiringly following the route I had planned. Up the hill, down to Clanfield, left onto the A3 ..... and so forth.

Some weeks later, as I dourly headed North towards the dreaded start of term, I decided to give teaching just one more year.

In fact that one more year became one more year plus one more term before teaching and I parted company for good.

But that is another Diana Moment.

Stopping golf.

What: I stop playing golf.

Where: Petersfield Golf club car park.

My age: 20

Once retired, dad took up what might be called social golf. He didn't enter any competitions that I know of or record a handicap. He strolled around Petersfield golf course a couple of times a week, sometimes on his own, more often with a pal.

The course at that time was nine holes clustered to the East and South of the Heath pond. It was open to the public, who wandered on the fairways and sometimes sunbathed on the greens.

Once, when we were playing, dad hit his ball into a bunker. "Well," he said: "at least we know where it is." This was an in joke, a reference to my habit of blasting my ball so off course it probably landed on the moon. It was a short hole, mostly downhill, with the bunker – with dad's ball – on the edge of the green. I hit my ball and scuffed it down the hill. With the following wind pushing it along it went OK. We picked up our golf bags and followed.

My ball was sitting up nicely. I got out my wedge, in the forlorn hope I might actually land it on the green, but fully expecting to scuff it again and end up in the bunker. At least then we'd know where it was.

For those with little talent – such as myself - golf is an unrelentingly cruel game. All you must do is hit the ball so it ends up in the hole. And that's it. A child of two could understand it. But for me, there was a gigantic unbridgeable gap between knowing what to do and actually doing it.

I stood over the ball, arms and shoulders tensing in anticipation of defeat.

I never did make the shot, for Dad's ball miraculously appeared from the bunker, arching up in a neat curve to softly land a few feet away from us.

Dad and I both stared at it, then towards the bunker. A bald head, fringed with dark hair and fronted by a pleasantly smiling face, emerged like a submarine surfacing. When he spoke, his accent was so strong it could have thickened soup.

To my astonishment, Dad gave a bark of pleased surprise. He strode over, saying (he told me later) 'Hello! Nice to see you!' first in Spanish, then Italian and finally in halting Portuguese.

The other man climbed out of the bunker. He was very short and round, with a spherical head perched on a spherical body. Paint him white and he'd be a perfect snowman. His smile stretched from ear to ear as he opened his arms and let go a machine-gun rattle of incomprehensible words.

Dad responded, likewise talking a somewhat more hesitant gobble-de-gook. I had forgotten his Cambridge degree was in modern languages. Italian and Spanish, I think.

He was always looking to practice his rusting language skills. And the amiable man in the bunker – and his equally amiable wife (also comfortably round, who surfaced a few seconds later finishing off a scotch egg) were absolutely perfect for him.

Within five minutes – less – they had exchanged names, established they lived only a few miles apart and written down phone numbers on a torn paper bag, previously used for sausage rolls. They had one left over, which Dad ate as we wandered on our way. I remember seagulls swooping down to pick up flakes of pastry.

I include this anecdote about dad because I feel I am not otherwise doing him justice in this memoir. He was very intelligent, extremely kind and sociable, with few affectations. So here he is, characteristically making a pal in the middle of a golf game. It never occurred to him to object to their settling down for lunch in a bunker.

But I did. I picked up my ball and – seething - went to the next tee. Because - for me - golf had become obsessive.

It was the summer after my second year at college. My first ever proper girlfriend was in the process of dumping me in slow motion and I was beginning to suspect teaching was not for me.

So golf became the ideal displacement activity. After all, all I had to do to improve was to improve. Just to hit the ball better with one of my motley mismatched set of clubs, found in the attic and carted around in a moth-eaten golf-bag.

But in truth, however hard I tried, I hit a good shot maybe just once every four or five times I played. The ball would fly straight, curving perfectly up into the air, landing far down the fairway or - with some backspin – on the green, to finish near the hole.

And these shots – certainly well less than one percent of the total – became, in my head, how I normally played. All the scuffing, the topping, the slicing, the hooking, the lost balls, the terrible putts, the five shots to get out of a bunker: they were but aberrations, temporary glitches in an otherwise near perfect progression from hole to hole.

But of course, under it all, I knew how rubbish a player I was. And I knew I would not improve, that all the practice and instruction in the world would never make me into – for instance – a better player than dad, a man then approaching seventy who seldom hit the ball more than a hundred yards but normally hit it straight.

And at a deeper level still, usually in the small hours when lying awake and tracing the faint outline of an old damp stain on the ceiling, was the certain, sober knowledge that golf was simply not worth it, that it was only a game: that real life, in the form of college and the future and being dumped: that was what mattered.

After all, sport is an activity so trivial you can afford to take it seriously.

I was so filled morose tension and self-hate that, when playing I'd become progressively more and more sulky, given to shouting and swearing and occasionally throwing clubs at innocent rabbits. I do not know to this day how dad put up with it.

And so we come to the Diana Moment. Dad and I have just finished yet another excruciatingly awful game. Two rounds of nine holes with dad plugging away, short arm jabbing the ball down the middle of the fairway or onto the green. Me being my usual sulking, useless at golf self, growing increasingly monosyllabic and full of self-resenting tension.

The boot of the car is open. Dad has stowed his clubs away. Mine are still slung over my shoulder. We have parked near some trees. A breeze is blowing and the sun is casting dancing shadows.

And from somewhere, a sane, reasonable part of me surfaces and takes control.

I find myself saying "I'm not playing anymore." I lower my shoulder, allowing the golf-bag to slip down. I grip the strap and it hangs for a second or so before I cast it into the boot of the car. Into darkness and out of my life. And as I do so, I feel at least one of the cares of my world has vanished.

Dad says "Are you sure?"

I say "Yes." and then needlessly add, as if it were not obvious: "I'm not enjoying it anymore."

Dad closes the boot and we go home.

That evening I wrote a letter to my (possibly ex?) girl-friend. It was full of noble sentiment and (I'm sure) other stupid crap. I did not send it.

And – having already put in two years at college – I shoved my doubts about teaching to one side for at least another year.

I never played golf again. Even now, retired and with both time and means, I am not tempted.

It's only a very stupid game.

Having a rant.

What: I go on a rant.

Where: Nottingham College of Education.

My age: 19

One of the patterns of my life is of slow adjustment. Whenever something new comes along it takes me a while to come to terms with it. I sometimes have the fanciful idea I'm like a white corpuscle, meandering along the bloodstream of my life. Every so often I stumble against something new. Then I need to surround it, smother it and ingest it. And in so doing, make it part of me. After which, I continue my serene, purposeless drifting.

When I switched from my private primary school to a secondary modern, it took me two years of acclimatisation before I felt - more or less – on top of things. And again, when I moved on to a grammar school, I only just fumbled my way to a single 'A' level pass.

And so it was when I went to Nottingham College of Education. My first year was academically rubbish and socially not so good. I went to lectures and thought I understood them, but my written work was not what was required, missing the point by margins so wide an aeroplane could land on them. My despairing tutor showed me a 'model' essay. I hated it, and swore I'd never write one like it. All those references! No imagination, no spark of creativity: it just regurgitated opinions and sentences that 'experts' had written down. I wanted my essays to be original, sparkly with ideas and concepts, not a flat boring rehash of dull thoughts from some chalky old bastard.

I found myself put into in a small group of likewise independently minded students. Or: to put it more accurately, students who missed the point. Or, to put it even more precisely, the bone-headed thickos who just didn't get it, whatever 'it' was.

Our special tutor was short, round, wore waistcoats, smelt of cigarettes and took no shit. His brief was simple: to instruct us on how to write essays of the required sort.

In truth, it didn't take him long. We had I think one session as a group and a couple of one-to-ones. I'm not sure about the others, but I responded well to his direct approach. In many ways he reminded me of Mr Brown, my old maths teacher.

His opening salvo was to tell us we could well be kicked out of college if we didn't improve. His next broadside was – slightly - more nuanced: "I've read some of your stuff, and I don't think you're dumb." His emphasis on the personal pronoun spoke volumes. A girl with frizzy hair gave a sniffle.

"All you need," he continued "is a template." He handed round some mimeographed instructions. "So, here we go. Paragraph 1: repeat the question. Paragraph 2: give an overview of your answer. Paragraph 3: note any related questions that haven't been asked and explain why you're not going to answer them. Para 4: -"

The girl with unfortunate hair put her hand up and spoke for us all. "I'm bewildered. Questions you haven't been asked?"

He looked pityingly at her. "No wonder you're in this group. By noting related questions that aren't there, you show you've thought about it and – more importantly – you can fill up maybe half a page with stuff that makes a good impression while being easy to do." He looked round at us all, frowning at the confusion in our faces. "For example, supposing the question is why are apples red?" He took a breath. "Para 1: repeat the question. Para 2: give a summary of your answer, whatever that is. Para 3: 'I am not going to discuss the general question of fruit colour, except where relevant.' Then you go on to discuss why you're not going to discuss it." He paused again, then sighed. "I tell you what, forget about para 3: promote all the others up one."

We diligently crossed out our para 3s and moved all the others up a place.

In retrospect, I am uncertain if he was just making it up as he went along, but at the time I listened with increasing interest and understanding. It hadn't occurred to me that writing an essay could be reduced to a process. There was no need for invention or good writing. There was in fact little need to be clever: all you had to do was follow the script. My resolve never to write a boring essay full of quotes vanished as if it had never been.

Those smudged, mimeographed, altered rules became a vital part of the scaffold supporting my scholastic endeavours. What pleasure there might have been in reading my efforts took a nosedive, while my grades had a corresponding leap upwards. They were never high, but sensibly stayed between fifty and sixty percent most of the time. In other words: good enough.

The extra tuition occurred about half way through the summer term. A few weeks later – as my grades and confidence were improving - we come to this particular Diana Moment.

It was a hot – very hot – weekend. End of term loomed and there was a sense of frivolity and devil-may-care in the student body.

The accommodation blocks were arranged roughly around a green sward. I was sitting - with some others - in our little first-floor common room. The window was open. I was probably reading.

There came some shouts from down below. On the grass, carrying buckets, a washing up bowl and a small watering can with a yellow rose painted on it, were six or so occupants from one of the opposing blocks.

They were all in swimming trunks and one was wearing a bandana with a feather tucked in it.

They were challenging us to a water fight.

One even said 'be there or be square,' a phrase so out of date it had started coming round again.

I got to my feet and leant out of the window. My voice might be nice; it can also be very, very loud. I let rip. "You stupid bastards, what the heck d'you think you're playing at, standing there looking like idiots, challenging us to a water fight – d'you think we're five years old, you absolutely moronic stupid cretinous bits of pond life … "

I ranted on and on, my voice – already loud – increasing in volume. Faces started appearing at windows and doors. The group below – good natured, nice people, out for a bit of fun – began looking shame-faced and shuffling their feet. I gave them no chance of reply, unconsciously adopting the old trick - used by politicians through the ages - of pausing for breath only briefly, and then in unexpected places. I finished with something like "..so bugger off, you insane bastards!" I slammed the window shut and sat down.

They crept off, taking their buckets and the watering can with them. The chap with the feather stripped the bandana from his head, as if suddenly ashamed.

I looked round: the common room now seemed empty, but then a fellow student stuck his head up from behind a chair, where he had been both sheltering from my tirade and making sure he could not be associated with the mad idiot shouting out of the window.

"Christ!" he said, "bugger me; what brought that on?"

I shrugged, for I did not know and – even now - I'm still not sure. But I remember it because it was a thing of unusual intensity and force and quite out of character. I had somehow stepped away from my usual diffident approach to life and stopped being the person who apologies when other people bump into him.

Quite often, in TV murder mysteries, the least likely person, someone on the periphery of events, turns out to be the killer. The postman, for instance, or a cleaner: characters who pop in and out of the action for perfectly legitimate purposes. And very often, when uncovered, the reason for their heinous act of violence was resentment building up over the years until it exploded into vengeance.

OK, so that's mere pop psychology, an easy way of providing a motive to justify a surprise ending in a drama with little connection to real life. But I tend to think of my out-of-character tirade in the same terms. I was nineteen years old. I had been struggling, academically and socially, for several years. My concept of what my life should be like was at variance with my life as experienced.

And then, right out of the blue, I was presented with a chance to express this resentment.

For a small group of inoffensive, near-naked people had issued a challenge.

In other words, they started it and – in waiting for a response – had passed the initiative to me, sitting high up, above their heads. In standing and leaning out, fully dressed and framed by the window, I had become like a king, reducing them to mere supplicants.

And so I let rip, as a monarch is perfectly entitled to do, tearing into them for I was tired of tearing into myself.

Afterwards, I felt a curious mixture of satisfaction and relief plus an overwhelming need to apologise. Which I never did.

Politics.

What: I learn of Francis Pym being sacked

Where: On the TV.

My age: 38

I am not going to write much about politics. For a lot of people it is a complete turn off, as it was for me for many years: it was just a thing that happened elsewhere with little relevance to my real life.

So I'm attempting to squeeze all my politics into this one tirade-filled – but hopefully entertaining – chapter.

Skip it if you like: no one will ever never know and I won't lose any sleep.

Many years ago my maternal Grandmother (Mum's mum: 'M.A.') was watching Harold Macmillan (the prime minister of the day) on the TV. Grainy black and white showing an elderly gent with a moustache. It might sound odd, but I remember not remembering what he was saying or indeed the subject under discussion. Perhaps I immediately dismissed it as completely unconnected to my life at the time – I would have been maybe thirteen. But what I do remember – after he'd no doubt spewed out some sonorous load of uplifting old tosh - is M.A. breathing in long and deeply and her chin lifting proudly. She said 'Hear hear!'

Even then, I thought: 'What?'

The years of my being hardly aware of politics trundled past. Sometime in the seventies there were power cuts, the three-day week and people milling around, shouting and holding placards reading '4% of nothing is nothing. We want 8%.' At that time I was living in an attic bedsit in Worthing and trying to be a writer. No, let's rephrase that: trying to become a writer who got paid for writing.

Across the upstairs landing was another bedside, mirroring mine. Living in it was a young chap. His name has long gone, so let's call him Ben. Logical thinking was not what Ben did. In truth, even 'thinking' is probably stretching it. If ignorance is a disease, he was raddled. I believe he held down a job, but as what doing what it is hard to imagine. He once went to an amateur dramatic play I was in and afterwards asked me, in all seriousness, if I had really learnt all those words, or did I just make it up as I went along.

The news was flooded with items about power cuts and exhortations to use as little electricity as possible. I had occasion to go into Ben's room. He had switched on every single one of his electric appliances: oven (with door open); TV; radio; kettle; a couple of heaters: everything. It was boiling in there and Ben himself was sitting in his underpants attempting - with Sellotape – to turn his toaster permanently on. He'd tried elastic bands, but they kept melting.

Not unreasonably, I asked him what he was doing and hadn't he heard of potential power cuts?

His reply was uniquely Ben and strangely unanswerable. He said, "well if there's going to be cuts, I'm going to use mine before any other bugger gets it."

Even in those heightened, angry times, I found politics boring: it took a few more years, the rubbish piled up in the streets, Margaret Thatcher stomping about, the Falklands war and the next general election before I sat up and took real notice.

And the Diana Moment for this was a BBC TV News item, a week or so after Margaret Thatcher had won her second term. I was eating some baked beans and wondering what else was on when the Newsreader said something about someone being sacked. I took no notice.

I was just loading a forkful when a politician I'd vaguely heard of – Francis Pym – appeared. An amiable looking chap, sitting down, with an elbow resting on a round table made of dark wood. He was saying – quite reasonably – that landslide election victories and large majorities were not necessarily a good thing.

Apparently, this was the straw that broke the camel's back, and why Thatcher had sacked him. It was also a tipping point for me. Even with my own lukewarm understanding of democracy, what he'd said made absolute sense. And yet that wretched woman had got rid of him! Yep, she'd shot the speaker of truth! A still of Thatcher appeared: head, shoulders, string of pearls, concrete hair and fake concern. To my now jaundiced eye it was an unpleasant, even loathsome, image.

I think it necessary to emphasise that, before then, I had an idealised notion of the democratic process. I believed politicians were driven by a civic duty to try and make life better for all citizens. Often it was unclear about what should be done to achieve this noble end. Therefore they discussed it. If they couldn't come to an agreement, they took a vote.

All very civilised and polite, founded on the assumption politicians were intelligent, fair minded, would courteously listen to opposing argument and – crucially – be willing to change their minds.

Yeah, I know: absolute balls: how I had managed to live to nearly forty (forty!) in this cloud cuckoo land of rose-tinted spectacles, soft soap and horse shit is astounding.

But this fantasy world was destroyed by Margaret Thatcher sacking Francis Pym. In that Diana Moment I realised she was not interested in anything other than dictating what should happen and to have it happen, regardless of consequence.

Not to mince words, I have hated conservative politicians and their God-awful policies ever since. Every single thing they do is driven by the ultimate aim of moving money and resources from the poor to the rich. Their perfect world is one where they are the masters and everyone else is a serf. Pretending to care for the lower orders (that's you and me) is a bit of chicanery they reluctantly drag out of the cellar near a general election, when they wrap it a heady mix of righteousness, patriotism and warnings of a dystopian future if they are not triumphant.

The sad and pathetic thing is, it often works. I am writing this in the Summer of 2020. We have effectively had a conservative government for the last ten years, with one appalling Prime Minister after another culminating in the absolute stupidity of Brexit and the vicious slaughter of the COVID-19 pandemic. I can't in truth blame them for the pandemic, but I do blame them for being lazy and incompetent in their responses, resulting in probably the highest death toll per capita in the world.

Often, I hate conservatives so much it hurts.

Not that other political parties haven't had their lengthy moments of my disgust, but the conservatives were there first, brutally breaking through my apathy and outraging me enough to forget my baked beans.

Authoritarianism is always ugly but – sadly – it is often the defining trait of the motley collection of politicians who aspire to the top job.

In fact I would argue – as many have done before me – that to want to be the Prime Minister should automatically disqualify you from being the Prime Minister.

After all, to any sensible, well-balanced person, being the Prime Minister is perhaps the worst job in the world. All that responsibility and decision making in various shades of murky grey, knowing that millions of people could be affected by the choices made? Who on earth would want that? It could only be sought after and welcomed by a warped mind.

The old saying that bad turds always rise is as true in Westminster as it is in Lima or Paris. But I don't think any country has yet developed a satisfactory democratic delivery system. Our 'first past the post' elections are plainly nonsense, while other solutions seem only marginally better.

So, soon after Margaret Thatcher inadvertently turned me into a socialist, I joined the labour party. And found many of them to be completely useless twats as well. It probably goes with the territory, it's hard to say. There was little to do and we all sat around in a circle whingeing about the dreaded Thatcher before going home to await the next call to arms. For me it never came, not even when – I assume – they needed some envelope stuffers at the next election.

After Thatcher was dumped and seen crying in her car (hooray!) there was dreary John Major, another conservative. I have to admit, I do have a slightly soft spot for him: he never appeared to believe he was A. Prime Minister or B. That he was up to it. Such a refreshing change from Thatcher's honking and destructive conviction politics.

But then Major went and trashed the railways and all my sympathy evaporated.

Even conservative robber barons run out of steam eventually, and Labour swept into power in 1997. The instantly forgettable, somewhat slippery, always grinning Tony Blair became Prime Minister. He did a good job of being all things to all people for quite a while, even winning an election or two but then put on too-tight trousers, went to war in the middle East and departed in a fart of his own self-importance.

Gordon Brown lasted long enough to save the banks (Good thing? Bad thing? The jury's still out) and pose with his family before he too fell into the arsehole of history and vanished.

And from 2010 on, things have turned increasingly bizarre. First there was the coalition, with 'take from the poor and give to the rich' rebadged as austerity, followed by Cameron vs Corbyn, otherwise known as twerp vs twaddle, with the twerp soon going down against the manky Brexit steamroller. Theresa May strutted about for a while but floated off into Nevermanageditland before the utterly deplorable Johnson, a man so useless he couldn't organise a fart in a cowshed, barged his sleazy way to the top.

It is even more appalling on the other side of the Atlantic, with an orange manfant avidly trying to destroy democracy.

And the big one which makes all human concerns as significant as tadpoles in an ocean, is just getting going.

Yep, I mean climate change: the real existential threat. I feel compelled to remind you that 'existential' means 'of existence.' Climate change truly threatens the actual existence of humanity. Without wishing to sound overly dramatic, that's you and me and billions of others, being eliminated by an indifferent mass extinction.

I don't have that long to live now: 5 years will take me to eighty, 10 to eighty-five. I'm aiming at ninety, but one can only call that wildly ambitious, and anyway, in my lowest moments, I have the feeling most of us will be wiped out by then.

We are, right now, quite literally, rubbishing the planet. Our only home. It would be easy to write that climate change is nature fighting back. But in fact it's much much worse than that. Nature doesn't fight back: that's mistakenly anthropomorphising processes we don't understand and can only – marginally – control. It gives the false impression that if, somehow, we manage to beat nature – whatever that means - all would be well. But nature is what it is, and will do what it does: it has no soul or consciousness and cannot therefore even notice that we are here and will not notice we are gone.

To us, time has meaning and importance. We measure it out in grudging spoonfuls like starving misers drinking soup. But nature doesn't give a shit. Years, decades, centuries, millennia: these words and concepts have no meaning to the non-sentient.

We will be squashed and cease to be. And nothing will regret it or even notice we have gone.

My daughter's beautiful children are only 2 and 4. And we are leaving them a wrecked world and an abysmal future.

Well, I've had my rant(s), feel correspondingly depressed and so will now stop.

My first flight.

What: I go up in an aeroplane for the first time.

Where: Gatwick airport

My age: 23

This memory came at the start of my first holiday abroad, and seamlessly blends into the Diana Moment that follows: 'The Idiot who couldn't swim.'

I was twenty-three and – as usual – behind the curve. For a couple of years I'd been hearing it was possible to just jump on a plane for a holiday abroad, but never thought this meant me.

But I was tempted by the marketing of luscious sun-drenched Mediterranean beaches and curvy bronzed girls in bikinis. And I was feeling restless, even reckless, so a holiday abroad, on a beach, it would be!

My budget was limited, so I looked in the small ads of the weekend papers, picked one at the bottom end of my price range and ended up going to Gatwick airport to catch a plane to Perpignan in France.

Ambitiously, I half expected to fly there by jet. A Comet, to be precise. My sister Judy had been on one and described taking off by saying 'whoosh!'

In the departure lounge I joined a motley collection of travellers, complete with motley items of luggage. At least one rucksack was festooned with an emergency supply of stout British loo roll, as if abroad people had nothing for wiping their arses. My battered old family suitcase with the busted lock tied down with string was perfectly at home. Out through the large windows, swish aeroplanes were enticingly parked, a couple of Comets among them.

When told, we all trooped out, excitedly headed towards a Comet, but disappointingly turned left and left again and there, on its own, like a shy, tentative aunt with halitosis at a barbecue, was the robust sight of a Dan-Air Airspeed Ambassador. Our transport to abroad.

The Airspeed Ambassador was as distant from a Comet as an arthritic warthog is to a greyhound. The Comet had sleek lines, jets built into the wings and on taking off went Whoosh! The Airspeed Ambassador had a reassuringly 'don't worry, I'll get you there' shape, clunky propellers with petrol engines and when taking off sounded like a demented tractor.

I wished to appear as if I did this boring flying thing every day, and loitered as we walked over the tarmac. Inevitably I finished up in an aisle seat. By craning my neck I could see out of the window and was rewarded with a view of mainly wing, with a small triangle of tarmac in the bottom right-hand corner. At least, I said to myself, I'll be able to tell when we leave the ground.

The seats were filled, the luggage stowed, the doors were closed and the engines started. The whole plane vibrated and I thought 'Wow! This is it!' Truly thrilling stuff, but then of course nothing happened for what felt like an hour or two, until there was a little lurch forward. Someone yelled 'chocks away!'

We slowly taxied past all the other planes and steadily kept on. The tarmac turned to concrete with weeds growing in the gaps. We seemed to be leaving all civilisation behind, but eventually, we stopped and turned. There was a brief pause before, in short order, the following things happened:

- The whine and vibration of the propellers increased until conversation became impossible.
- The cabin crew sat down, fastened their seatbelts and grabbed something to hang onto.
- An amplified voice echoed some indecipherable words. (Probably about flight times and the weather, but could have been 'Here we go, cross your fingers everyone!').
- The pilot seemed to release the handbrake, for the plane suddenly jolted forward and gathered speed.
- And the man sitting next to me turned and looked out, obscuring my view.

We hurtled down the runway, rattling on and on for what felt like forever. It seemed impossible the runway was that long and I was trying to remember if there were trees at the end when, surprisingly gracefully, we took off.

My companion sat back and opened a book. As we banked and turned, I had a thrilling triangular glimpse of shrinking houses, moving figures smaller than marionettes and cars like Dinky toys.

Then, we went into some clouds and everything became grey, which was sort of exciting.

Then, we were flying in sunshine, with the clouds beneath us, which was very exciting.

Then, I discovered the one immutable law of flying: it's boring.

It's no wonder passengers drink on planes and eat the plastic chicken and the what-on-earth-is-that! Pud. It passes the time. My companion – obviously an experienced flyer – had a book with a lurid cover, great wodges of text and – as far as I could see – no chapters.

I had a book, but it was in my suitcase, lodged somewhere in an overhead rack. I lacked the courage to try and retrieve it. So I sat and sat and sat and sat and sat and sat and sat. The clouds remained clouds. The woman in front had a big nose which remained a big nose and the chap across the aisle had to move his leg when the drinks trolley came along and then again when they dispensed the food. I ate a lukewarm something or other, managed to have a pee and sat and sat and sat and sat and sat and sat and sat and sat.

After a subjective year or two the voice said something indecipherable again and soon afterwards the following things happened:

- The plane banked a bit, losing speed.
- The seatbelt light came on, the cabin crew were suddenly busy locking things away and checking we were all strapped in.
- Outside became grey as we dropped down into the clouds.

- There was a clunk and the whine of wheels wheezing into position.
- The cabin crew sat down, fastened their seatbelts and grabbed something to hang onto.
- The mist vanished and my companion put his book away, clutched the arm rests, leant back, closed his eyes and reassuringly said 'Oh God, I hate this bit.'
- At wing level, tops of trees appeared, moving incredibly fast.
- Large sheds whizzed by.
- There was a small lurch, and we had landed.
- Everyone on board breathed out a relieved sigh.

We were in France, and I had learnt never to go on a plane without something to read or with a full bladder.

The idiot who couldn't swim.

What: A chap nearly drowns a few meters away.

Where: Spain

My age: 23

Note: if you haven't read it, I suggest you read the preceding chapter: 'My First Flight' as a prequel.

This was a lesson on not taking anyone at their word. Or – to put it another way – people can lie about small things and then – ridiculously – literally almost die trying to cover it up. A valuable life lesson and one of the very few I have learnt, although over the years it has transmogrified into the realisation many people, much of the time, just talk crap.

From Perpignan airport we were transported by the advertised 'luxury coach' (a minibus) to a small Spanish fishing village busily turning itself into a tourist destination.

All told, there were five of us. We were dropped near the seafront. The driver said something about something and drove off, leaving us standing in a little group.

I put the family suitcase down, then worried it might immediately be stolen and picked it up again. In truth, apart from some traveller's cheques secreted in Mum mandated underpants, it contained little of value. But I did have a roll of loo paper, as Dad – ever alert to such things since his prostate op - had said, somewhat conspiratorially: 'You never know when it might come in handy.'

The others wandered off, vanishing into a nearby bar. Scared of missing whatever had been planned for us, I stayed put, pretending to be absorbed by the view of beached fishing boats, other tourists and a man frying an egg on a primus stove by a gorse bush.

Eventually a brisk lady with a clipboard arrived, announced herself as the part-time holiday rep, gathered us up and trooped us around, cheerfully dispensing us into various houses as if she was doing us all a favour. After maybe ten minutes there were two of us left: myself and tall chap of about my own age: he had spots and an over-eager grin. We will call him Terry.

We ended up sharing a room which – as the holiday rep pointed out – was mentioned in the small print as a possibility before adding, over her shoulder as she marched off: "Enjoy your stay. Bye-eee!" We never saw her again until the very last day, when she herded us into the luxury coach (still a mini-bus) and waved goodbye.

Terry sat on a bed, knowledgably testing the softness. "I've had worse," he declared, "playing football in Bulgaria."

He lived in London and this cheap holiday was a last minute, spur of the moment thing as for some obscure reason he couldn't go to his usual hotel in the Caribbean. He filled the small bathroom shelf with medicated, anti-acne soap (with its own little soap-dish), anti-dandruff shampoo, a safety razor and some expensive shaving cream smelling vaguely of farmyards.

In casual conversation, Terry would let drop small hints and sideways allusions of places he'd been, people he'd met, things he'd done.

He really was an expert at giving the impression he'd been and done more things than you could possibly aspire to. As an example – and this will become relevant later – he casually mentioned he was considering swimming the channel, maybe next year, 'if everything comes together.'

On the whole, I sort of believed him. I kept quiet about this being the first time I'd been abroad, or that I lived in a tiny flat over a one car garage in Amersham. And when he talked about his car (a new mini Cooper of course) I definitely did not mention I drove a 1952 side-value Morris Minor with a split windscreen.

Sharing a room meant – to begin with – we hung out together. But, fairly quickly, he began seeking out other companions and the relationship shrunk to the odd friendly wave or chat and sometimes a beer in the sunshine.

Not being gregarious, I just mooched around or lay on the beach listening to my hair turning golden. But, somehow, I managed to meet a girl. She had long legs, long hair and – towards me - a dull, flat character. We duly embarked on a sparkless, unenthusiastic and somewhat boring holiday romance. We'll call her Lilly.

She said, a couple of times: "this isn't going anywhere, is it?" To which I had no real reply.

But inertia is powerful, she was soon returning home, and we both looked reasonable on the beach. So we stayed together.

Once I'd hooked up with Lilly, Terry turned up almost daily. He'd be importantly walking past and give a little start of surprise we were sitting where we usually sat, outside the bar we normally frequented. He'd be en-route to meet someone, but always had time for a quick drink and to monopolise the conversation, with himself as the main topic.

I'd heard most of it before, and Lilly - so she told me - just switched off.

The day before Lilly was due to go back, energized at the thought of it all ending, we hired a pedalo and set off, plunk-thumping our lazy way out to sea. There was a slight breeze that created some ripples, which gave a nice sparkly effect to the whole enterprise. Lilly settled back and I found I was doing extra work to keep the pedals turning. I said she wasn't trying, and she said why should she, and we progressed for a while in silence.

The harbour was defined by a long mole stretching out into the sea: it had a walkway on top and large rocks underneath.

As we reached the open sea there was a shout from the end of the mole. Terry - in his swimming trunks – had climbed down and was standing on a rock near the waterline. Above him, a couple of uninterested spectators were admiring the view.

The distance between our pedalo and Terry was perhaps 7 or 8 meters. Certainly not more than 10. Absolutely no distance at all for someone thinking of swimming the channel. The waves were minimal. I could have swum it, and I'm no swimmer.

Seeing him, I thought he might help to pedal the pedalo. And Lilly probably thought the same.

He was so close we hardly needed to raise our voices. I said "C'mon Terry, give me a hand" and Lilly chimed in with "Yeah, c'mon: there's room."

Terry, I remember, seemed reluctant to swim over. So we encouraged him a bit more. The spectators, attention caught, formed an audience. Terry glanced up and saw them looking down. And then back at us again.

He should have said: "Oh, I dunno: looks a bit cold, I think I'll give it as miss." And clambered back up.

But he didn't. Instead, with a suicidal, wide-eyed, accusatory stare in our direction, he launched himself from the rocks, belly-flopped into the water and promptly sank out of sight.

I thought he must be swimming under the surface and would suddenly pop up in front of us, his head appearing as if by magic between the floats.

But Lilly was more perceptive, and for the first time ever, I heard her swear. "Shit shit shit! He can't swim! Shit shit shit shit!"

I said "What!?"

"He can't swim! Look, he can't swim!" She took a breath and yelled into my face: "Do something!"

For perhaps another second, I did nothing but stare at her. Her habitual languor had evaporated. She was now animated: her eyes were bright and the top half of her bikini was swelling up and down. A strand of hair had blown in front of her face.

Christ almighty! She had become monstrously alluring! What had I been missing?

She shrieked again: "He's drowning! Do something!"

Open mouthed, I looked round. Towards the mole, the calm surface of the sea was still completely Terryless.

And that was the Diana Moment: a weird combination of unexpected, sudden lust and total disbelief that someone would be so cavalier with his own life. Terry might have died trying to uphold a simple untruth, not even a proper lie: just a few casual words said to impress. And what made the situation even more dumbfounding was that - by diving into the sea and possibly drowning - Terry had exposed the lie without room for doubt.

Basically, what an arsehole.

There was a small upheaval in the water: abruptly, Terry's bewildered, scared head popped up, like an astonished meerkat. He was doggy-paddling frantically to keep his head above water and – as a secondary objective – to move towards us. If anything, he was actually going sideways.

Why he didn't try to get back to the rocks (at most two meters away) is a mystery. And after we had laboriously plunk-thumped the pedalo round and rescued him, it was something we never discussed.

It took him a while to clamber on board, but recovery was swift. Soon Terry and I were in the engine room while Lilly, framed by the glittering Mediterranean Sea, her hair slightly blowing in the breeze, stood proudly front and centre as we paraded slowly up and down to the evident and jealous admiration of some of the assorted sunbathers.

I am sure it was the high point of Lilly's holiday. Maybe even Terry's as well.

However, for me, a small but significant tear had occurred in the fabric of my understanding of human nature.

And when trust leaves and is replaced by cynicism, the world is diminished.

I give up teaching.

What: I decide to stop teaching.

Where: A classroom in Bristol.

My age: 23

This Diana Moment was unusual in that it resulted in immediate, life-changing action, done without thought or due consideration. It was in some ways comparable to my minor Damascene moment in Petersfield golf club car park, when I gave up golf for good. But golf is only a game. Teaching was my livelihood.

I am in a classroom, standing at the front, holding a stick of chalk and behind, scrawled on the blackboard, is one of those bad, messy diagrams unprepared, uncaring teachers specialise in. It is October, and I have been teaching (or failing to teach) at this school for only a matter of weeks.

A shaft of sunlight angles through the window. The chalk dust in the air sparkles. The pupils (for once) are silent. Everything looks old and tired: even the pupils, at 13 or 14 years old, have turned into generic blobs representing all the future pupils I will be teaching for years and years to come. I will be standing in front of their uninterested, uncaring, bored faces this time next year. And the year after. Nothing will change. And when I get back home at the end of the day, it will be the same as now: I will have a headache and spend the evening doing nothing much.

It is infinitely depressing, and I have felt, to a lesser degree, the same on most teaching days. But this is an intense Diana

Moment, and it is vivid and meaningful. For a few seconds I hold it close and get the fanciful impression I am barely controlling a monstrous force, guiding me remorselessly along a set course of action.

Without saying a word, I leave the classroom, walk along a corridor and around a corner. The building feels oddly silent and deserted. I go past the school secretary's office: the door is open, and I catch a glimpse of her white shirt. I stand in front of the headmaster's closed door and without pause I knock: rap, rap, rap.

His pleasant, somewhat distracted voice says, "come in?"

I open the door, take a couple of steps forward, say his name and add: "I've decided to leave at the end of this term. I'll bring you a letter tomorrow."

And once I say these words, the Diana Moment vanishes, its task complete: I had been booted out of my rut.

I cannot now remember what his response was. Did he try to dissuade me? Did he ask why? Or perhaps he said nothing, just tilted his head to one side and waited for me to explain.

I can't recall if I said anything more. I probably mumbled something.

The next day I handed the school secretary my resignation in writing. I had absolutely no idea what I was going to do next. Whatever it was, it would not be teaching.

This was – of course – the somewhat dramatic culmination of several years of growing unease in the direction my life was taking.

After leaving college I found a job at Great Missenden secondary modern school, supposedly teaching maths. I was there for two years: during that time I do not recollect teaching any pupil anything. So I resigned during my second summer term. I told myself I needed a new start, with fresh pupils who didn't know how useless I was.

Accordingly I applied for – and got – another teaching job, in Bristol. Why Bristol? Well, someone had once said it was a nice city, the job there seemed reasonable, a romance I was in was spluttering to a stop, so why not.

Really, I should not have bothered as I was only there for one term.

My dad – who's career as a schoolteacher was hardly more distinguished than mine - once told me in his experience it took just five minutes for any class to see through any pretence of confident competence and realise you were essentially mincemeat waiting to be fried.

Five minutes was probably an exaggeration. In my case it was about a week before all the old cracks began appearing again. The pupils took less and less notice of me and I became burdened with an all too familiar sense of failure.

I was never convincing as a teacher because I never really believed I had anything of importance to say, or that it was necessary for every single one of my pupils to learn what I was trying to teach. Why does the average fourteen-year-old require knowledge of (for instance) square roots or algebraic equations? The answer, of course, is they don't. I taught maths, so I knew, but I don't think that knowledge has helped me one iota as I've haphazardly blundered my way through life.

Also, and this is undoubtedly the practical crux of the matter: I couldn't keep the little buggers under control. They knew my heart was not in it, that I didn't really care if they learnt something or not. At root, all threats of punishment – even when carried out – were fundamentally spurious.

But, driven by that serendipitous Diana Moment, I got out.

It is usual to say that when a big decision has been made and implemented, a great weight is lifted. Your shoulders stop being bowed and your steps get lighter. There might even be the singing of joyful songs as you do the washing up.

And d'you know what? It's true. That evening I sat happily in my car pigging out on fish 'n chips, eating with my fingers and joyously realising I could now do anything!

I spent the next few weeks thinking what I should do. In the end I decided to become a salesman.

After all, both teaching and selling were a species of performance art with a high bullshit quotient. But as a sales rep, I wouldn't have to deal with of 30 or so snotty little bastards and I might get a company car. So: win win!

Oh, well, some lives are defined by mistake after mistake.

Thicko!

What: I realise I am not as clever as I thought I was.

Where: In a hotel somewhere

My age: 23

I started applying for jobs as a salesman a couple of weeks or so before Christmas. On paper I could make myself look good, so in the new year I did get a fair number of interviews.

Eventually I managed it: I became a sales representative for a firm making building fixing devices. I had a good salary, performance related bonus and a company mini. However I didn't have a clue, sold nothing and crashed the car. My career as a salesman lasted about four months, if that. Not a great success.

But this Diana Moment occurred right at the end of the second interview for a company distributing pet food.

The first interview was a departure from the norm. Instead of being dribbled in one by one to see the interviewer, we all went in together – all 10 of us – to sit round a circular table, be given a felt-tipped pen and a sheet of A4 paper and told to make a name plate and prop it up in front of us.

Mine was a bit uneven, but the letters were large enough to be legible to everyone.

The chap opposite me must have studied calligraphy as his script was both beautiful and unreadable, while another just laid his paper flat on the table so only the people sitting alongside him could read it (upside down).

We all thought: "Idiots! They won't make it. 8 left."

In charge were two vaguely menacing men. One was tall and angular, sharp-suited and with the disturbing habit of suddenly becoming motionless, like a snake about to strike. The other was older: short and tubby with that unfortunate combination of bald head and greying whiskers that declares a lopsided ego. You just knew he always wanted to be thought of as a belligerent professor.

They explained they were trying a new type of first interview process, so we were guinea-pigs. But – they hastened to assure us – it was all genuine, and at least two of us would go through for another interview, to be held in a week or so.

One guinea-pig asked: "D'you mean just from this group of ten, or from the total round of first interviews?"

And we all thought 'Oh, I wish I'd thought of that. I wish I'd had the balls to interrupt. I bet he'll go thru.'

But the professor – eyes glittering - pounced: "And how does knowing that make a difference to your behaviour here and now, in this process?"

To which the reply was a crushed and mumbled "I just was sort of .. Thinking, maybe ..."

And we all thought "Hurrah! He's out. 7 to go."

A flip chart was unveiled. On it was written: 'WHY ME?'

The tall, reptilian one said "Right, let's start, shall we? You want to be salesmen. We want you to be salesmen. So we'd like you to sell yourselves, as salesmen, to us. Tell us why we should employ you to sell cat food and dog food and budgerigar seed. Not forgetting – of course - sandwiches for tortoises." He became momentarily still, waiting for prey. Someone laughed a strange sort of snort. Bad move. A finger pointed. "OK, you can start: off you go, why should we employ you?"

The professor's bristles bristled. "We are waiting on your every word."

And we all wondered if it would go round the table, and if so in which direction and how long it would take to get to us.

And so it went on. In retrospect, I could see it was staged: a choreographed performance with the intention of revealing the kind of ballsy young men they believed was required to sell their products. As they said at one point: "we're after proper salesmen, not mere order takers."

After about an hour of going round the table and egging us on to verbally nut each other, they changed tack.

The professor stepped forward. And smiled, looking almost genial. "Well, that bit's over. Thank you." He violently ripped the top sheet of paper from the flip chart, revealing the single word: '**WORK**.' He paused to make sure we'd all read it and re-read it. Finally he continued: "my colleague and I will now be taking a back seat." he nodded at a couple of chairs quietly parked in a corner "and you will discuss this topic: 'WORK' for about half an hour. Oh – one bit of advice:

it works best if you have a chairman." He took out a notepad and a child's pencil decorated with elephants and redundantly added "We'll be taking notes!"

They went into the corner, occupied the chairs and said nothing more until it was time to finish.

We all sat and tried hard not to look at each other.

We all thought: 'go on, say it: just say you'll be chairman; that's what they're waiting for. It's there to be claimed Go on, go on, say it, say it!'

But no one did. Even after an hour of being aggressively poked and prodded, we were still too polite and diffident.

Finally, someone suggested someone else, who proved to be totally useless. We all thought we could do better, but no-one launched a coup. I think by then we were past caring. I did chip in occasionally with what I believed were pertinent comments, but all in all it was a miserable experience, and we were glad when it finished.

I accredit being called for a second interview to mum. I remembered her advice from six or so years before: "It doesn't really matter what you say in an interview: just say it clearly and don't mumble." There was quite a lot of mumbling in that room, but none of it came from me.

But in truth I expect they needed to fill a quota and just randomly picked my name out of a hat.

The second interview took place in an instantly forgettable hotel in an instantly forgettable town with a small, dapper, middle-aged gent in a well-cut silver-grey suit. He never said what his position was exactly but gave the impression of being pretty high up.

He was waiting for me near the reception desk. After introductions, he twinkled at the receptionist and asked for coffee and biscuits.

We went and sat at a small round table in an alcove.

He looked invitingly at me "Well," he said: "what did you think of the first interview?"

I said it was different and went on to lie about how "I'd quite enjoyed it, actually."

He said "yes, that's what I heard." I had the feeling he'd said that many times before. The coffee and biscuits arrived, and we had a relaxed conversation about me and the company, their requirements and my abilities.

He was very skilled at putting people at their ease; interrogating without seeming to interrogate and giving enough space for nuanced answers.

I think I did reasonably well. He nodded and smiled and twinkled away and when I tried a witticism, he threw his head back for a moment and laughed.

After about twenty minutes I sensed the interview was coming to an end: the coffee had been drunk, the biscuits eaten, and he had – or so I thought – got all he needed.

He piled the coffee cups onto the tray. "One more thing," he said: "a little test for you." He moved the tray to the side and turned to a fresh page of his notebook. He had, I realised, taken no notes yet. "There is a boat floating in a harbour, moored to a buoy." He helpfully drew a picture of a steamship, complete with a funnel, tied by a long loop of rope. "There is a rope ladder going down from the deck to the water." A ladder appeared, complete with evenly spaced rungs. "The rungs of the ladder are one foot apart, and the ladder stretches down far enough to reach the water." A water line was drawn. He counted the rungs above it. "There are six rungs above the water, and the tide rises at one foot per hour. Got it?"

"Yes."

"Good. Now the question I would like you to answer is: once the tide begins rising, how many rungs will be above the water after four hours?"

He sat back and folded his arms.

I stared at the neat little picture. I knew it was a trick question. I knew he knew I knew it was a trick question. I said, "It's a trick question, isn't it." A statement rather than a question.

He shrugged slightly but said nothing.

I tried to force myself to think, but I just couldn't see it. The water would cover one rung at the end of each hour, so after four complete hours, it would have covered four rungs of the ladder. There were originally six rungs, so there would be two left.

But I knew that wasn't the right answer. I puffed out my cheeks and asked something silly about if the water was exactly just over the bottom rung. Again, he said nothing.

The tray with the coffee detritus was removed.

I sighed, looked away, opened my mouth and told him there would be two rungs left.

There was a pause. I looked up. He was regarding me. And that's what I remember: the Diana Moment: a fleeting, half-second glimpse of his face: neatly shaved, lined, modestly tanned, well looked after and intelligent but (and isn't there always a but?) overlaid with a profound disappointment. For whatever reason, he had wished me to succeed. But the question had been a showstopper.

And I had failed.

His voice was flat and neutral. "The boat," he said, "floats. It goes up and down with the tide. So does the buoy. There's always the same number of rungs above the water." He closed his notepad and slid it into an inside pocket. He smiled a professional smile. "Well, I think we're done."

Outside the hotel we exchanged the usual words about how the company would let me know in due course, shook hands and separated. He went back inside, and I walked off.

I'd always considered myself as clever. And whenever that cleverness let me down, I re-classified myself as intelligent which was – I told myself – at a higher level. I even had a useful distinction between the two: cleverness is for tactics, but intelligence was for strategy.

All very facile and smugly ya boo sucks to the rest of you.

But now, I knew I simply wasn't bright enough to sell cat food, dog food, budgerigar seed or even sandwiches for tortoises.

I was officially considered a thicko by a pet food company.

I was not feeling buoyant and optimistic as I drove home.

But the next day I received an invitation to yet another interview, for yet another sales job.

And of course I went.

Crash.

What: I crash my company car

Where: near Ludlow.

My age: 24

It's odd how things don't work out. I managed to land a job as a salesman but - when it came to it - I was rubbish. I was even worse at selling than I had been at teaching.

I lucked out with the interview. It was scheduled for three-thirty on a Friday afternoon, and they were running late, so it was past four before we started. The interviewer – a pleasant chap smelling of toothpaste - plainly wanted to wrap things up. He gamely listened to a minute or so of my carefully rehearsed lines on why selling was my passion before interrupting to say he was going to trust his instincts on this one. And offered me the job.

Of course, I accepted.

He shoved a business card at me, said "ring on Monday and we'll go through the details" and sprinted off. He was out in the car park and away before I left the room.

The company sold building fixing devices directly to the trade. Or – as one of the salesmen later put it – plastic plugs to men in sweaty vests.

To start, there was a week of training. Six of us in a hotel somewhere in the middle of nowhere. There was a farm nearby: you could hear the cows in the morning.

Our tutor in the art of selling was a bouncy man of about thirty, full of vim and vigour, intent on turning us all into clones of himself. After all – as he frequently informed us – he was the company's top salesman. We'll call him Jasper.

Jasper was absolutely fizzing with energy, tricks, techniques and advice. He set us questionnaires and essay subjects and gave us demonstrations of how to sell ice to an eskimo ('Do you know where your huskies have been peeing? Our ice is pure. Guaranteed! You can always put our ice into your Martini!'). Upselling came as natural to him as breathing ('You'll need twice as much ice when Granny starts boozing, ha ha!') and the very concept of a no sale was absurd.

He'd jab his finger at us. "You're selling building fixing devices to a man who spends eight hours a day fixing buildings! Of course you have something he wants. You just need to find out what it is. Then he will buy."

We all wanted to be like him. Unconsciously we imitated his rapid walk and thrusting hand movements.

On the last day, one of us went missing. A friendly chap: we all liked him. We had breakfast as usual, but half an hour later, when we assembled in the training room, he wasn't there.

We asked Jasper, who'd been seen talking to him in an otherwise deserted corridor.

Jasper was uncharacteristically reticent. Eventually, he said "he didn't make the cut." He blinked and added: "you always need to look at the small print: you only get a job with us if you make it through this week. He didn't."

The last day was somewhat sombre.

I started my life as a salesman not – as I expected – driving around in a brand-new company car, but in an open plan office ringing up people who hadn't ordered anything for a while and trying to sell them something. Anything.

There was a big blackboard listing our names on the left and increments of £10 to the right. Every time you made a sale, you went to the blackboard: eyes followed you as you picked up the chalk and carefully, opposite your name, filled in one square for each £10 you had just sold.

At the end of the day it was immediately evident who had sold the most. And who had sold the least, which was usually me.

The best salesmen had light, friendly voices, were quick and confident with their answers and always probed away, looking for a link to be made. "Oh, you're renovating? Lots of plasterboard I bet. We have a special nail for that: galvanised and ribbed, with a slightly oversized head. Better than anything you can buy at a builder's merchant, guaranteed. And as we sell direct to you, cutting out the middleman, it's cheaper. I can have a delivery at your door on Thursday. Or if you want it sooner, I should be able to make it Wednesday. Which suits you best?"

They made it sound so, so simple! I would lie awake at night, rehearsing into my pillow, trying to emulate that easy confidence, that imperceptible swerve – taking the customer with them - from proposing they buy to assuming it was a done deal. And I couldn't do it. I'd always end up monotonously plodding through the script and when they said 'no, I don't need anything' I'd feel a great sense of relief at being able to hang up.

After a few weeks of this hell, the manager called me in. I went expecting to be sacked.

He confirmed I wasn't that good on the telephone.

More for form's sake than anything else, I said I thought I was getting better.

He shook his head. "No James. Sorry, but you're not cut out for it. I've done this job for years, and – believe me - you're just not suited." I felt immensely relieved and wildly hoped – although the notice period was a month – that I could go right then. I could walk from his office, along a corridor, out into the carpark and drive off. I wouldn't even stop at my desk to pick up my biro.

But he went on: "We feel you'll be fine talking face to face. On the road." Unbelievably, they were giving me a car and an area in the midlands. "Virgin territory: we've done a few sales, but you'll need to work it up."

Wow! Did I feel good? I'll say. I'd stopped listening after 'company car.' A company car! What could be better!

And so I moved to Birmingham and joined the Midlands sales team. I had an area vaguely to the south of Telford. I was told the larger building companies already dealt directly with our head office: my job was to find new clients. Effectively, I was a bottom feeder, scurrying around, attempting to sell plastic plugs to the sweaty vested small fry.

And that's when things really went tits up.

And the main reason for this was simple: I was (and continue to be) very reluctant to meet anyone I haven't met before. Not a good closed loop for a salesman.

At the start – for the first few days – I managed to retain an optimistic outlook until about lunchtime. Then I'd sit in a layby eating a porkpie, glumly staring at an empty order sheet and dreading the afternoon. After a week that dread had extended from breakfast through to teatime. A week more and it was always there, a relentless backdrop to whatever I was doing, making me twitchy, uncertain and miserable.

I knew exactly what Jasper would do. Jasper would relentlessly hunt them down, trap them in a corner and not release them until they'd ordered at least a year's supply of plastic plugs, drill bits, electric drills, plasterboard nails, wood screws, masonry screws, frame fixers, toggles, woggles ……. Christ, I can't remember half the stuff in the catalogue, but by the time he'd finished they'd have bought the sodding lot.

But me? No. Half the time I couldn't get hold of them – they'd be out somewhere and the wife didn't know where or - on the rare occasions I did manage to see one – he'd say it was more convenient just to pop down to the local builder's merchant and anyway, where would he store a year's supply of plastic plugs?

I would have used up all my vim, vigour and confidence getting hold of him in the first place, so I'd just nod my head in agreement and that would be that. Another no sale.

I began to deliberately take longer and longer on the road, plotting my course for the day in the most inefficient manner possible, driving miles and miles hoping they wouldn't be there, then miles and miles back, zigzagging along meandering country lanes and frequently ending up in a farmyard.

But I still hung on. I'd dug a trench so deep all I could see was the sides. I couldn't think of what else I could do. I'd make excuses and lie to myself. I'd tell myself all I needed was some friendly faces and a couple of sales: that would be the spark to ignite my career.

But I was way too submerged for that: even the friendliest of faces appeared furtive and hostile. Inevitably, the sales never came.

Being in this moribund, dismal condition is not conducive to happiness. Or indeed to what – nowadays – would be called mental health. At one point I had sunk so far into depressed misery I drove to the top of Wrynose pass in the lake district and – in a half-hearted, half-knowing fashion - pretended to myself I'd stay there, without food or water, until I either died, was rescued or went into a coma. It was March, and bitterly cold. The landscape was appropriately bleak and deserted: not once did I catch a glimpse of another human being.

But I always knew it was just a gesture to myself; an acknowledgement of the state I was in. So, after one uncomfortable night curled up on the backseat, shivering in a skinny sleeping bag, I started the engine and drove back.

And in an echo of when I sat in a tree as a child, no-one had noticed I wasn't there.

A few days later I became aware the bed was hard and the sheets crisp. A figure stood and walked towards me. It was surreal. It was real. It was a Diana Moment.

She said "You are in hospital. You had a car crash. You have been unconscious for a day. You are probably concussed, but that will pass. You didn't break any bones. It is now Wednesday afternoon."

She was middle aged, thin, with brown eyes and a large nose. She had been reading 'The Reader's Digest' and still held it in her hand, bent back to keep her place. I could see *'Word Pow'* before her thumb chopped off the rest.

She smiled. I asked what had happened, and she replied she knew no more details. I sunk back to sleep.

They said the memory of the actual crash might come back, but over fifty years later I'm still waiting. In fact the whole day has been lost. A complete Tuesday eradicated from my memory as if it had never been.

What I do know is second or third hand, mainly from a policeman who came in the next day. I told him I couldn't remember a thing. He said he didn't know much either, except a car had shunted me into a lamp post. My car had been wrecked: they required a tin opener to get me out.

He seemed rather disappointed I knew even less than he did, and left after about ten minutes.

And that's it. Undoubtedly, I was very, very lucky (again). This was late 1960s: no one wore seat belts, air bags were virtually unknown and as for crumple zones, forget it. Apart from having half my hair shaved off so a great big gash in my head could be stitched up, I was fine.

They discharged me the next day and my company gave me a couple of weeks off to recuperate.

So, with two black eyes and my head swathed in bandages, I took the train home to East Meon, to mum and dad.

The crash wasn't a near-death 'experience' as I remember nothing: no shining lights or tunnels to another universe with figures waiting for me at the other end: just a prosaically functional hospital room with a kind nurse reading a magazine.

But it did give me pause. And after a monster headache that lasted nearly a week, I accepted the inevitable and resigned. Selling was manifestly not for me.

Seeming to have few options, qualifications or an aptitude for anything much, I decided to become a writer. Well, why not: at school my essays and compositions had always done well.

All I needed was a typewriter, and there was an old one of those – built like a battleship - in the attic.

Being unable to type didn't seem to be much of a drawback.

I hauled it down, dusted it off, oiled its ancient mechanism and began to practice.

The querk.brwn fox kWump s, over ^he laZy dag11!.

Photographs: young man to IT guy

Circa 1964. I grew my beard as a student,
but didn't tell anyone, so big surprise when I came home.
In those days it was a bit of an effort to take a photo (you
required a camera!) so this is the only picture I have of me
as a student.

Circa 1966. Summer.

The newly qualified teacher relaxes on the beach before starting at his first school.

Circa 1966. Christmas.
After one term of teaching, gloom and doom has overtaken my life. From the left: me, Peter (back from N.Z.), Dad, Mum, Judy.

Circa 1974. From the left: Peter, me, Dad, Mum.
This is the only photo I can find from my years as a writer. It's the hair that gives it away.

Circa 1980. Judy sitting at the dining table
in Dad & Mum's bungalow, working on an illustration for
one of her books.

Circa 1988. The IT guy starts his first job at Rex Software. Over the next few months the suit was discarded and
the tie ditched.

1991: The IT guy (46) on a day off.
Lizzy used to call this '*Ol' blue eyes*' but I always think I should have shaved.

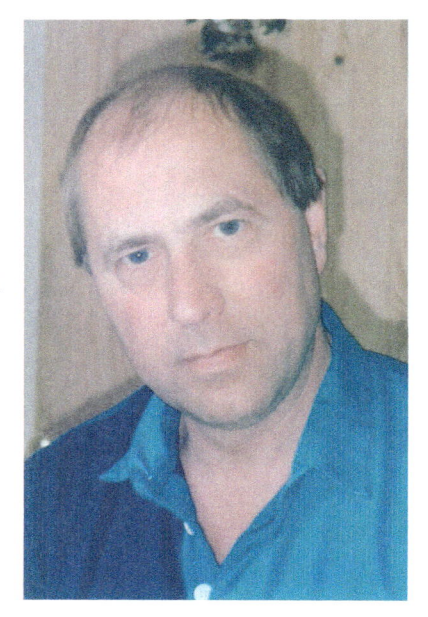

Keys.

What: Lizzy loses her keys.

Where: Her flat, Southampton.

My age: 37

Here, in my current world of 2020, I have just finished writing the Diana Moment *'Crash'* which ends with how (and possibly why) I started writing, after failing as a teacher, then as a salesman and crashing my car. You may have just finished reading it: or perhaps you have not. I do not know; nor am I sure if it matters.

But – however bleak my life then – the crash was a turning point. Which leads me, inexorably, to another turning point: Lizzy. And in between the two there are some twelve or thirteen years. So later (or perhaps sooner) I will be writing about my writing, which overlapped the beginning of my career in IT. But – right now - I have this compelling urge to write about Lizzy.

So I will.

Lizzy lived in a small flat in Southampton. Clever with her hands, she worked in a sail loft. For the most part she made dodgers: those waterproof screens and hoods yacht owners use to proudly declare the name of their boat and – seemingly as an afterthought - keep out the spray.

To get to work she walked. Her stride was distinctive: head slightly down, body leaning forward, legs taking rapid steps.

I worked as a programmer for an IT firm. Mainly, I wrote code for a small IBM mainframe system. Usually, to get to work, I left the car and biked. About three or four times a week, our paths would cross: she on the pavement, I on the road.

After a while - as one does – we started to acknowledge each other. First, maybe a nod. Then, a week or so later, a nod and a grin. Another week and it'd be a nod, a grin and a hand raised.

All in all, it took maybe a month before she said – just as I was passing - "How's it going?"

I jammed on the brakes and stopped a little way further on. She waited while I backed up.

And we had our first conversation. Awkward and a bit shy but at one point she said 'Oh, I'm Lizzy,' as if it completely explained who she was, what she did and how she lived. I found her certainty of herself very appealing.

She told me her number and I pedalled furiously off, mumbling it over and over to myself: for forgetting it would feel like a betrayal.

Two days later, we ate at Mr C's which was down the side of a hotel facing a small park opposite the city hall and library. I can't remember what we had. I can't remember what we talked about.

But I do know the date: November the 4th, 1982. It was a Thursday.

Afterwards – it being autumn – we walked in the small park and kicked dry leaves.

And then I took her home. A sweet smile, a quick kiss on the cheek, another date arranged, and she had gone.

Some weeks later, in her small flat, she came in from the bedroom and looked vaguely around, picking up a book and seeing what was underneath; moving one of the saucepans in her kitchenette; searching through her bag.

I asked if she'd lost something.

"Yes." came her reply: "My keys."

I was astounded at her casual tone. For me – then as now - losing keys is a catastrophe, up there with the end of the world or being late for an appointment. Regardless of circumstance, I'd turn the place upside down and would be unable to stop until they had been located.

But Lizzy seemed unconcerned.

Bewildered, I asked if she was not worried.

Her reply was so uniquely Lizzy, so completely out of kilter with my own closed existence, my heart gave a lurch.

Her answer, when asked if she was not worried about losing her keys, was "no: I haven't looked in the fridge yet."

For her, it was no more than a casual, throw-away remark, tossed out as she rootled through the contents of her bag. It was of no more significance than - for instance – an observation it might rain tomorrow.

But to me it was a game changer. I stared at her profile: the regular features, the smile lines at the corner of her mouth, the slight squint as she peered down. My Dad always said – of Lizzy – that she had good bones.

I said, "The fridge?"

"Yeah." She didn't look up; her long black hair cascaded down her back. Outside a lorry trundled past: the windows rattled. I was in her flat, a place where – delightfully - keys could reside in fridges. I pondered on what that meant, for it was both absurd and logical, as well as casually assuming everything would be fine.

I felt as if she'd extended a welcoming hand, reaching through from her world and into mine.

Yeah, OK: that's all a bit OTT on the metaphor front. But, simply put, regardless of what would happen, I knew I'd made – at the very least - a friend. For life.

In the end her keys were discovered not in the fridge but on the mantlepiece, carelessly tucked behind an imitation Dresden figurine of a shepherdess.

"There." She smiled. "No reason to panic."

I propose.

What: I ask Lizzy to marry me.

Where: Carrefour-that-was, Eastleigh.

My age: 38

Lizzy was 9 years younger me. More interestingly, her birthday was exactly a day before mine.

So on our first birthday(s) together we established a tradition.

On her birthday we sat up, waiting for midnight. With about fifteen seconds to go, we started singing together.

I'd sing: "happy birthday to you, happy birthday to you, happy birthday dear Lizbob, Happy birthday to you."

And she would sing: "happy birthday to me, happy birthday to me, happy birthday to meeee, Happy birthday to me."

The clock would click over to midnight and we'd start over.

This time she'd sing: "happy birthday to you, happy birthday to you, happy birthday dear Jimbob, happy birthday to you."

While I sang: "happy birthday to me, happy birthday to me, happy birthday to meeee, happy birthday to me."

'Lizbob' and 'Jimbob' had evolved from either 'The Waltons' or 'The little house on the prairie' both of which she had seen and both of which I had not.

I borrowed £1,500 from my Mum (we didn't tell Dad, but I suspect he knew) and used it as a deposit for a flat just round the corner. Lizzy moved in and – from a cat charity - we obtained a kitten. We called her Rocious (short for Ferocious) and had a cat flap installed.

And with Lizzy came friends. We went surfing, cycling, walking, eating out, rough riding, camping and playing games of an evening.

Her parents lived in Portsmouth and every few weeks we'd drive over to see them. On leaving Southampton, by the railway bridge, there was a gasometer. The top was often right down, leaving a circle of girders sticking up.

One weekend, as we passed it, I casually said "Um: everyone's cooking a Sunday roast."

She was puzzled. "What?"

"The gasometer's down: everyone's cooking a roast."

"What?"

I explained about gasometers going up and down, to keep the pressure constant. I finished – rather pedantically "That's why they've got little wheels on the side."

"You're joking!" She often thought I was pulling her leg. Often, I was not.

"Nope. They go up and down."

By now the gasometer was way behind us and couldn't be examined. I later got her dad to confirm gasometers did indeed rise and fall.

And Lizzy said "really? You talked to dad about gasometers?"

I said "yeah, it's important!"

She patted me on the head. "Yes, yes: it's important gasometers go up and down."

Of course, there is a hackneyed narrative here, the stuff of many films and stories: that of the lively – often the word 'ditsy' is used - girl meeting the serious-minded chap. Fun enters his life and some rigour enters hers: both have their horizons expanded and - after a few mandatory romantic ups and downs - they trip off happily to a bright future.

And, to some extent, with Lizzy and I, that is what happened. Except Lizzy wasn't ditsy or indeed always lively and I wasn't necessarily serious minded: sometimes – particularly with her - I could be inordinately silly.

From the get-go, it was a relationship that appeared both completely solid and yet worthy of nurture. After nearly a year I found – settling gently into my mind and emotions – the conviction my future should be our future. It was a strange, almost alien realisation, both frightening and comforting at the same time.

We had fallen into the habit of shopping once a week at Carrefour, in Eastleigh, just North of Southampton.

As an aside, that Carrefour is now an ASDA, but to retain the link to this Diana Moment, we now call it Carrefour-that-was.

Lizzy and I were incompatible grocery shoppers but went together anyway: we rather enjoyed squabbling over out of date apples or green bananas or if we really needed custard.

Once our trolley was full, we'd park it and take the escalator up to the diner for lunch. With luck we'd get a table overlooking the shoppers below: ideal for spotting hairpieces.

We had been together for eleven months. A time of remarkable, exciting, ordinary things.

Food fetched, we sat down opposite each other.

Lizzy had a salad: a shredded iceberg lettuce; a fluff of grated carrot; some cucumber spirals; coleslaw, potato salad and a slab of white chicken breast. I had sausage, mash, peas and a splash of gravy.

I munched, as usual eating fast.

She munched: as usual, she ate much more slowly than I.

When my plate was empty, I carefully arranged my knife and fork and said "I've been thinking about this. Will you marry me?"

Her hand stopped in mid-air. A bit of carrot dropped back onto her plate. "What?"

"I've been thinking about it for a while. Will you marry me?"

She said "Yes." She blinked twice, then turned to a couple on the next table. "He's just asked me to marry him."

They stopped eating. The woman said "Oh," in the sort of tone one uses when you want to appear more excited than you actually are. The man grimaced, caught my eye and – slowly - shook his head.

Lizzy said "yes. I said yes." She turned back to me. Her fork was still in mid-air. "Yes." She grinned. "Yes! Wow."

I reached over and touched her hand. "Good. Now eat your salad."

She lowered her fork. "Eat my salad? Eat my salad??!! Now?!"

We didn't finish the meal. A restless urge to tell people consumed us. We left the trolley full of shopping and tossed a coin to see who we would tell first. My parents were heads, her parents, tails.

It came down tails so, there and then, we drove to Portsmouth. Her parents had just finished lunch, but – in honour of the occasion - her Mum heroically produced tea and cake. She and Lizzy then vanished into the front room for two hours. Two hours!

Overcome by comfort eating I demolished six slices of cake but would have murdered for a bacon sandwich.

When we departed to tell my parents, her Mum said "Don't forget. How many."

I put the car into gear and off we went. "How many what?"

"Guests of course."

"Guests?!"

"Of course." She looked at my blank face. "From your side. For the wedding."

"Oh."

I hadn't thought further than the proposal. That was a giant step in itself, so needed its own space. If I thought of 'the wedding' at all it was of some vague, fuzzy and relatively unimportant event that might – or even might not – occur sometime in the distant future.

But Lizzy and her mum had taken my proposal as a launchpad: an immediate and imperative springboard into organisational nitty-gritty.

It was as if the start button had been pressed on a giant steamroller on top of a hill. And immediately it had begun to descend, gathering speed and momentum with astonishing rapidity, spewing out great steamy belches of things to do, items to consider, people to contact, stuff that must not be forgotten. Guests! Cake! Venue! Dates! Caterers! Presents! Seating! Speeches! Lists! More lists! Lists of lists!

I found it exhausting, even though my input and involvement was slight.

I borrowed a library book on weddings and looked up 'groom's responsibilities.' As far as I remember, all I needed to do was to find a best man (I asked my brother, he said yes) and pay for the honeymoon (I suggested Cornwall, but we ended up in Tunisia).

And, three or four months later, Lizzy and I were married at Portsmouth registry office and held the reception at a nearby pub.

I will not be writing about either the wedding or the reception as such. There were no Diana Moments and it all went – more or less – according to plan. But it is tempting to construct a fictional comic set-piece of mishaps, drunk uncles, late arrivals and inadvertent strip-o-grams, but that would be contrary to the spirit of this book.

Except: Lizzy was dressed in blue, had a small flare of white flowers in her hair and looked completely wonderful and radiant. And I knew, when I saw her waiting for me, that what we were doing was absolutely and completely the right thing to do.

Which it was.

I sell my first play.

What: The BBC buys 'Cerdic and the outside world'

Where: Southsea, Portsmouth

My age: 29

Like many would-be writers, I began with THE NOVEL. It was called something along the lines of 'Rita love I, Alex.' (Don't ask. This was fifty odd years ago and - even then - I didn't understand it.) Bashed out with an ancient typewriter and corrected with Tipp-ex, it only had one failing. It was rubbish.

But I believed this was the masterwork that was going to capitulate me – in a couple of months at the most – to fame, fortune and a lifestyle to cherish.

It didn't happen, of course it didn't happen, but I kept on. Magazine stories, short stories, another novel and a steady drip drip drip of TV plays, radio plays and comedy scripts.

It still didn't happen. No novel was published or taken up by an agent. No play garnered any sort of interest. No magazine submission sparked anything other than a generic rejection slip.

I'm sure mum and dad thought I was wasting my twenties, but I cannot remember either of them, at any time, passing a derogatory comment on how I was living. They truly were astoundingly good parents to have.

I've often thought about why I kept going, moving from one bedsit and low-paid job to the next, spending my weekends and evenings tap-tapping away. I think the reason was simple: I was now happier. I had found both teaching and selling stressful, unrewarding and seemingly offering nothing more than the most mundane of futures.

But writing was far more akin to constantly doing the lottery. It allowed you to dream that one day all your efforts might bring forth a wonderful cornucopia of riches. All you had to do was stay the course and keep going.

Slowly, one bedsit, town and job at a time, I worked my way along the South coast, starting in Worthing and finishing in Portsmouth. I had many jobs: on a civil engineering site; in an office; as a waiter; at a bowling alley; as a gardener; as a taxi driver; as a supply teacher (yep, OK, I was desperate) and (probably) other things I've now forgotten.

Money was tight, but really, I was only playing at poverty. Every so often mum and dad would visit, bringing a food parcel, which always included loo rolls from dad and a £5 note from mum.

So I was never truly hungry, except for one time I ran out of funds on a Friday, with nothing further expected until Monday. All I had was a very large white cabbage, some mayonnaise and a bunch of grapes so far gone you could drink them.

I binned the grapes and heroically lived for two and a half days on coleslaw. By Sunday evening I was farting so frequently I couldn't sleep. It truly was the night of the hovering duvet.

As each explosion rent the fetid air, I told myself this was all grist to my writing mill.

But by God, the place stank.

I was living over a naughty knicker shop in Southsea, Portsmouth, when I sold my first piece of work. It had taken me five years.

'Cerdic and the outside world' was a radio play. A short (thirty minutes), picaresque comedy with a big cast, no subtlety and little plot. It traced the brief career of Cerdic, who leaves his dad and the circus to venture forth into the outside world. An innocent, he stumbles from one absurd situation to the next, meeting a variety of unlikely characters. There were nine actors and between them they played over twenty parts.

'Cerdic' by the way, is not a misspelling of 'Cedric.' Cerdic was the first king of Wessex and I probably chanced across him when reading about Alfred the Great. I was considering a play centred around the woman who got her cakes burnt.

When I opened and read the acceptance letter from the BBC I remember thinking to myself: *'this is a historic moment. I must treasure it and never forget.'* But I don't think this memory of a resolve to not forget quite qualifies as a Diana Moment: there is no real intensity; nothing vivid; in fact it's possible I'm just retrospectively making it up. It was the sort of thing I would think, so perhaps I did.

No. The Diana Moment came a couple of hours later when I was walking along Southsea sea front and met a bird. A seagull, to be precise.

I can't remember the time of year: the sky was blue; the wind bitter and few people were out. So I would guess early spring. I sat in a small shelter, shoved my hands into my pockets and stared out at the sea, at the dull waves endlessly flopping themselves against the pebbled beach.

I closed my eyes and let out a long, long sigh.

Abruptly there was a rush of air and a harsh squawk. Startled, I looked up. The seagull was hovering in front of me. It was large and intimidating: its quivering, outstretched wings were more than twice as wide as my shoulders.

It was all I could see.

For a long, intense moment it hung there, just a few feet away, inspecting me. Then - after ascertaining I held no ice cream or sandwich or sausage or in fact anything edible - it wheeled and flew off, dipping low over the waves, heading rapidly to destinations unknown.

I stood and walked home, the truth sinking in. I was now a proper writer, officially validated by the BBC script department.

Goodbye Dad, Goodbye Mum

What: My parents die

Where: Hampshire

My age: 51 and 55

This chapter is unique in that it records not one Diana Moment, but two.

For I find it impossible to think of one without recalling the other.

In my mind and memory, they are always linked: mum and dad, dad and mum: my super, ever loving, ever supporting, parents.

They both went in the winter, from pneumonia: dad aged 92 in 1996 and mum aged 88 in the year 2000.

If this book was a sentimental family film, there would now be a series of small, heart-rending scenes depicting happy family times: memories to cherish topped and tailed with myself and other family members standing by a joint grave, with trees casting dappled sunlight as a blessing over us all.

All very chocolate box, tear jerking, cliché-ridden and tired. But I know if I watched it, my eyes would moisten.

For my emotions here are very mixed. I knew they were tired; I knew they wanted to go, but I feared the loss, of them not being there, of Peter and I becoming the oldest. Becoming the next in line to die.

Dad had a stroke when he was in his mid-80s. The left side of his face became slack and unresponsive, his speech slurred into near incomprehensibility and he needed to use his right hand to move his left arm.

I remember visiting them: we had a meal, a Sunday roast. Normally Mum would put the food on the table, Dad would carve, and we'd help ourselves to veg. All very traditional. But this time she loaded the plates in the kitchen and bought them through two at a time. Dad flopped his left arm down, picked up his fork with his right hand and began to eat. I realised Mum had quietly cut up his food for him. When he dribbled slightly, she wiped it away with a damp tea-towel she discretely kept for the purpose. We ate in near silence.

I helped Mum wash up while Dad, in the front room, dozed gently in front of the TV and Lizzy – then pregnant with Hannah – put her feet up.

Mum stared out at the garden. She said: "The doctor says it'll all come back." I concentrated on rinsing a plate. She went on: "It just has to join back up. The nerves and things. I know he's very clear in his head, but he slurs his words."

I couldn't think of anything to say apart from "d'you think he might like a game of chess?"

"You could ask."

But when I mentioned it, dad just shook his head.

The doctor was right: over the next few months his face tightened up, his talking became clearer and his arm began to function as normal. He even resumed golf, but not as often and seldom more than three or four holes.

He went on for another seven years, finally going in January, that damp, joyless old people's friend.

A week or so after Christmas he had trouble breathing. The doctor prescribed a course of pills – presumably antibiotics – but to little effect.

Dad was moved first to hospital and then to a nursing or care home. In truth, it was a hospice.

The Diana Moment came after he had been there for a few days. It was a Wednesday, in the afternoon. It was soon after 2, but already getting dark. The building was old and rather grand, with a great sweep of gravelled drive and a portico designed to impress.

Dad's room was on the ground floor and had a pleasant view of trees. The sheets were ironed, maybe even starched.

He was half sitting up and looked so very very small, worn out and tired. He leant forward when he saw me. The smooth pillow behind had been dented by his head. His pyjamas – bought from home – were for a larger frame, the seams for his shoulders now hanging down his forearms.

His voice was thin, our conversation awkward. He was pleased to see me. Yes, the food was OK. The staff were cheerful but a bit bossy, the doctor had seen him this morning and Peter would be coming tomorrow with Mum.

He was hoping, he said – and here he looked straight at me, as if asking a question - to go home soon.

His eyes were watery, his breathing heavy, his skimpy, discoloured chest effortful as he breathed. Peter had said Dad now required bedpans and bed baths.

It was the Diana Moment. To this day, I do not know if I said the right thing, only that I said it.

I said "You won't be going home, Dad. Mum can't cope." It was the first and last time I ever said 'Mum can't cope.'

After a pause he said, "thank you for being honest." He looked out at the trees, then back to me. His voice hardly changed. "I think," he said "I'll just pop off now."

I drove home. Lizzy was there with Hannah, Beth and Josh. All my life I have been surrounded by people better than I deserve.

Dad died two days later.

*

Mum's going was the same but different. As ever, she set the agenda.

After Dad went, she had a bit of a renaissance. As I'm sure many carers find, people don't appreciate how tiring and dispiriting caring can be. We didn't. I don't think Mum did either: his slow decline masked her ever greater commitment. She probably only realised when – finally - Dad wasn't there.

She became very active around the village: dressing smartly and putting on her little hat. She went to Church for the sociability, the shop for daily necessities and a couple of times to New Zealand to visit Peggy, her sister.

The last time she went, the flight was almost too much. Her feet swelled up and she spent the first week or so in hospital. Flying back, insurance provided a nurse with an oxygen cylinder: Mum felt very pampered.

Peter said: "I've just been going through Mum's finances. God, she needs so little." I now think – and this is typically Peter – he quietly kept her going with a monthly sub, but never told me.

At her request, we did our 'Christmas visit' early in December. Peter had gone into her attic and retrieved a small artificial Christmas tree about eighteen inches high. It had spray-on snow and tiny baubles glued in place. Sitting smugly on her mantelpiece it was her only Christmas decoration. She gave small presents to the children and allowed Lizzy and Hannah (now 11) to organise tea.

She looked OK: her usual self, but she admitted to feeling tired at times.

We went out for a walk and when we returned, she was asleep in Dad's old chair. Her face was relaxed, her mouth smiling gently. We decided to go home without waking her, but loading three children and the usual support gear of toys and games into the car proved too noisy.

She stood outside the back door and waved as we reversed out into the lane.

We all waved back, I gave a short beep and we drove off.

A couple of weeks or so later, Peter rang. Mum was in Winchester hospital. Pneumonia. We both thought of Dad, but didn't mention him until later.

Mum had let down her hair. Normally, she kept it tidied away in a bun. I had forgotten how long it was. I had not realised how white it had become. It cascaded like foam over her shoulders, shining against the slightly off-white of the hospital pillow.

The knuckles on her hands were large and red, but her palms were as warm as ever.

She said: "My boys."

I said "Yeah, well -" and stopped.

Peter said, "you're looking great, mum."

She asked us to stand together at the end of the bed. We did so. I felt almost as if we were actors in a play she had written.

"My boys!" she said again. "I'm so proud of you both." Her words sounded almost rehearsed, and I realised that indeed, we were in a scene of her own construction. She said: "I'm sorry about taking so long to die."

It was the Diana Moment. My indomitable Mum wasn't going to hang about hoping to get better and begin yo-yoing between hospital and home. She knew her body was giving up, and she was organised and ready.

Peter and I stood in Winchester Hospital car park. He said, "I'll see how she is tomorrow."

I said I'd come up. He said not to worry, it was easier for him.

It was two days before Christmas when the expected call came. Peter again. He sounded tired, relieved and immensely sad. "She's gone."

I was sat with the twins and Hannah at the kitchen table. I can't remember how I told them, but I do remember the numbness.

When her parents died, Lizzy had said "I'm now an orphan."

When she returned, she immediately knew what had happened. Middle-aged orphans both, we hugged and wept.

The man on the stairs.

What: I listen to a midnight monologue

Where: Worthing

My age: 26

Early in my writing career I washed up in Worthing and lived in a bedsit in a large and once substantial Edwardian house, now carved into single rooms. There was unreliable plumbing, shared bathrooms, coin-operated meters and stair lights that went dark after thirty seconds.

My room was downstairs, with a double bed, small kitchenette, thin curtains, draughty sash windows and two electric sockets hosting a trailing jumble of extension leads.

In short, it was much the same as most of the places I lived in during that period. Better than many as the mattress was only a couple of years old and still comfortable, albeit on a repaired bed of such ancient lineage it was probably slept in by Noah.

I was working at a small civil engineering site, helping to build an underground pumping station. For once the wages were good, so I banished my old battleship of a typewriter back to my parent's attic. Now, I spent my evenings plugging away, writing scripts on a new compact portable machine. The physical act of writing became easier, but the quality hardly improved.

Over time, I got to recognise some – but not all - of my fellow residents. There was a divorced chap who cleaned himself up once a month to see his children; an old lady who ignored you, even if you opened the door for her; a pretty girl on the top floor who showed absolutely no interest in me and the caretaker and his wife living in comparative luxury in half the downstairs floor with – listen to this – a proper kitchen and bathroom.

Also, somewhere on the first floor I think, there lived a small, tired looking, musty man with a bent back, who moved slowly, dragging his leg, lurching along with his head hanging low.

I had been there about a month when, going out through the front door, I found him standing on the step, fumbling for his keys. From his arm dangled a white plastic carrier bag containing the distinctive shape of a can of corned beef.

I said "Here y'go!" and held the door open.

His head turned up towards me, his balding pate replaced by a face that was surprisingly moon-shaped, with one watery eye. It was difficult to guess his age, but if pushed I'd say around 40.

He smelt of loneliness.

I stood to one side, the easier to let him pass.

He stayed where he was, blocking the doorway. Without preamble he said: "I was in an accident. No compensation, nothing." His voice was thin, complaining and unpleasant. He took a long breath and looked pleadingly at me, wanting a conversation so badly I felt repelled.

I said, indifferently: "Oh," turned my shoulder and brushed past him, guiltily heading to the outside world.

Over the next month or so I got into the habit, before going out, of glancing through my window, which gave a good view of the path to the front door and the pavement beyond. And if I saw his bent back and downcast head coming towards the house, I would retreat into the shadows, waiting for his key in the lock and his slow, hesitant lopsided tread up the stairs. And even then, I would slowly count to ten before quietly going out.

He had said eight words to me, and received little more than a grunt in reply, but now I avoided him like the plague. For somehow – and take this how you want – I felt assaulted by his needy loneliness. I told myself I wasn't a bad person, but I felt guilty for not being a saint, for not being charitable and inviting him in for a chat. But then – I was sure – if I did share a few minutes with him, I'd never get rid of the bugger.

The crunch came a few weeks later still.

It was about midnight, and I was in bed, drifting off to sleep. And then I heard a voice. A thin voice, unpleasant and immediately recognisable.

"Hello. It's me. The chap in the small room tucked away at the back. I'm the one you wait for on the stairs. You all know me. I was in an accident. Well, I haven't seen anyone or spoken to anyone for a week now. So I thought I'd come out and see if anyone wants a chat. Hello, anyone? I'm sat here on the landing with my little teapot and two cups, one for me, one for someone else. And milk, I've got milk. Doesn't anyone want a cup of tea with me?"

My first reaction was one of affront: I'd managed to avoid him for weeks but now, here he was, invading my life again. In fact, he was invading everyone's life. We'd all be awake, the residents of the house. The divorced man, the old lady who ignored you, the pretty girl on the top floor, the caretaker and his wife and probably three or four others I had glimpsed but sparingly.

All of us: now awake and listening in the small hours to this needy, whining, whinging voice spilling out the emptiness of his life from the landing on the stairs.

He went quiet for a while and the house settled back down, like a giant but nervous flounder on the seabed.

Of course – either by accident or design – he started up again precisely just after a collective - but silent - sigh of relief, felt by everyone, had quieted the house.

"Hello? No-one here, except me. Still on my own. I said to myself, I can't go another day without talking to someone. Yet another day without a chat. Couldn't do it. I waited up 'till midnight. You can't tell me you wouldn't like a cup of tea. I've got milk. And sugar. And sweeteners, 'cause I know some people don't like sugar. I got sweeteners especially, in case someone joined me. Anyone?"

And I had a sudden urge to switch on my light, throw on some clothing, open the door and clamber up the stairs and say something. What, I didn't know. Nor did I know if I should I say - whatever it was I was going to say - loudly, so other people would hear and breathe a sigh of relief and know I had martyred myself for them to get back to sleep.

But I hesitated as another thought struck me: with the thirty-second timer on the lights, he must be sitting there in near darkness, like a little mysterious gnome in the gloom, with his little tray and his little teapot with matching and grubby (they were bound to be grubby) milk jug and cups.

Or perhaps he had jammed the timing mechanism with a splintered matchstick? I glanced at the base of my draughty door: no light shone through, so he must be sitting in the dark. And with this excuse, my thin resolve faltered and died.

And still his voice droned on. By this time I had stopped noticing the small variations in tone: his words had become a sort of mental toothache: impossible to accommodate, impossible to ignore and impossible to stop.

Somewhat disturbingly, he changed tactic, making it personal.

"Hello, the man in number 6, why don't you come out and join me? You seem friendly. I told you about my accident, didn't I? There's a cup of tea here for you, if you want it. Number 6, I'm talking to you, hello. Another chat, that would be nice. Hello? Number 6?"

There was no response and after a pause this sad, pathetic, infinitely irritating man continued.

"I'm sorry, I don't know your names, I don't know anyone's names. Not here, in this house. Hello number 7. Number 7, hello? You're that kind looking lady, aren't you? You smiled at me once, on this very landing. I was coming up; you were coming down. You smiled. Do you like tea? Come and have a cuppa. I have sweeteners, did I say I have sweeteners? And sugar."

He waited for a while for a response from number 7. I couldn't place her, but I got the impression he'd been banking on the kind looking lady in number 7. She might have been the one all this was for: as he couldn't ask her directly, he'd wrapped it up – like some insane Christmas present – in layers of lonely neediness.

Eventually, he gave up on her. "A week now without a chat. A whole week. The lady at the post office, we always say a few words to each other. I wait outside until there's no queue. I always buy stamps. 3. second class. And she says 'the usual?' And I say 'yes please, 3 second class stamps.'' She gives them to me, but she never asks why 3. Second class. But I have a story prepared, just in case she does. Three nephews, I'll say, one in Wales, one in London and one in Bristol, that's what I'll say. Wales, London and Bristol, but she never asks. And I should mention I have Garibaldi biscuits. We used to call them squashed fly biscuits. I thought of cake, but I don't have a cake tin and anyway, some people don't like marzipan."

He subsided again, back into quietness. I imagined him staring down at his cold tea.

And as I lay there, in bed, on top of my comfortable mattress and under the warm duvet, with my head nestling down, a thought came, like a treacherous assassin in the dark.

'This,' it told me, *'this could make a great TV play.'*

I imagined all us listeners, our heads on pillows in the half-light, faces reflecting a range of emotions from irritation through indifference to guilt, while this wretched man droned on and on.

It could be a tour de force of wonderful writing and acting. The BBC's 'Play for Today' would lap it up. The critics would go wild. Commissions would come pouring in. I'd be asked to open shops and give lectures. Beautiful young actresses would queue up to visit me in my luxury hotel room and -

But the voice, seeping miasmically under my door, was not to be denied.

"Hello, Hello, 1A. 1A, are you listening. You held the door for me once, remember, and said 'here y'go.' That was nice of you, 1A."

1A was my room: he was speaking directly to me, so my ears had sat up and paid attention. My cosy dream of untrammelled lust and riches vanished.

"And I have biscuits. 1A. Garibaldi, everyone likes Garibaldi. Why don't you come out and join me. The tea's getting cold, but it would only take a moment to boil some water. I could make a completely fresh pot. Nothing like a fresh pot of tea, 1A. Hello? hello?"

Abruptly, the caretaker's voice, so loud he must have been standing by his door, boomed out: "Oi! You! Just shut the heck up, would you?"

The drip drip of words from the landing stopped, as if the tap had been abruptly wrenched closed. There was a long, hurt pause until – finally – small clattering sounds signified the cutlery being stacked and carried away.

And all became still and quiet.

In the morning, the landing showed no evidence of occupation: no spill of milk or tea on the worn carpet. I know this, because I checked, hoping the pretty girl would turn up and we would have something to chat about, but she didn't.

Over the next few days my overwhelming feeling was one of relief, mixed with guilt for my own lack of charity. Also – and this was perplexing – I found it uncomfortable the caretaker did not use the man's name when he called for him to shut up. 'Oi! You!' is generic and could apply to anyone: man, woman, even a dog.

Which made it seem the man on the landing had made such a negligible impact on those around him, even his name had vanished.

Which in turn – of course – made him seem even more pathetic.

I never did write that play: I think I instinctively knew it would require a degree of skill and finesse I did not possess. And later – when I thought of it – I could never shake off the conviction that one person, vomiting out his loneliness for an hour, could be anything other than boring.

And as for the man himself: he must have moved almost immediately afterwards, for I never saw him again: he dropped completely from my existence, as if he had never been.

But since then I have carried — and continue to carry — this sad, lonely, guilt-ridden and pathetic incident, popping up every so often like a malignant pimple, reminding me of my own lack of charity.

I receive my Mantra.

What: I take up transcendental meditation

Where: Portsmouth

My age: 32

I have been happy many times in my life. Usually, it creeps up on me without my realising. For instance:

Many years ago I noticed our shed roof needed repairing. So, one summer afternoon, feeling optimistic and energetic, I climbed up with a roll of tar felting, some clout nails and my bag of tools.

The sun shone, birds sang and the hammer made a satisfying sound as the nails were driven home. I realised afterwards I had been whistling.

The shed was small, so it didn't take long.

I heard a cheerful voice: "How's it going?" I looked down. Lizzy, with a couple of mugs of tea. She went on: "I could hear you coming along the road."

I grinned. "I haven't been along the road!"

"Oh, ha ha." She put the tea down on our cheap plastic garden table. "D'you want a bit of cake with that?"

"Too right I do!" I banged in a final nail, trimmed off the surplus and descended. Lizzy and I had tea and cake in our garden, warm in the sunshine, with birds singing, a slight breeze and a repaired shed.

And in bed that night, contentedly reviewing the day, I realised I had been happy that afternoon.

But – and here's the crux of the matter – had I thought at the time *'I'm happy'* I doubt the mood would have lasted. For – like many moods - happiness can shrivel under inspection.

Notwithstanding, I - like everyone - have sought out things – stuff - that might increase my happiness.

I had a spliff once: it made me feel so ill and dizzy and wanting to vomit I've not tried another. And drink just makes me obnoxious, losing myself in music is not reliable, exercise is intrinsically boring and being with people stressful.

Early in my thirties, on the suggestion of the same pal who later told me I'd be good at computing, I decided to have a go at transcendental meditation, still riding on a bit of a wave from the Beatles a few years earlier.

Some weeks later I found myself with a like-minded group in the front room of a small terraced house with wind chimes at the door.

The walls had a macrame decorations, a framed picture of a man with a beard and a colourful rainbow painted directly onto the plaster. I'd been half expecting gloom, scented candles and quiet farts, but I'd been wrong: it was all cheerful and bright. Uplifting, even.

Our teacher (instructor? Leader? Guru?) was sat on a beanbag. Let's call her Martha.

Martha was around thirty, had light brown hair and wore a tie-dyed skirt and an embroidered waistcoat over a crumpled white shirt. She referred to transcendental meditation as 'TM' and asked us all to share why we were here, what we hoped to gain from TM and – to break the ice - she would start.

She spoke in well organised, rounded sentences, with little grins and flashes of humour, telling us how TM had changed her life, from one of chaotic, tension-filled meaninglessness to her present calm, creative, stress-free state.

When she had finished, we all felt as keen as mustard and ready to meditate like mad.

Martha tilted her head slightly and said: "now, people: your chance to share."

It turned out we all – to one degree or another – suffered from headaches, anxiety, stress, tiredness and depression. Martha assured us TM would help, and smoothly moved on to how the course would work.

We would have lessons and practice sessions and little chats.

And at the end we would individually receive our mantra: a unique, internal sound, carefully chosen and tailored – by Martha – to fully release, for you and you alone, the power of TM. This wonderful password to a better life was never to be shared or even spoken out loud.

There was a bit more instruction and we finished with a practice meditation session.

I fell asleep. Martha said this was often the case and quite normal.

A girl said she now felt energised. Martha said this was often the case and quite normal.

Someone else said they didn't feel any different. Martha – with a grin – said this was often the case and quite normal.

We started laughing and it was very jolly: I was a big, big Martha fan from that moment on.

I can't remember how many practice sessions we had – maybe three, perhaps four - but towards the end I thought there were too many. I was impatient to have my one-to-one with Martha and receive my hand-made, bespoke mantra and strike out on my own.

Time trundled on – as it always does, even for those practicing TM – and the great day arrived.

Martha, for this auspicious occasion, made an obvious effort. Gone was the tie-dyed skirt and the embroidered waistcoat: instead she was draped in a white robe that gave her a solemn, priestly air: to my admittedly slightly adoring gaze, it was breathtakingly impressive.

We sat opposite each other. I was acutely conscious of her knees being very close to mine.

She said something, I said something. We sort of stared at each other for a short while. She bent towards to me to whisper in my ear.

And this is the Diana Moment: her calm, symmetrical features nearing, then moving to the side, presenting me with a sliding, close-up view of the left half of her face.

She smelt of oranges, had pierced ears and — startlingly - was wearing eye make-up and rogue.

The oranges and ears I half expected, but make-up? And applied so skilfully it was barely noticeable a hand's breadth away? My admiration stalled and fractured: I had always thought of her as without vanity of any kind and therefore scornful of cosmetics.

I hardly heard the mantra she whispered in my ear.

She said it again, and this time I caught half of it, I think. But I didn't dare to ask for a repeat.

Walking back, I decided a flawed Martha was better than no Martha: not that it mattered, as I never saw her again.

When home, I settled down to meditate, diligently pinging my half-remembered half-mantra around in my mind; and as I did this, I felt it warping and growing and changing into a new - and in many ways more personal — internal sound.

Later, thinking about it, I really wouldn't have been surprised if Martha — and perhaps other TM teachers — just said the same 'seed' mantra to all new acolytes. A sound that is sufficiently bare boned, malleable and meaningless it can be contorted into whatever works for the meditator. That's what happened to me: I ended up with a two note, rather pleasing base 'sound' impossible to say out loud. When meditating, I allowed this to pulse in my mind, to become the centre of attention: and after a while it would dissipate into nothingness, along with my thoughts.

And after a timeless time (more prosaically, maybe ten or fifteen minutes) it would return like an echoing heart-beat, and slowly guide me back to the here and now.

I gave TM what I felt was a good go: for a month or so I religiously did two sessions a day.

But I didn't really notice any difference to my life: I wasn't any happier or calmer and my headaches and sleep patterns remained erratic. And the next time I had to go to the BBC for a couple of days I felt too self-conscious about it and stopped.

And on returning home I allowed it - as I knew I would - to lapse.

Transcendental Meditation didn't really work for me. Maybe I should have had a better hold of my mantra, or perhaps I didn't try for long enough or treat it with sufficient seriousness. But I am sure – for many people – it is a blessing. So if you are of that mind, try it. It might work for you and – if so – good.

And to finish up: even now, if I dig around inside my mind, my mantra awaits: it will spring – like a neglected puppy - into existence. And I will – perhaps - meditate for a while.

And – most probably - fall asleep.

Opening the wedding presents.

What: Lizzy and I open our wedding presents.

Where: Drayton, Portsmouth.

My age: 39

So, Lizzy and I got married at Portsmouth registry office on a cold March day in 1984. The reception was in a local pub and afterwards we set off on our married life together in my trusty, rusty, little old yellow car. A Datsun 100A, if you're interested: I've been a fan of Japanese cars ever since.

We didn't go far: just drove around the corner and down the road a bit, before stopping and walking along the seafront, where the paving stones are laid in a pattern that echoes the battlements of the nearby castle.

We did this as a kind of pilgrimage: for in the past we had both lived in Southsea, and our times had overlapped. Also, for both of us, this part of the seafront had been a favourite, but we had never met or noticed each other. So there was an appropriate and pleasing synchronicity to doing this together now, on our first day as a married couple.

We parked by the little fun-fair and set out: to our left Southsea common was a green sward; on the right the pebbly beach ran down to the sea and above, the sky was grey and dull.

It could hardly be called exciting. We had planned to perhaps get as far as the castle, but the wind was bitter, so at the Naval War Memorial we turned back at a run, holding hands and giggling, to drive – as arranged by Lizzy and her mum - to her parent's bungalow.

I was expecting a relaxing time: tea, cake, perhaps a nap. But in the front room was the assembled ranks of Lizzy's side of the family: aunts and uncles, cousins once or twice removed and - I'm sure - a black sheep or two. Lizzy's mum presided over stacked cups and saucers, sandwiches, cake, more cake and the largest teapot in Portsmouth, while her dad stood by a table of glasses, bottles and a small crate of beer.

When we entered everyone stopped and stared.

I have never been comfortable in any sort of crowd, and instantly began to panic. I whispered to Lizzy 'I need to go to the loo!' but she grabbed my hand: her voice was fierce: 'No you bloody well don't!' She was not going to have her newly acquired husband skulking off and vanishing for the next hour or so.

Her dad appeared, handed us both a small glass filled with a brown liquid, turned to the assembled multitude and said 'to the happy couple!'

Everyone raised their own glasses or cups or bottles or whatever: 'the happy couple!' And we all drank. As did I.

It was sherry: truly the drink of the devil. Even the finest quality sherry cannot disguise the vile taste of it being sherry. I felt as if I were drinking a stagnant something or other left over from the Christmas before last. In my stomach I could feel it clawing its way through the greasy lunchtime chicken.

Feeling queasy, I looked round. After a couple of blinks, things fell into place: the vast crowd of relatives was largely a product of my panicked imagination: there was perhaps only seven or eight of them, all amiable and welcoming.

I was handed another glass. I was past caring so drank it down. Sherry again! As if there wasn't enough pain in the world.

Neatly stacked in a corner were our wedding presents. Beside them were two pouffes. Lizzy was sat on one. She patted the other. "C'mon Jimbob!"

"His and her pouffes!" I said in what I thought was a wise and witty manner but almost certainly wasn't. A black sheep, or more likely an uncle, chuckled appreciatively.

Pouffes are difficult to navigate: there is a certain point in the descent where you just have to trust you have aimed your backside correctly. I hadn't, and swayed precariously, one cheek on, one cheek off. I said 'Whooooah!' kicked a present out of the way and managed to jam a foot against the skirting board and – amid some hilarity – got myself upright.

We opened presents, with everyone commenting and saying 'Oh, look at that!' And 'That'll come in handy,' or 'I hope they've kept the receipt for that' in the sort of tone that pleasingly condemns with small praise.

And as Lizzy and I sat there together, untying string, ripping paper and often giggling, a strange and welcome happiness descended upon us as a couple: the events of the day had – at last – caught up and become real: we had just got married and were now opening presents in a group of friendly relatives; the room was warm and soon we would be eating cake; tomorrow, we would go on honeymoon and lo and behold – a four slice toaster! Could life get any better?

That happiness: unique, shared, exquisite and wonderful, is the Diana Moment of this chapter and indeed of the whole day.

Yep, OK: maybe I was slightly drunk and discombobulated, and perhaps getting through to that point without great mishap gave an overwhelming sense of relief, but so what? Whatever the reason, it was a Diana Moment, shared with Lizzy: it sits there now, in my mind: a moment to cherish.

And yet another lesson

What: I learn a lesson from my first TV play.

Where: Southsea, Portsmouth.

My age: 32

It is odd, how sometimes, things work out in ways you didn't expect. It's the law of unintended consequences, which is another way of saying nothing is certain.

When I sold my first and only TV play, I hoped – despite previous experiences - that I was made. Fame and riches would surely follow. I had served my apprenticeship and my writing had become (I thought) confident, economic and fluid. Twenty or more radio plays had been written, bought, produced and broadcast, ranging from absurdist comedies through tense emotional dramas to supernatural thrillers.

I had been up and down to broadcasting house many times, staying in the background, rewriting, adding and cutting, but often thinking: *'this is my plot, those actors are saying my words, all from my fertile imagination!'* And, occasionally – no more than every hour or so - *'none of this would have happened without me!'*

I would stay with my sister Judy, who had a small house in Chiswick and – I believed – rather enjoyed fussing over me. Sometimes, if I managed to get a seat on the underground, I'd pull out a script and – somewhat obviously - annotate it with a BBC biro.

It was all very ego-boosting.

But the truth of the matter was, I never got out of bedsit land. My name might have appeared in the Radio Times and there had been a phone interview with a local radio station (they must have been desperate) but mum and dad still visited with food, loo rolls and a five-pound note.

My earnings from writing enabled me to take slightly longer breaks between temporary jobs, but not much else.

And then BBC TV contacted me! Let me write that again: BBC TV CONTACTED ME!! I received a letter saying they were developing a new series of 'Second City Firsts' - a season of short plays by new writers, produced from Birmingham (the 'second city'). And they wished me to submit a script.

Oh Wow!

Someone had been paying attention! My brilliance had been noticed! My long slog had not been in vain!

Now all I needed was a plot. And characters. And a location. And to make it visual.

Over the years I had developed the habit – when needing an idea – of smearing glue over my Formica topped table. After carefully replacing the cap, I would spend an engrossing twenty minutes or so peeling the drying glue from my fingers then another twenty – with the aid of a pin – removing it from the table.

I thought of it as a form of meditation instead of just another displacement activity. Or maybe meditation is a displacement non-activity.

But who cares? As so often at that time, when my mind had little else in it but ideas - it worked.

I had a title: 'Postcards from Southsea.' And a plot, characters and location.

After three days I had a finished script and sometime later I found myself in Birmingham. There was a set with a stylised beach, a stuffed seagull and some fine actors. I inadvertently annoyed the director by saying I thought one of his cherished ideas was naff. Even at the age of 32 I was still – underneath it all – a little prat.

'Postcards from Southsea' was not a masterpiece. Nor was it absolutely terrible. It was an instantly forgettable TV play saddled with radio play dialogue.

Allow me to expand. Dialogue for radio plays inevitably has more work to do than the TV equivalent, as it needs to carry the visuals as well. So there tends to be quite a lot of extra lines of the 'Oh, don't raise your eyebrows like that' variety. On their own, on radio, they can pass without being noticed: it is the way things work because it is the way things must work. But the accumulative effect in TV drama can be deadening. Like wearing wellington boots when running a marathon: sure, you will get there in the end, but the effort will make you feel twice as knackered.

And this – or rather my realisation of this - was a Diana Moment which fed into my decision - a year or so later – to give up writing. But I get ahead of myself.

The people in Birmingham did their bit: the producer produced, the director directed, the actors acted, everyone else scurried purposefully around and I was largely ignored, which was undoubtedly the best way of doing things.

And a month or so later it went out on national TV and vanished – like a single drop of rain – into the vast ocean of media history.

As written, the play ends with a couple of characters having a conversation in which nothing much is decided. This peters out, the camera tilts to a darkening sky and there is the sound of seagulls and waves while the credits roll.

Yeah, I know: totally naff.

But when 'Postcards from Southsea' was broadcast to the nation, there were no seagulls or waves.

Nope: they had been cut. Instead, under the credits, you heard the unscripted chatter of the two actors as they waited on set for the all clear.

Just mundane talk about this and that.

Yep, OK, it might have been directorial revenge for my early comment about naffness but – and here's the thing - it was way, way better than all my carefully honed and scripted radio dialogue. To return to the marathon metaphor: when the end credits were rolling, the play finally cast off its welly boots and began running properly.

My mouth dropped open. It was the Diana Moment. If the best I could do wasn't as good as two people shooting the breeze, what was the point? I was OK at radio stuff, but that was probably it. I looked around at my bedsit. It was a nice bedsit, as bedsits go: bed, table, chair, a couple of bean bags, kitchenette, wardrobe, chest of drawers, telly and always a draught from somewhere.

Was this it?

Old people might live in bedsits. Young people under 30 might live in bedsits. But I was 32 and wanted more.

Two years later – for it takes that long for hope to be squashed – I gave up writing.

Goodbye Judy.

What: My sister Judy dies.

Where: In a hospice.

My age: 53

As I have remarked before: it is shameful, the memories that are missing from my mind. Pivotal moments I know must have happened have vanished, obliterated by following events, like a single wave being overtaken by a tsunami.

I offer no excuses. I remember what I remember, not what I expect to remember. And I have no more control over the process of forgetting than I would have over smoke from a bonfire in a wind.

And so it is with Judy. She became poorly and went to the doctor. After tests and more tests she was diagnosed with pancreatic cancer. I don't remember how I learnt that fact. Dad had died a year or so previously, so undoubtedly the news came from my brother Peter or my mother or possibly Judy herself. Or maybe Lizzy, having fielded a phone call.

The moment has gone.

We had a friend, Hillary, a doctor. We sat around our kitchen table: Lizzy and I, Hillary and very possibly the cat. And I asked about cancer of the pancreas. And I know she knew I was not asking idly, but she answered as if I had.

And she said, it's one of the bad ones. There was little chance of a cure and usually only palliative care was offered. Patients are normally given about six months or less to get their affairs in order, and/or make peace with God and/or tick off items on a bucket list.

I asked it if could be sudden? I meant, could they ignore it until bang – it happened and was over.

Her reply was sometimes that might happen, but often there was too much deterioration of bodily function: it couldn't be ignored.

I said we are talking about my sister. Somehow, without a change of expression, her eyes became compassionate. She touched my hand and said "I thought we were. Talking about someone close."

And I said, as if somehow it made a difference: "Half-sister. By Dad's first marriage."

Hillary was fairly accurate with her prognosis: Judy lasted another eight months. But she was less accurate about no treatment: Judy did a course of radiotherapy which – I suppose – might have added those two extra months.

The summer came and with it Judy's slow, inevitable, depressing progress from home to hospital to care home to hospice to grave.

Peter: as reliable and as kind as ever, visited more frequently than myself. Sometimes he took Mum, but usually he went alone. Judy – always a great walker – was forced to cut back as her life closed in. Conversation was normally about the past and old friends: her hand would shake if she tried to pour tea and her cheekbones became more prominent.

We waited. All of us waited.

Judy and I were sitting outside the care home, which was on the south coast, but a little way inland. Seagulls could be seen and heard, but not the sea.

She said "I cracked, y'know, yesterday, or it might have been the day before. Or even the day before that."

I said, "Cracked?"

Judy said: "The nurse said she had been waiting for it." I might have said something, but I don't think Judy was listening. I remember her exact words, and the stunning, intimate passion with which she spoke. "About it. It. I cracked. I screamed and yelled and said how unfair it was, how unfair it really was, this thing, this fucking thing, growing inside me, killing me."

She had placed her hand on her abdomen: her palm must have been only a few inches from the monstrous, blind, borrowing beast that was killing her.

The hospice was very pleasant: tucked away in tranquil grounds, with closely mown, flat lawns, trimmed hedges and disciplined trees. Even the signage was muted and respectful.

Judy's room had a view of that lawn, and the hedges and the trees. The curtains were suitably bland and without excitement, as if ashamed of witnessing the constant parade of bed-ridden occupants waiting to fade away.

With a growing sense of futility, Peter or I would visit every couple of days. Often, Judy – now on palliative morphine -

would be asleep and there was nothing much to do unless you took a book or wished to watch a small TV perched high on a bracket on the wall.

I usually lasted about half an hour: I don't know about Peter: possibly the same. For although Peter and I talked on the phone, our conversations became routine about who would go on what day and if she was the same and had the doctor said anything.

Until, on a Friday evening, he rang at an unaccustomed time. The doctor had been in contact: as far as they could judge, Judy would not last until the morning.

Peter and I met in the neat carpark, and stood in moonshine on the raked gravel beside the straight-edged border. He had waited for me, or I had waited for him: neither of us wished to go in alone, to possibly face a concerned nurse, asking us to wait while she rang someone more senior to impart the bad news.

I asked if mum knew.

He said no: he had taken her once to the hospice and, driving back, Mum had said she only wanted to know when it was over.

Judy – unconscious - was breathing in great spasmodic gasps, as if underwater and only occasionally reaching the surface. Each gasp was long, and came with a groan: and was only ever outward or inward, as if her body, having made the effort to exhale or inhale, needed to gather strength before completing the breath.

And sometimes the gap between stretched to seeming infinity and Peter and I would look at each other, wondering if our sister was due to take air in or let air out or had stopped altogether.

And occasionally she would be restless, and sit up, the light coverlet cascading down, her nightie awry, a thin, naked shoulder exposed. And one of us would tell her unseeing eyes 'it's OK Judy, it's OK, lie down, it's OK.'

And she would subside at an angle, with her head dangling over the edge of the bed and one of us would straighten her out, drawing up the cover and restoring her to decency.

We had begun in the late evening: possibly ten or eleven o'clock. And right through the night little seemed to change and we got used to being in this small remote bubble. Even Judy's irregular breathing became mundane; we dozed and found some magazines to read. I watched – with muted sound - 'Waterworld' with Kevin Costner and wondered why the reviews were bad.

And in the morning, I kept watch while Peter went off to his London flat, to come back a couple of hours later showered, fed and refreshed. His flat was only 25 minutes away, but in those pre SatNav days there was absolutely no chance I could find it through London traffic.

So I washed as best I could and found a small café and had breakfast.

And nothing changed. A doctor had come in when I was out. Peter had asked if Judy knew we were there. And the doctor had shaken her head and answered it was hard to say. But probably not.

And so we continued to wait.

Sometime in the afternoon, Peter said what we were both thinking. He looked at our sister, lying on her hospital bed, her pitiful chest awaiting the next upheaval. "Look," he said: "what's the point of this vigil?"

And we both knew exactly what he meant and how the conversation would go and precisely what the outcome would be.

That we would leave. The constant vigil would be over. We would go home and feel guilty and say we would come back later: and we would, but the chances were Judy – now - would die alone.

So we had a circular conversation, justifying doing what was easy rather than what was hard.

And left.

Peter rang the following morning: the Sunday. No change and he didn't think he could get in that day. I said I wasn't sure I could either and Peter said he'd ring the hospice that evening and get back to me if there was any change. And I said that was sensible.

Our sister Judy, at the age of 72, died overnight. Alone.

She did not – according to the doctor – regain any sort of awareness. But I ask: **how do they know?** Judy was checked every hour or so, and at some point, she was found not alive. So how did they know she didn't wake up and discover she was alone?

The simple truth of the matter is, we don't know: no-one does. But to live – to go on - we tell ourselves plausible stories to make truth palatable, then bury them in the past.

Because of guilt and a feeling I should pay my last respects – whatever that means – I drove up and parked for the final time in that immaculate car park.

It was the first time I had ever seen a corpse. She was flat on her back, her body decorously wrapped, her legs and arms neatly arranged, her face in repose, her expression neutral, her eyes open.

I only stayed a few minutes. I touched my lips to her forehead. I knew she would be cold but somehow, when I felt it, I was repulsed. I could not bear to touch her eyelids, to close her away from the world.

And that image of her sad, vacant body, staring unblinkingly at the ceiling, is the image I remember.

I mumbled 'goodbye Judy,' and left.

The Heinz Wolff look-alikes.

What: I take a programming test

Where: A hotel in Bournemouth

My age: 34

In case you're wondering, in the 1970s Professor Heinz Wolff was often on TV and looked exactly as a professor should: great balding domed head with tufts of hair above the ears, intelligent features, glasses, accent and bowtie. In any BBC science program he'd be present, enthusiastically communicating complex stuff in simple terms. I was a great fan.

I was playing chess with a pal when I found myself saying: "I think I need a career change. Check."

He said: "Oh, bummer, I never saw that. You're good at chess, try computing."

And I said "Yeah. OK: might as well. Check Mate!"

And he said "Oh, bollocks."

A few days later, in the labour exchange, I was interviewed by a tired man behind a desk.

He asked me why computing? And started looking through my CV.

I began telling him how my writing career was going nowhere, how my ideas had dried up since 'Postcards from Southsea' eighteen months before, and my general feeling that I had to do something different, right now, to get out of bedsit land, and -

He cut me off. "I see you taught maths." I nodded. He hardly noticed. "There's a computing course you can do." He riffled around in a drawer. "But you have to take an aptitude test first." He handed me a few sheets of printed paper. "Here y'go, good luck, bye."

It seemed that computer programming required a particular turn of mind, adept at solving logic puzzles.

And to put you off applying, there were some examples, none of which I was able to do. Undeterred, I applied anyway, secured a place and bought some books on intelligence tests and how to boost your brain power.

As a benchmark, I did one of the tests and scored an extremely disappointing and deflating 105: barely above average, if that. Before this, on good days, when feeling smart, I'd always thought of myself as capable of joining MENSA, but hadn't because they all seemed too needy.

The test would be at a Bournemouth hotel in two weeks. I settled down to boost my brain power, doing every test in every book, and when they ran out, buying more books. It became obsessive, a bit like when I was playing golf, only more fun.

Steadily, my brain power – as measured by books - climbed, eventually peaking at just 120.

Still not MENSA material but – possibly– good enough.

I got to the hotel with two minutes to spare: even with boosted brain power my bump of location was smaller than a walnut. An irritated looking woman wearing blue gave me an insincere smile, ticked my name from a list and ushered me through.

I found myself in the hotel conference hall, a vast space normally used for ra-ra meetings of middle managers. It was packed with circular tables, each with seating for five would-be computer programmers.

The woman had followed me in and closed the door. She pointed into the far distance. "I think," she said, "there's a place over there."

I set off, edging gingerly between the tables and saying sorry. Meantime, the lady mounted a podium and tapped her finger against the microphone. Tap-tap. Her amplified voice echoed disdainfully. "When we've all got seats ... we'll begin."

A couple of hundred pairs of eyes followed my progress. I found the table, sat down and settled myself, laying out sharpened pencils, an eraser and two biros. I also had an intimidating slide rule I didn't know how to use, but I chickened out from putting that on display.

Once I was sitting, she spoke. She was commendably forthright: there were some 247 applicants in the hall and only 74 places. So roughly two out of three of us would be unsuccessful. She added 'sorry' as an afterthought and paused for a moment to let it sink in. Then she gave the schedule: the test would last 90 minutes, followed by an hour's coffee break while they were marked. To finish, the names of those that had passed would be read out. She made it sound like we'd be attending a funeral service after a violent massacre. The test would be starting in five minutes and don't turn over your papers until then.

A couple of minions appeared and began distributing test papers, placing them carefully upside down.

And for the first time I looked properly round the table at my competitors.

There were four of them. And they all – more or less - looked like Heinz Wolff, but with more hair and only one bow tie between them. In other words, they all gave the impression of being formidably logical and intelligent. I felt doomed: with guys like these in the mix, what chance had I got?

There came the tap-tap again. "You may turn over your papers and begin."

The test was a thick wodge of some 20 or so pages. An industrious silence settled over the hall. From my practicing, I had a system which served me well: sweep once through, start to finish, answering everything that looked straightforward. Then another pass to have a bash at everything else and finally a third skim through making random guesses at any I hadn't answered.

After all, I might get some right and there was – as far as I understood it – no penalty for being wrong.

After my first pass I flipped back to the start and took a sip of water. Glancing up, I saw two of my companions staring glumly at me. With a sudden starburst of insight, I realised they thought I'd finished! Not only finished, but finished in double quick time! It was the Diana Moment: they might resemble mega big brain Heinz Wolff, but that was probably the all of it: underneath they were just ordinary people hoping for a job.

So maybe, just maybe, they weren't as good at this stuff as I'd assumed.

Maybe, just maybe, they were ill prepared and without a plan.

And maybe, just maybe, not everyone else in the hall had one either.

Which meant that maybe, just maybe, I could make it.

This revelation seemed to boost my logic circuits. And as I again worked my way carefully from page to page, many of the problems that had seemed impenetrable before, now yielded an answer.

I had just finished my final skim-through when - tap-tap - "You have 3 minutes left."

In 'Enter the Dragon,' (a very enjoyable martial arts film with little artistic merit, laughable storyline, bad acting and brilliant action sequences) Bruce Lee – after destroying an army of opponents – is suddenly imprisoned by descending steel shutters. There is no escape, so he sits down, neatly arranges himself, puts his hands on his lap and calmly awaits the future.

OK: I'm not Bruce Lee and I know completing a 90-minute pencil and paper test is not quite the same as maiming and slaughtering a multitude of karate killers, but at the time I felt it was.

So, while the Heinz Wolffs were desperately trying to finish, I neatly squared my answer papers, pocketed my writing equipment, put my hands on my lap and calmly awaited the future.

Which duly arrived in the form of lukewarm coffee and uninteresting custard creams.

The names of those that had passed were read out in alphabetical order. So 'James Brook' was high in the list. I stood, walked to the front and waited while – one by one - the rest of us geniuses were assembled. Not a single Heinz Wolff was called.

I was now, officially, one of the one in three who had a quirky enough mind to become a computer programmer.

Which I duly became and – in one capacity or another - I remained in IT for the next 30 years.

Computing, to a diligent slogger like myself, is seldom exciting.

Which is why many of my Diana Moments from that point on are not work related.

First child: Hannah.

What: Our first child is born.

Where: Princess Anne Maternity Hospital, Southampton.

My age: 43

Our beautiful daughter Hannah was born in March 1988 at Princess Anne Maternity Hospital, Southampton. A few days before, at a check-up, our baby was deemed small, and not showing any enthusiasm to turn: it was likely she would come out bum first. So there was talk of C-sections, or just sections. I knew what they meant, so in my head, I thought 'Caesarean.'

One was arranged for Friday, at 9:20 am. So the day before, on Thursday, after supper, I drove Lizzy, looking stout and sounding cheerful, to the hospital.

Sitting up in bed, comfortable in a crisp clean bed jacket embroidered with small blue flowers, she was outwardly calm.....ish

"Oh, Jimbob," she said. "Tomorrow!"

I took her hand. "Lizbob, tomorrow, yes."

I was feeling sick and nauseous, my stomach wanting to spill upwards while my guts made it clear they wanted to unload downwards.

Lizzy touched my white, cold, sweaty forehead. "You OK?" I couldn't answer. "D'you want to go?"

"Sorry, yes."

Her fingers were tightly entwined with mine. "You'll be here tomorrow?"

"Yes, of course." I stood. "Sorry."

"You will be here?"

"Yes, promise."

"Love you."

"Love you."

I got back home at eight or so. I couldn't see the cat but put out some food anyway.

There is an old joke: a sea-sick man is vomiting over the side of a ship. Another man comes up and pats him gently on the back. "Never mind old chap," he says: "you'll be fine once the moon comes up." The sick man stares at the waves. "Oh God," he replies: "has that got to come up too?"

And for the next ten or so minutes I knew exactly how he felt. Then I drank some water and went to bed, falling instantly asleep.

In the morning I felt fine and was at the hospital in good time. I donned some protective kit, made possibly of paper. Everything had started to feel surreal, as if I'd entered some parallel universe, halfway between the real world and a TV medical drama.

Lizzy was wheeled in, I was positioned at the non-business end and told to stay there.

She patted my hand and smiled. "You OK now?"

"Yeah. You Ok?"

She took a breath. "Yeah. Butterflies."

"Me too."

We moved into the operating theatre, with lights, equipment and medics. Lizzy looked down, watching herself being shifted onto the table. "It's happening, Jimbob, it's happening."

I pressed her fingers. "Yeah." The medics gathered round and a sheet was put up, stretching across, concealing her lower half. I could have looked over, but didn't.

I lowered my head but not my voice: here, emotions were not embarrassing. "Love you, Lizbob."

"Love you Jimbob."

Over the sheet a masked face appeared. I recognised our consultant from the formidable eyebrows.

"All OK up there?"

"Yeah," I said. "Thanks."

Lizzy said "Thanks, yeah." Then, with barely a hint of tension: "go for it."

"Righty-ho!"

He vanished and we felt the mood changing into one of industrious efficiency. After a minute or so Lizzy was tilted to the left, then to the right. There was a quiet, business-like mutter or two beyond the curtain: orders issued, crisp responses.

She closed her eyes. I whispered "here we go!"

She ignored me. She often did when I stated the obvious.

She was rocked some more; it was quiet for a minute or so before the midwife appeared. She carried a small bundle wrapped in a towel. Lizzy, eyes wet, held out her arms.

Our baby had arrived, bang on time, right on schedule and - as these things go - with minimum fuss. Lizzy looked down at the tiny, peaceful face. "Hello you. We've been waiting for you for such a long time."

I moved a flap of towel to get a better view. "Hello Hannah. So, so good to see you at last."

The eyebrows appeared again. "All seems to be fine. A couple more minutes and you'll be wheeled off."

I said "Lizbob, you've done it."

Her smile was undiluted joy. "Yeah." She gave an enormous sigh, letting out the tension of our five years of trying. "Yeah, we've done it."

Hannah was so, so perfect. Our eyes were ravenous, devouring her as we made an inventory. We counted her toes, her fingers, her legs, her arms, her elbows, her knees, her eyes, her nose, her mouth, her ..... oh, you get the idea. Everything about our fresh new perfect daughter was poured over and remarked on and assessed as if we were explorers in a cavern of delights.

Finally, Lizzy said, "you need to make those calls."

I thought of grandparents and sighed. "Yes."

"And you need to eat something: I know you."

"Yes. Are you eating?" I was still looking at our daughter, hoping she would grip my finger.

"Jimbob: you need to make the calls. And have something to eat."

"You'll be alright?"

"Yes. Never better." She glanced at the clock. It wasn't yet 10:30. "I need to sleep."

"I'll be back at 2?"

"Yes, that would be fine." She closed her eyes. "Love you."

"Love you." I said. And then to Hannah: "love you." And to Lizzy's already relaxing face: "All welcome after two? Grandparents? Everyone?"

She didn't answer, but a weary hand waved bye bye.

I sat with Hannah cradled in my arms for a minute longer, then asked a passing nurse – or midwife – or anyone really – what I should do with this tiny baby. And Hannah was gently placed in her crib.

And in the afternoon, it was grandparents and relatives and photographs and trips to the vending machine and more inspections of this wondrous baby: the first grandchild for both sides. Often, I found myself redundant, and sat outside, leafing through old copies of 'Hello' and 'The Nursing Times.'

And as dusk settled in and Lizzy and Hannah eased into sleep, I drove home, thinking 'tomorrow - or maybe the day after – we will have a baby in the car. A baby!'

I ate and went over to some nearby friends. We drank wine and chatted; I'm sure I mentioned more than once how perfect Hannah was, and how she had ten toes, every one of which I had counted.

Walking back, the day and the wine caught up. I stood for a moment, feeling pinpricks of cold against my face. I put out a hand and supported myself against a lamppost.

And realisation came: Lizzy was – now - a mother; I was – now - a father; we were - now - parents. The nursery (finished only two days before – don't ask) would be occupied. And the future we had so endlessly discussed would become real: the pram in the hall, the baby seat in the car, the steriliser in the kitchen and bottles of formula in the fridge. And further ahead: Hannah would grow, we would get old, she would have children, we would become Granny and Grandpa.

But, for now, we would take it in turns when she woke in the night and spontaneous evenings were unlikely to happen.

It was the Diana Moment: the belated recognition our world had – for ever - tilted on its axis.

A man shambled towards me and paused. He smelt of poverty, mildew, old clothes and shoddiness. His hand - held out, grubby palm upwards – was thin, almost skeletal.

His mouth was in shadow and his voice mumbled: 'spare fifty pence for a cuppa?'

I gave him all the money in my pockets: a ten-pound note and some change.

I left him staring at it while I – whistling – went home.

Tom.

What: What not to say to one of the Gods.

Where: Fawley refinery

My age: 43

I went into computing (as IT was then called) to change my life and my life was duly – and fundamentally - changed.

Here's a potted history of my ten years of writing:

1. I lived alone in a series of bedsits.
2. I needed food parcels and money from mum and dad.
3. I got so tired of trying to pull ideas out of my head all fun and excitement evaporated.
4. I realised I just was not good enough and had to change.

And here's a potted history of the ten years after going into IT:

1. I took out a mortgage and bought a flat, later upgraded to a house.
2. Lizzy and I got married.
3. I evolved from being a 'new computer programmer' into an 'experienced computer consultant.'
4. We started a family.

In other words I swapped the selfish life of a penniless, responsibility-free writer for marriage, mortgage, commute, office work and children.

Or, to put it even more simply: it was a very good change that worked for me.

In 1988, I started working for Rex Software in Eastleigh, and stayed with them until I retired over twenty years later. Their basic business was hiring out computer consultants to clients so – by default – I became a 'computer consultant.' Accordingly, I felt rather grand as I drove down to Fawley refinery to begin work in their IT department.

Fawley refinery was vast. Hundreds of acres of gasometer sized tanks, odd smells, occasional flares from the top of mysterious towers and about a zillion miles of pipes connecting everything to everything. It had its own power plant and to get to the canteen was a five-minute walk along pipe-lined roads.

Reception made a phone call and I sat waiting to be fetched, watching people going in and out of industrial strength revolving security doors.

A tall, studious looking chap appeared and introduced himself. We'll call him Tom.

Tom was a doctor (but of what I do not know) had 4 or possibly 5 children, rode a bike with a little flag sticking out to make sure passing cars gave him enough room and was one of the most pleasant managers I ever worked for.

We reached a small open plan office with half a dozen or so desks, two potted ferns, four people staring at monitors and aluminium framed windows giving a view of parked cars.

Tom said "This is James." There was a chorus of Hi. Tom led me over towards a young chap hunched like a hermit over his keyboard. He possessed a big discoloured nose and looked as if he'd wandered in by accident from a homeless shelter. I could hear him muttering to himself, but the only word I could make out was 'bastard!'

Tom said "This is Richard. You're his replacement. Richard, here's James – all ready for the handover." Richard didn't look up, but said 'bastard' twice more. Tom leant over his shoulder. "Problem?"

Richard stabbed his finger at the screen. "The overnight batch has gone down again." He scowled at the monitor, then swivelled round, looked at me and abruptly grinned in a friendly manner. "Don't take too much notice of me, I'm just grandstanding. You're going to love this stuff."

Tom said "What does support say?"

"As usual, they don't have much of a clue," was the disdainful reply. "They have raised a ticket and will look into it."

Tom included me in the discussion. "We get a batch update every night from the States."

"Huston." Richard added. "Bloody Huston."

I asked: "Oh? What does it update?"

He shrugged. "Oh, I dunno: some management system I think."

As if on cue, the door opened and two men walked in. Their stride was purposeful, their shoes polished, their suits well cut. They stank of opulent offices, carpeted corridors and elegant girls sat behind desks too small to hide their legs. In short, the two men oozed management.

It was as if a chill wind from the Artic had suddenly blown in. The friendly, industrious atmosphere vanished and everyone paid immediate attention.

Tom muttered 'Oh .. shit' and walked towards them. His back was straight, his smile broad, his whole demeanour welcoming.

"Hello!" He singled out the slightly less svelte of the two. "Jonathan: what brings you here?" I later learnt that Jonathan was Tom's bosses boss. The other man was Tom's bosses boss bosses boss. That's five or six levels above Tom: right up there in the stratosphere, where satellites orbit the earth. Unfortunately, my arrival had coincided with his annual circuit of the serfs, probably undertaken as a penance for his company Jag.

Tom shook hands with them and they all smiled practiced smiles.

They went to the first desk. Tom said: "And this is Mary." Mary stood and almost curtsied. "Any problems? All OK?" asked the head honcho, looking over her shoulder as if the wall behind her was more interesting.

"Oh No, no problems," Mary spluttered. "All fine."

"Good!"

They moved on. The same question was asked at the next desk, with the same reply. This was repeated once more and then they came to Richard. And me, standing at his side.

Tom introduced us: "And this is Richard. He's leaving in a couple of weeks. James here is taking over."

"Ah! I see." The boss of bosses of bosses turned his face towards me. His eyes focussed on a distant horizon. "Any problems? All OK?"

I said "There is a problem: the batch transfer from Huston has failed."

You could have heard a pin drop. In the background I could see Tom, his face frozen as if auditioning for a live performance of 'The Scream.' Yep: this was the Diana Moment: Tom's tortured face in the middle of a silence as profound as death.

For an instant the eyes of the boss of bosses (aka God) scanned me, then moved away. His voice was firm and dismissive, making sure we all knew his celestial existence had not been disrupted. "Good, good."

He sniffed and the group moved off. I glanced towards Richard and lifted my eyebrows in what I hoped was a 'what a plonker' expression, but he ignored me.

The door opened and closed, leaving Tom behind.

He came over and looked at me. They all looked at me. I found I had backed up against Richard's desk. Tom gave a deep sigh. "James" he said "when your immediate boss – in other words, me - asks if you have a problem, you tell me about any problems you have." He looked round. "If anyone here, working in the same office, asks if you have any problems, you tell them about any problems you have. You might even find it is useful to tell about problems before being asked. Often, you will find this is very very helpful. You may at this point nod."

I nodded.

"But," Tom continued "if a member of management asks about problems, the answer is always – and forever - 'No, there are no problems. Everything is fine.' Even if world war three has just started and we're all going to be blown up in four minutes, if management asks anything at all, you say everything is fine. You may nod again."

I nodded.

"If there is a problem, we fix it. We don't tell them." He frowned for a moment before adding: "The basic truth is – and James, you really, really have to understand this – is that they – management – are absolutely uninterested in our problems. We exist at too low a level. If a problem is big enough then I – not you, but me – will move it up a notch. Understood? Nod your head again."

I nodded my head.

Richard said "What Tom means is they don't give a shit." Everyone nodded in agreement.

Mary muttered: "nope, not a shit."

Diplomatically, Tom ignored them. He was standing with his back to us, looking out of the window. His voice became reflective. "I tell you: we are as barnacles on this massive Fawley tanker. We don't matter, and they know we know we don't matter. We could all be scraped off and replaced tomorrow, but the tanker would just keep going. So we don't stick our heads above the parapet, as the chances are it'd just get shot off." He looked down as his shoes, as if contemplating the mysteries of the world. Then he turned to face us and became brisk.

"OK, mixed metaphors apart, let's do a coffee run." He handed me a small plastic tray with 6 holes in it. "The handover starts now!" He grinned. "You'll have to remember who likes what coffee when. Mine in the morning is black, no sugar."

Richard looked up from his monitor. "I've heard from Support. They reran the Huston batch and it went through OK."

Tom paused. "Any idea why this time and not last?"

"Nope." Richard shrugged. "And the ticket's been closed, so that's it."

Tom sighed. "And so it goes."

Hello twins.

What: Josh and Beth are born

Where: Princess Anne Maternity Hospital, Southampton

My age: 48

To begin after it was over: I have in my possession a dress. It is tiny, scarcely larger than my hand. It is made of cotton and has a simple, cheerful pattern of blue flowers on a yellow background. Lizzy – bending over her sewing machine, her agile fingers guiding the material under the needle – created it from an off-cut in less than an hour.

She held it up as if on display in a shop window. "There we go," she said: "Beth's first dress."

For some reason, we had got into the habit of occasionally slipping into an exaggerated mock Nothern accent. I said: "A week old, and t' lass gets a dress? You spoil our children, mother. It'll be a suit for that there Joshua next."

Lizzy grinned. "I, 'happen it will!"

The dress appeared impossibly small. More suitable for a doll than a baby.

The next day we visited the twins. In his incubator, through the clear plastic top, Josh looked like an old man shrunken inside his skin. His eyes were closed and his face as calm as that of a pharaoh. Attached to him was yet another tube, leading to a giant syringe in a cradle, with a motor slowly, slowly driving the plunger, pumping fresh blood into the body of our son.

Lizzy, guiding Beth's tiny arms through the miniscule armholes of her dress, said "he needed another transfusion."

I knew this, but even so I found myself asking: "Is that normal?"

"Yes." She arranged tiny socks, hardly bigger than my thumb, on Beth's feet. "They told us about it. Jaundice."

I looked up at the sterile laboratory walls, the row of incubators, the machines, the tiny, tiny babies.

"Yes," I said and fell silent.

To take a step back, let us start again.

Lizzy is lying on a cushioned hospital examination table. Her jeans are unzipped and her shirt hoicked up, exposing her naked torso. She is stout, but does not look pregnant.

It might seem crazy, but I cannot now remember clearly if we thought Lizzy might be carrying twins and this ultrasound scan was for confirmation, or if we did not suspect and got to know when the technician said something along the startled lines of: 'O! And there's another one.'

Or perhaps it was not the ultrasound at all: it might have been another, simpler scan, listening for a single heartbeat, but finding two.

For I simply cannot recall – now - exactly how we got to know about the twins. Nor can I recollect when or why the doctors insisted Lizzy should come in for weekly check-ups.

I do remember, after seeing them, Lizzy and I had a late-night conversation, a neutral space in the half dark, where the elephant in the room was not so formidable.

For our doctor had mentioned Lizzy's age (pushing 40) and linked that to the possibility of Down syndrome and seamlessly (for she was well skilled at this conversation) linked this to a test and percentages and possible termination.

And we had remained uneasily silent.

In the half light of midnight, Lizzy's face was averted. The streetlight threw long shadows on the ceiling. I found the idea of knowing frightening. Knowing might mean making a decision. Life or death for a newly minted small person: a desired small person.

As I write this, I realise it must have been before we knew it was going to be twins. So perhaps this muddled chronology will need to be altered. But not right now.

I know I told Lizzy I didn't want to know, but I can't remember what words I used. I would have said knowing everything was OK is all fine and good, but knowing it wasn't was a prospect too brutal for me.

I remember the relief in her voice as she said she agreed.

And so it was settled: we would take what we were given. I said a friend of mine – a man who always beat me at squash (before my back became too wonky for me to play) - his child had Downs; and he had quickly added she gave so much back in terms of love and affection it was inconceivable they should wish her otherwise.

And Lizzy had said "Yes, I have heard that too." And we never discussed it again, never talked of it.

The kindly, middle-aged technician has warmed her hands by rubbing them together and is now applying KY jelly across Lizzy's torso. She winks and says: "good stuff this." She wipes her hands clean and begins sliding the scanning device from side to side, up and down and round and round, building up small jelly waves as if she were driving a particularly blunt-nosed tugboat.

The device is linked with wires to a box and then to a screen. Shapes appear, but they mean nothing to our untrained eyes: shifting blobs and squiggles made of shadows and gossamer.

But later (how much later? I do not know: hours? Days?) we told Hannah that in due course there might be two more children in the family. And she painted a picture of five blobby people: two parents and three children. Later, we framed the picture and hung in the hallway.

The weekly checkups revealed something or other: I'm not sure what: Lizzy was put on a daily regime of pills.

Around week twenty-six or maybe twenty-seven on Easter Saturday morning, we were visiting friends.

Lizzy went to the loo and then she called me. I think, she said, it's happening. They're coming.

We left Hannah with our friends and drove to the maternity hospital.

They administered drugs to stop the labour. Received wisdom is you could safely go up to a certain dose, and we got to within 5% before the labour stopped.

Had they been born then, our twins would have been so, so small. The treacherous word 'unviable' comes to mind: even now, over 25 years later, my thoughts always skitter around this small knuckle point of our history. There are too many alternatives here: Too many 'what ifs'; too many pathways for imagination and fear to needlessly follow.

But the labour did stop. And they talked in terms new to me: of Special Care Baby Units and Neonatal Intensive Care Units and vacancies and reservations.

And I sat there, holding my wife's hand. Wanting to understand but unable to do so.

And later, I watched as an administrator: tired, with short hair and bitten nails, started ringing round. She was, she said, calling the nearest maternity hospitals first. Hospitals, she added, with Special Care baby units as – right now - there were none to spare in Southampton: too many ladies were having too many premature births. Eventually she located what was required, in London: St. George's Hospital, Tooting. About eighty miles away.

She rang off and smiled at me. "Good: now we're getting somewhere." She picked up the phone again. "So let's find you an ambulance."

And with quiet, efficient efficiency, it was organised on Easter Saturday afternoon in the middle of spring, 1993.

This was before SatNavs, and as we approached London the medic pulled out a map and began looking at street names and routes to Tooting. And when we were stopped at traffic lights, I could see them: the driver and the medic outlined against a wide arc of dashboard instrumentation, their heads together as they discussed where we were, where the hospital was, and the best route between the two.

And now my memory goes blank. I cannot remember what happened next. I surmise Lizzy must have been taken to a ward and that I watched as she was tucked in and settled. And I know I must have got home, but when and how no longer exists for me.

I know Hannah stayed overnight with our friends, as she remembers they organised an Easter egg hunt the following day (Easter Sunday).

But I have lost that time: everything has gone: it is as if it were a reverse Diana Moment: just too intense, too worrisome, too full of tiredness and stress: too incoherent to form a memory.

I think I must have gone to my sister Judy: I would have rung her up from a payphone in a hospital corridor and she would have been full of love and concern and raided her fridge and made sandwiches or cooked something and treated me like royalty. And I feel treacherous as that generosity has now vanished: it is merely a surmise I am constructing because — now — it appears the most likely scenario.

I would have sat in Judy's small Chiswick house, in the knocked through back room/front room separated by the diagonal flight of stairs to the two small bedrooms above and made phone calls: to parents and friends, telling what had happened, and how Lizzy was and to reassure Hannah things would, eventually, return to normal.

But that is all conjecture.

Further, to add to my confusion, I have two fixed, indisputable dates in 1993 that I know are correct, but feel are entirely wrong. They are: the seventeenth of April and the fifteenth of May.

The first date is Easter Saturday, when Lizzy went into premature labour and we ended up in London. The second date is the day the twins were born.

These dates are only four weeks apart. And if you unpick it a little further, I know Lizzy came back to Southampton midway between them.

So it cannot be disputed: she was only in London for about two weeks.

But in my mind, those two weeks have stretched into a long, black, bleak time of: many, many car journeys to London and back, Hannah and I listening to a tape of Roald Dahl's 'Matilda'; of giving keys to borrowed au-pairs so they could deliver or fetch Hannah from school; of dashing home from work; of hurried meals and of enormous, all-encompassing tiredness and stress so real it felt as if it were made of lead.

And Lizzy, propped up in her functional and lonely hospital bed, her eyes frightened for the future, for the twins, the tiny fragile tucked away twins nestling inside her.

And Hannah, not always knowing who will be looking after her or where, and knowing Mummy was away but not understanding, really understanding, why she was not there.

I know I turned up at my brother's house one evening and stood dripping tears onto their doorstep: my sister-in-law gave me a long, long hug and they put me to bed and I slept for twelve hours straight.

And I kept telling myself, one way or another, it will soon be all over, for pregnancies run their time and cannot last, it's not as if Lizzy had an illness that could go on forever.

But after a fortnight, within a couple days, the clouds parted: special care baby units became available in Southampton and Lizzy, complete with her precious, precious cargo, returned, and was no more than a ten-minute drive away. And a day later, from abroad, Jackie arrived, a close friend, complete with her two daughters: the oldest the same age as Hannah as their Mums had met in antenatal classes, sitting in a circle watching a midwife demonstrating birth using a grapefruit as a substitute baby's head.

They moved into our spare bedroom and – being vegetarians and newly back from Fance – filled the fridge with smelly, cheesy things.

And – boy oh boy oh boy – we were so pleased to see them!

Life became less formidable, more controllable, shared and predictable.

And on May the fifteenth, 1993, exactly four invaluable weeks after that epic Easter Saturday when Lizzy was ambulanced to London, the twins were born: premature, tiny and vulnerable, but Lizzy had managed – with the help of doctors and specialists – to keep them in, growing and developing: and as each day dragged out and completed, first in London, then at Southampton, 'unviable' morphed to become – eventually - 'viable.'

It was a caesarean again. Beth came out first: a tiny, tiny baby, briefly shown to us: but Josh was smaller still. We did not see him as he was immediately placed in an incubator and wheeled away.

Lizzy lay there, being stitched up. Her eyes sought mine. She said: "Jimbob: I don't want to do this again."

And I replied: "Lizbob: nor do I."

And to conclude in the present: the twins are now 27 and I have in my possession some photographs, sent electronically and viewed on laptop, phone or monitor. The wonders of the internet!

One set of 'photos and texts are from Beth: there are pictures of her, sunning herself on Bondi beach, Australia, where she is now living, working and studying. She is tall, elegant and slim, wearing something I know must be fashionable, for to Beth appearances are important.

The other set are from Josh. It shows him and his super girlfriend wild camping in the New Forest: they have a small tent and got there on bikes. They are smiling and happy, Josh grinning through his beard, enjoying the open air and the basic basicness of it all: for Josh, appearances are not so important.

Our beautiful, beautiful twins: both look healthy and happy, and that is all that parents can hope for.

Photographs: Lizzy, marriage and the family

1984. Lizzy and I share a quiet moment at our wedding. Dunno about him, but she looked wonderful.

1984. Cutting the wedding cake.
The knife they gave us would have had trouble cutting butter: the icing completely defeated it. Amid much hilarity it was whisked away and something more industrial used to reduce it to the traditional small squares. We kept the top tier in the attic for years, but somewhere along the line it got lost or became mouldy and thrown out.

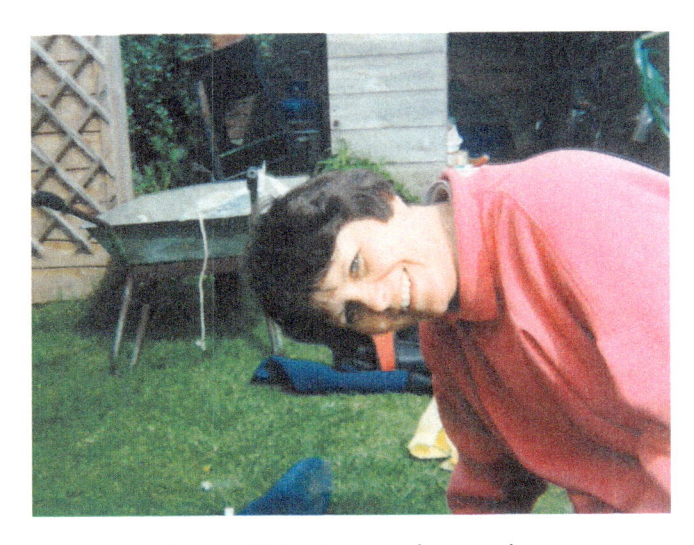

Circa 1990. Lizzy in the garden.
This is my favourite photo of her: having fun getting in the way of my view of a rusty old wheelbarrow and what looks like a discarded wetsuit.

1988. Lizzy, pregnant with Hannah, in the garden.

1988. Dad and Hannah.
She was the first grandchild.

1988. Lizzy, Hannah and I.
In her parent's garden.

Circa 1994. The twins having a whale of a time.
Beth on the left, Josh on the right.

Circa 1997. Josh (5). In the garden with a toad.
Or it could be a frog.

2000. Beth (7), ever watchful.

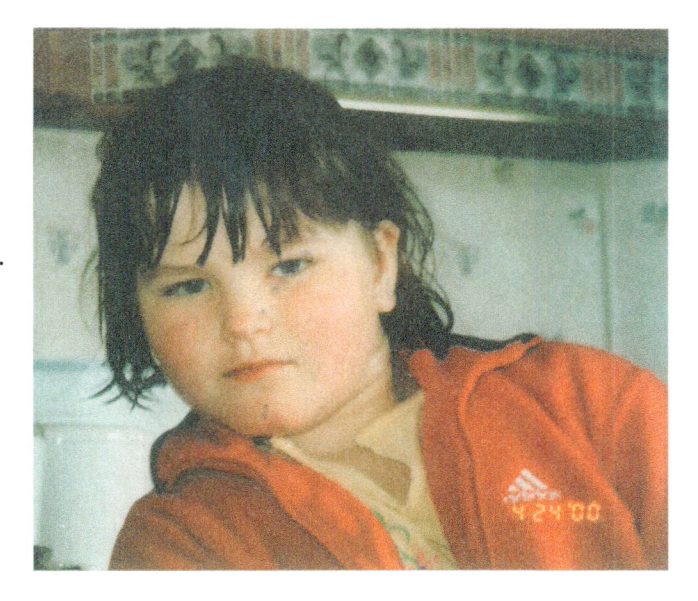

Goodbye Peter

What: My brother Peter dies.

Where: New Zealand

My age: 61

For me, one of the depressing and thoroughly dispiriting aspects of writing an autobiography is that it is necessarily centred on myself. I find the prospect of being under scrutiny unappealing, even if I am the one conducting the examination. After all: it could be argued who better than me to ask me the awkward questions. (Equally, it could also be argued, who worse...)

And when constructing a memoir - like the one you are reading now - where each short chapter is driven by an intense, never forgotten shard of personal memory, it is very hard to escape yourself. In fifty or so years of off and on writing, I have never used 'I' so frequently.

It seems inescapable: I am on stage all the time. Other people tend to be seen only as actors with walk on parts: they come into view, have an interaction with me and then vanish.

But these 'other people' are not creations woven from words on paper, whistled up out of nowhere to populate the story of my life. They have lives too. And in their story, I merely have the walk on part.

And so to my brother Peter. Older than myself by some eighteen months, he had a much more interesting and fulfilled life than might appear here, on these pages where - once we get past childhood – he tends to show up only during those old stalwarts of births, marriages and deaths.

But unquestionably, through age and parentage, he occupies a unique and special place in my life. Not that we were similar characters: Peter was outgoing, energetic and sociable whereas I was (and remain) shy and socially awkward. He always had friends and activity: I always had a book.

Enough: he is gone now, and painting memories into fixed, broad-brush immobility is seldom useful.

From his time in New Zealand in his early twenties, Peter had dual UK-NZ citizenship. He once described New Zealand as 'like Surrey, but with mountains and better weather.' He also repeated the old canard that – on arrival – the announcement over the aeroplane tannoy was: *'You are now landing in New Zealand. Please set your watches back thirty years.'*

Once Mum went, Peter and his wife (Mirabel) made plans to move their whole family (they now had three children) there, to New Zealand. Looking back, it seems clear they had almost certainly decided earlier - probably after Dad died - to do this.

By then they were affluent after years of hard work and shrewd property speculation. I visited him once and found him in his office (a back room smelling vaguely of hay) sitting at an old desk of planks stretched across a couple of filing cabinets. There was a telephone, a stack of paperwork and some files on makeshift shelving: even though it was the late 1990s, there was not a computer to be seen. I can't remember how the topic came up, but I asked him what he had done with his share of our sister Judy's inheritance money. 'All gone,' he'd said, pointing at large sheet of paper stapled to the wall. On it was a hand-drawn grid in thick marker pen, with pencilled in numbers decreasing as they went down the page. Over the years he'd spent it all, mainly on school fees. In many ways, that scrubby bit of paper epitomised the difference between us: I would have spent hours creating a spreadsheet, taking delight in formulating algorithms to auto-update the numbers. Peter just spent five minutes drawing lines on some paper, pinned it up and, over time, filled it in with pencil.

This gave him time to concentrate on what he enjoyed and was good at: meeting people, making deals, seeing ahead to possible profit.

His method was simple: take out a mortgage to buy an old property and do it up, then rent out to pay the mortgage and wait – sometimes years – for the property to gain value and then – maybe - sell it on. Sounds easy, but isn't. Lizzy and I, inspired by Peter and numerous TV programs, bought a nearby flat in Southampton. After about ten years, with the rent having only just covered the mortgage, we sold at a loss.

Before Peter and Mirabel went to New Zealand, they sold up. Once there they bought some land and began property development again, but now with mountains and better weather.

By then, of those we grew up with, only Peter and I remained. Old age had claimed Dad and Mum while both our sisters had been taken by cancer.

And now we come across – yet again – one of the recurring themes of this book: that memory is tricky and difficult: it can cling tenaciously to unimportant incidents and detail, while letting slip others of more import. Undoubtedly, for me, some denial is taking place; but I see no reason to chase that particular hare.

In short: once again, I cannot now recall how I learnt someone close to me – this time Peter – was seriously ill.

At some point I knew something was wrong, so I rang. His voice – as always - was confident and upbeat. He told of the alternative therapy he was having, which – as far as I could tell – consisted of attempts to flush accumulated toxins and poisons (most probably from his time working on a farm) from his body.

He was fine – he said – nothing more than a temporary blip.

I told Lizzy, and she said: "that sounds odd."

And I replied: "oh, I don't know. He seems to be doing OK."

My brother got worse, then better. Driven by uncertain motives, I booked us all a holiday in New Zealand. We hired an MPV and toured around the tourist spots and visited relatives.

Inevitably, we finished up at my brother's new house, in the hills a short distance from the Pacific coast, some miles south of Napier.

It was truly, stunningly, beautiful.

Peter looked tired and thin. Mirabel had organised a big family get together in a vineyard. All our NZ cousins and children came along: a big happy bunch: there must have been over twenty of us in total, sat at a long table under the warm autumn sky. Peter was in good form, smiling, laughing, being attentive.

We left the next day. As we were piling into the car, Mirabel came out to wish us bon voyage: she said Peter was still sleeping and she didn't want to wake him.

But he did manage to appear, looking fragile. It was the first time I had hugged him for many years. Under the thin fabric of his shirt, his chest was scarily insubstantial and bony.

As we left, I could see them in the rear-view mirror, standing in front of their house, with the rolling hills behind. Then we drove down little more than a lane to join country roads, dual carriageways and – eventually – the wide highway to Auckland airport.

A few weeks later, back home in the UK, I spoke to Mirabel on the phone. I cannot remember if I rang her or she me: it might have been I called intending to speak to Peter, and she answered. Even from half the world away, her voice – as always - was clear and precise. The words dropped, one by one, into my ears. "It's cancer. Small cell cancer."

I was more numb than surprised. I found I already knew, and had known for a while. I just hadn't wanted to assemble the evidence into the inescapable, depressing conclusion.

In early September, after chemo and radiotherapy had roller-coasted hope through the New Zealand winter, the oncologist gave permission for him to travel. Mirabel organised a valedictory trip: friends, relations, all the old haunts.

As children we lived in East Meon and went to school in Petersfield. From his teenage years, Peter had played cricket in nearby Steep: a well-hit six, it was said, could land halfway to the Harrow Inn, the pub they used before, after and sometimes during matches.

I last saw him there, in the Harrow, holding court, welcoming old friends, looking extremely happy, in the crowd.

Before I left, Mirabel and I hugged for a long time in the car park. I drove home to Southampton and my family: Peter and Mirabel went to Corfu with friends, then back to New Zealand.

The reports from New Zealand tightened and rapidly became worse.

My brother Peter died in Mirabel's arms in late November, 2006. He was 63 years old.

The news reached me at about 9 in the evening. I spent most of the night listlessly trying – and failing – to find a flight. In the morning I went to a travel agent and in half an hour was booked to leave Heathrow in the afternoon.

I was flying – for the first and probably only time - in business class. The seats went flat and we had pillows and sheets: a blanket if required. I slept deeply, but not for long.

And as I edged back up into consciousness, a Diana Moment occurred in that place where dreams and uncertain reality mix.

When we were children, Peter and I shared a bedroom. Sometimes we would try to communicate with a string stretched between two empty cans. We would pretend whispered messages could be heard and set great store in saying 'over' at the right time and sign off by saying 'over and out.'

Of course, in reality, our beds were only a few feet apart: even whispered words could be plainly heard without our make-shift telephone. But holding the tin can – first to the mouth then to the ear – rendered our conversations secret, private and special.

And the Diana Moment, in that half-life between sleep and wakefulness, was very simple: my brother's distinct, childhood voice whispering in my ear: 'over and out.'

Apologies for sounding mystical: the whole experience was the undoubted child of sadness, stress and lack of sleep. I don't believe in an after-life, but I do believe your mind can comfort you by pretending into existence things that are not there.

I sat up, pressed the button that converted the bed back into a chair, pulled across the little dining table just the right size for the plastic branded airline tray, took out my notepad and wrote: 'You don't always know what you have lost until it's gone.'

And half an hour later my eulogy, for my brother Peter, was finished.

There is little more to write: the landing at Auckland was mundane and the drive to Napier tiring. Mirabel was coping and – like my cousins – was kind and hospitable.

And in a small chapel we stood in a circle round his coffin and said the words we had planned to say while – outside - the beautiful New Zealand sunlight lit the trees.

That Diana moment.

What: I learn Princess Diana has died.

Where: Southampton

My age: 52

Well, here y'go: the only 'true' Diana Moment in this book.

It was a Sunday morning, and I was having a lie-in. Lizzy was looking after the kids. She came in and shook my shoulder.

"Jimbob, Diana's been in a car crash."

"Diana?"

"Princess Diana."

"Oh."

"They're saying she's dead."

"Oh." And I went back to sleep.

For, to me, it was hardly a 'Diana Moment' at all. I only remember it for the fuss everyone made and how it filled the world. It didn't matter what you were doing or where you went, people were saying things like 'Dreadful,' and 'I never thought,' or 'they say the driver was drunk,' or 'those papa-whatsits should be shot,' and so on.

The next day at work I kept mostly silent, pretending a grief I did not feel. When I detected quiet people with tears in their eyes or even just a sad face, I would reinforce my own doleful look and do my best to avoid them. I suspected most people were like me, just going along with it out of some residual herd sensibility.

But when I got home, I found next door had bought an enormous wreath, packed all their children in their big family estate car and driven to London to place said wreath outside some palace or other. Frankly, I was astonished. I was willing to trundle mournfully around for a few hours, but spending money on flowers and petrol seemed well over the top. Maybe, I thought, most people had taken it to heart, and I was the one out of step.

I asked Lizzy if she felt sad and she said: "Yeah, course: it's very sad."

I asked if she wanted to buy a big wreath and take it to London, and she said "Oh God, no."

So – in public - I kept my sad face on for a couple of days more.

When I was about 9, I was in Petersfield, waiting by the station to catch a bus home. My head was down, watching my shoes as they scuffed the ground. When I looked up, I found the pavement was crowded. It was as if everyone had magically appeared out of thin air. There was a general air of excitement and evidence of flags. It was most peculiar.

From just down the road, a cheering started, getting louder as it approached. Bodies leant out, arms extended, flags fluttering, hands waving. I bent forward to see and my foot strayed onto the road. An indignant, shocked voice in my ear said "get your foot off the Queen's highway! She's here!"

And indeed she was. A great big shiny black car, moving as smoothly as a battleship. hove into view, and inside was the actual Queen, with her actual hand doing that distinctive royal wave. It was exactly as on the newsreels. She looked straight at me, I know she did: straight at me, a small, belligerent boy, glaring back, with one hand waving a little, the other thrust firmly into a pocket.

The Rolls serenely progressed over the level crossing, past the brave souls packing the footbridge, and sailed onwards, out of sight.

There was a collective sigh and we all felt – even me – cheered and uplifted at this wonderous visitation.

That evening I asked my dad what would have happened if a train had come along: would the gates close? Would the rolls have stopped? What if the signalman had been distracted and there was a crash?

My Dad pondered the question for a while, then said he wouldn't be surprised if they had timed things so there were no trains.

My mother, knitting away, said "of course they'd stop the trains. She's the Queen."

Which seemed to me rather unfair. Why should she be different?

And – essentially - for many years this is what I thought.

But of late, my attitude towards the royals has mellowed. As individuals they hold no interest: there's not one I'd invite round for a cup of tea. But I'd be a lot more sympathetic if they got rid of all the flim-flammery: the jewels and medals; the ball gowns and frock coats. And while they're at it they should ban bowing, curtseying and all the rest of that deferential nonsense and insist on informality. I rather like the idea of the Monarch rescheduling some state occasion because they're too busy digging turnips.

Hey-ho: bang goes my chance to refuse a knighthood.

Melvin (the bastard)

What: I meet Melvin (and wish I hadn't)

Where: Southampton

My age: 38

After a few years in IT things were making more sense and I felt ready to step up to bigger projects. So – apparently – did my boss, for one morning he called me in. With him was a chap I'd occasionally seen hurrying importantly along corridors. He carried a leather briefcase adorned with '**MB.**'

My boss – a friendly chap given to selling dubious stuff from the boot of his car – said: "This is Melvin." the other man waved his hand in a sort of semi-salute. "He's developing a system that needs to be fast-tracked."

Melvin chipped in. His voice was deep and rapid. "Yes. Fast tracked."

My boss stood and gave a quick grin. "And I've told him you're the man to do it." He glanced at us both. "So, I'll leave you to it. Use my office for a while if you like: I must sell some ping pong balls. Any takers?" He paused for a moment, got no response and - his duties as a manager finished - he left.

Melvin was in his mid-thirties, with a thickset body, large head, a somewhat aggressive expression and disconcertingly shrewd eyes behind large, square, black-framed glasses. He was wearing a blue suit, black shoes but no tie. The watch on his wrist looked expensive. He had an alarming habit of looming over you.

He put his briefcase on the bosses' desk, sat in the bosses' chair and waved a gracious hand. "James, isn't it? Do sit."

I did so.

His fingers were short and stubby, with wiry black hairs growing between the knuckles. The briefcase was opened and a box file produced.

He said: "this is the result of nearly a year's work. Go on – open it."

I did so. It contained yet another file, with 'The Just in Time Modular Maintenace Management Order System by **MELVIN BAGSHOT**.' printed on the front cover. And inside that, separated neatly by coloured page dividers, were flow charts, screen layouts, a database design and program specifications.

It appeared a substantive, thorough and very impressive piece of work.

In retrospect, his name in **BOLD CAPITALS** should have given me a clue regarding Melvin's self-regard. But it didn't. After all, he had been fast tracked and looked and sounded important. As if he knew what he was doing. And – to be fair – he probably did. Which was for me to do all the work and take the blame for any failure, while he – of course – took all available credit.

I had barely glanced at the first page when he said: "Well my friend, what d'you think? How long will it take you?"

"What?"

Melvin sat back, swivelling round so he could see out of the window. His hands steepled judiciously under his chin. "As I see it," he said "it needs to be written as a modular construct, capable of easy expansion, for when the LAN is up and running and for when we can add more and more bits of kit. You've heard of the LAN, of course."

"Er-"

Melvin took little notice of my hesitation. He was now doing what he did best: bullshitting.

"God, the LAN will revolutionise things! The time of the Mainframe is ending. Believe me, technologically, we're in a backwater here. But with this -" he half turned and laid a meaty hand on the folder "with this we'll be right at the forefront, leading the way, the go to people."

And then, like a chef giving a cooking lesson without doing any actual cooking, Melvin swept me into Melvinworld, a place where all things were possible, where Melvin was so full to bursting with wisdom, sagacity and sheer wonderfulness all problems and technical limitations vanished as if they had never been.

He was expounding on our blindingly bright future when his eye caught the time.

"Sorry - we need to wrap up here. I've another meeting in five!" He went to the door. "Test system ready in 2 months, OK?" And without waiting for a reply, he had gone.

And so I became Melvin's developer. His writer of code and – inadvertently – his interpreter of business requirements. At the beginning, still buoyed by his wonderous vision, I was somewhat chuffed. But that turned increasingly sour as the days then the weeks passed.

It was so, so frustrating. His ideas looked impressive on the page and his use of fonts ingenious, but to actually work from them I found more and more difficult. Logical wormholes were left dangling in mid-air, the database had bits missing and the proposed screen layouts demanded features I didn't think possible. I realised it had probably been cobbled together over a month of long weekends, with more attention to presentation than to detailed logic.

And as for Melvin himself, well he was always away in Liverpool, or London and – when at Southampton – usually worked from home. If he did come in, he was constantly at meetings or out to lunch. I would wander by his office, hoping to catch him in, and discovered he was hardly ever glimpsed after three-thirty in the afternoon.

I began to have sleepless nights.

Lizzy found me at three am gloomily having tea and toast. She sat down.

"Jimbob, you've got to tell someone."

"I know, but I keep thinking …."

"What?"

"Well, I keep thinking I'm on the cusp of understanding how it's meant to work, but ..." I took a sip of tea and confessed " .. but maybe me not understanding is me being thick."

Lizzy – as ever – didn't think much of my self-indulgence. "Well, if that's what you want to think, that's what you'll think." She gave me a kiss and a hug and went back to bed.

A day or so later my boss called. "James, come in would you please? And bring Melvin's stuff."

He was waiting for me. So was Melvin, looking suspiciously cheerful.

He gave a big grin. "Hi!" The grin remained but became sharklike. "I hear my specs are giving you a problem."

My boss put up a hand. "Wait a second, Melvin." Then, to me "Take a chair and let's have a look, shall we?"

I sat, passing him Melvin's wonderfully impressive folder. I felt sick, as if I were on trial. All my detailed thoughts of what I might say to Melvin when I finally managed to corner him went out of my head.

My boss flicked through, skim reading a few pages. "Ummm." He sat back. "OK, tell me what isn't clear."

My mind remained blank. "Well ..... er..."

Melvin suddenly loomed over me. "Yes, what isn't clear?" I hesitated, trying to get my thoughts straight, trying to remember. Melvin sighed and turned to my boss. "I really can't waste too much time here, on this. I've a meeting in five!"

My voice abruptly came out with a disconcertingly childlike wail. "That's just it! You're always busy! I need to ask you things and you're not here!" I realised my hands were clenched, my fingernails digging deep into my palms. My eyes felt wet and I needed to blow my nose. I felt absolutely humiliated: me, a man of almost forty, close to tears.

My boss regarded me. Melvin – with a satisfied, smug look on his face – stared relentlessly.

Eventually my boss said "Right, what we'll do is this. Melvin: I want you to schedule a 30-minute weekly catchup meeting with James. James: make sure you have your concerns to hand. Write them down and send them in advance to me as well as Melvin." He gave a pause and added "Right, I think that's it. Off you go."

That evening I told Lizzy what had happened.

She said "Good." A grin. "I'm glad my phone call wasn't wasted."

I said: "I did wonder. But I didn't know you knew him."

She said, "I bought a space hopper from him." She hesitated and added "Was it OK?"

I nodded. "The space hopper? You tell me." We kissed. I added: "Lizbob? Let's get a take-away and go early to bed."

A smile. "Jimbob, let's do just that!"

And later, I said: "Y'know, I think I need to change jobs anyway."

And her reply was: "yeah, I think so too."

The way things worked out, there was only one catchup meeting with Melvin, which took place a couple of weeks later. It didn't go well. I had already started applying for other jobs so I found it hard to take an interest. And his capacity for explanation was severely limited by his indifference to detail and his obvious scorn of my abilities.

After about ten minutes we'd both ceased to pretend, and the space between us became heavy with the atmosphere of a failed project.

He went uncharacteristically silent, then nudged the colour-coded pages, pushing them away from him as if consigning them to oblivion. He stared at me as if I were an unwanted insect, his heavy features full of scorn, his mouth twisted into a sneer. He removed his glasses, revealing naked eyes as cold as ice. His voice was vicious. "Oh, for God's sake: you expect me to think about this shit? ME!?" He headed for the door, stopped, half turned. "That was your job. YOUR JOB. And you failed me." And he was gone, busily walking to his next meeting.

For form's sake I drew up a long list of questions requiring answers, sent it to both him and my boss and stopped working on the project altogether. I heard no more from him.

I heard later that Melvin had spun the whole debacle as a failure in the IT department, which really required a complete top-to-bottom reorganisation.

For which – of course – he had a very impressive colour-coded schematic.

But even before then I had found another job. When I handed in my resignation letter the boss said: "Was it Melvin?" I nodded. He sighed and remarked. "You're not the first."

Our first grandchild.

What: Lizzy and I hear our first grandchild has been born.

Where: The Algarve, Portugal.

My age: 70.

On my 65th birthday, in 2010, I retired. Lizzy – almost exactly 9 years younger – immediately whisked me away on a surprise trip to Iceland, where we stayed in Reykjavik.

The highlight of the trip was to see the Northern Lights, so we stood about on a hillside (twice) staring upwards (twice). But no-one saw anything (twice).

Nor was there much snow.

But the people were friendly, the museums good, the blue lagoon unique and a coach tour interesting. And – worth the whole Iceland trip on its own - we discovered the joy of having two single duvets on a double bed. Solves at a stroke duvet hugging, different tog requirements and the draught caused when someone goes for a pee.

I had been ambivalent about retiring. On the one hand I liked that work provided both a role to fill and a comforting structure: things to do, people to see, scheduled events to happen. But on the other hand was the drudgery of driving 55 miles there and 55 back to do stuff I was finding increasingly difficult.

For the harsh and brutal truth was my skill set had fast become redundant, the systems I looked after were being retired or replaced and my mind wasn't agile enough to adapt.

But for a few days, after retiring, I hovered around the phone and checked my emails every other minute, waiting for someone at work to have a problem that no-one else could solve but me.

But it never happened. It was as if all my thirty-five years of IT work – the thousands of lines of code, the pages and pages of analysis, the projects, the meetings, the unscheduled weekend work – had just dropped out of my life and vanished.

And, in truth, within a week, I had stopped missing it. I felt less tired and worried: in short, the pressure was off. So I cast around for other things to do. I tried cooking (too stressful) and gardening (too slow). So I just pottered for a few months.

Lizzy went with friends to the Algarve (Portugal) and rather fell in love with the place, so we bought a part share in a small house (casa) fifteen-minutes from the beach.

And along the way Hannah became a midwife and at 25 married Jonny, on the hottest day of 2013. The couple were handsome, the twins smart, Lizzy stunning and I, in my obviously hired baggy suit, gave a father of the bride speech I like to think - with little evidence – was rather good. I ended with an admonishment not to believe the old joke about marriage being like a long boring meal with the pudding served first.

And Hannah – with her usual planned efficiency – became pregnant eighteen months later. Which brings us – some eight months later still - to this Diana Moment.

With five weeks to go before our first grandchild was due, Lizzy and I thought it would be OK to have a week's break in Portugal. We should be back in plenty of time to fuss away when the birth actually happened.

Five minutes' walk from our casa was a small restaurant, with outdoor wooden tables, palm trees and cheerful staff. The food was OK, the service prompt and – often tired after a day doing nothing much - we had got into the habit of strolling there for our evening meal perhaps 2 or 3 times a week.

On the Saturday evening we were waiting for our main course. The sun had set and the air warm. We could hear cicadas chirruping, the occasional clatter of knives and forks and a pleasant murmur of conversation.

Lizzy sent Hannah a text: 'I can see the moon. Can you?'

And the answer came back: "Can't see the moon as no windows in the delivery suit!"

Lizzy gave a little shriek, short and sharp, followed by "Oh God!"

I found I was on my feet. The manager and a waitress came dashing over.

Lizzy said: "Oh God: Hannah's in hospital!"

I said: "What?"

The waitress said something in Portuguese.

The manager said "Hospital?"

And Lizzy's phone rang. Hannah calling.

Lizzy answered and wandered off. I hovered, wondering what to do with my hands. The rest of the world hung back to give us some privacy.

Lizzy said "OK" a couple of times, nodded her head, listened intently, said "OK, love you" and rang off. She said to me: "It's OK, they're all fine." Then, to the interested people: the manager, the waitress and assorted nearby diners: "Nothing to worry about. Our first grandchild is being born a bit early, that's all."

I said, "So she's OK?"

Eyes wet, Lizzy replied: "She's fine, fine, just happening early, that's all. Early."

The manager beamed and translated for the waitress.

The diners resumed dining, the cicadas continued chirruping and the normal sounds of a placid, warm Algarve evening returned.

When we got back to our table, our food had arrived, with a complimentary bottle of wine.

I said "I know grandparents are meant to stay out of the way, but Portugal?"

Lizzy said "Oh, Jimbob, our first grandchild."

My voice was thick. "Oh, Lizbob, yeah. Our first grandchild."

We ate, but not particularly well and the wine remained untouched. I found myself suddenly superstitious and left it, telling the manager: "thank you. Tomorrow. For luck."

We waited for news. Lizzy said it could be hours, first babies can take a long time, we should take it in turns to make sure we didn't miss the call, that I should go to sleep. I lay down, but she remained sitting on the edge of the bed, her form a dark shape outlined by the thin Atlantic light coming through the window.

And this is what I remember, a Diana Moment: Lizzy: my lovely wife of over thirty years: so kind, such fun, so loving; the mother of our children, the heart of our family, sitting there, in our part-owned Portuguese casa, waiting for her phone to twitch into life and inform us we had become Nana and Grandad.

I offered to make tea and toast, but she said no, go to sleep. It was about eleven, quiet and serene. I think she was attracted to the synchronicity of resolutely staying awake while — a thousand miles away — our eldest daughter resolutely gave birth.

I fell asleep.

And instantly opened my eyes when her phone burped into action. Lizzy answered so fast it barely had time to ring.

"Yes? OK?" She stood and walked to the window.

I sat up. It was one in the morning: the dark small hours, when cats go marauding.

The room was so quiet I could hear Hannah's distant voice, but could not understand the words. Lizzy said 'Umm' a couple of times, then turned to me and gave a thumbs up.

I said, with exaggerated mouth movements miming the words rather than talking: "BOY? GIRL?" She mouthed 'BOY' and continued umming down the phone as she listened to the long and detailed details.

Eventually she said, "Here's Dad." and passed the phone to me.

Hannah sounded tired, drained and happy. "Hi Dad. All OK?"

"I'm meant to ask you that."

"Yeah, we're fine."

"It's a boy?"

"Yeah. Beautiful."

"You've counted all the fingers and all the toes?"

"Yeah, they're all there."

"Well done sweetheart." I could feel her tiredness seeping along the electric airways. "Love you, HannahB."

"Love you Dad."

So that day had stretched into the next and ended downstairs, with newly minted Nana and Grandad having tea and toast.

We were back in bed and fast asleep when the sun rose.

Hello George

What: We get a dog.

Where: Southampton.

My age: 65

The idea of getting a dog grew on me as retirement approached. I mentioned it to a pal at work, and she said it was a good idea. Then, a week before I left, she gave me a book. It was called 'First Dog,' or something like that, written by a vet who was the father of a TV outdoorsy chap I'd never heard of.

I read a chapter or two and learnt dog owners were happier and lived longer. So it looked good. And after a few weeks of retirement, I said to Lizzy: "I think we should get a dog."

She mentioned we already had a cat and a tortoise, and did I remember what happened to the hamster after it escaped and had a showdown with the cat?

Our cat then was old and arthritic, but – at 2am - managed to trap the rogue hamster in a corner of the dining room. I had been woken by the noise of the conflict and found the two of them facing off, the hamster on its hind legs throwing ferocious punches, while the cat was having a little rest to gather enough strength to finish the job.

I banished the cat to the kitchen and managed to get the hamster back into its cage without disturbing the kids.

We were woken at six the following morning – maybe earlier – by small people wailing: the hamster was dead. I went downstairs to find a matchbox or some other suitable hamster coffin and found the cat also dead.

More wailing.

So – in our project dog discussion - I said: "Hamsters are in the past, we'll get a puppy and I'm sure the cat won't care."

Lizzy could get an amazing amount of scepticism into a single grunt. She did this now.

I said: "And the kids want one. And it'll get me out of the house."

Lizzy grunted once more before pragmatically accepting the inevitable. "OK then. But I don't want a dog that barks, or moults, or puts its front paws on the kitchen table and pants at you."

"OK," I said: "done deal!" and put on my coat.

"And where are you going?"

"To the common: dog research!"

She grinned. "Good luck, Fido hunter!"

I found dog research surprisingly sociable. It suited me because there is no need for small talk, which I have always found difficult, awkward and usually boring.

A dog would come bounding up, I would put my hand out for sniffing and say "Good boy, good boy!" And then – to the owner - something like: 'I'm thinking of getting a dog.'

And we'd end up talking dog in the same way parents at school gates talk children.

This went on for a week or so, with no dog quite right enough to present to Lizzy as a solution.

And then – almost when I thought to ease up with project dog for a while - I saw a large, lugubrious chap staring morosely into some scrubby bushes. He carried a lead and wore a tie: he seemed depressed enough to be a teacher.

Almost by reflex I stopped and said: "Oh. Lost your dog?"

His voice was gloomy. "It's said 'you might lose your dog, but your dog won't lose you.'" He continued to regard the gorse as if it were a personal enemy. "I seem to be testing that to destruction today."

"Oh. What sort of dog is he?"

His tone remained morose. "A bichon. Small, fluffy, cheerful, fun."

From seemingly nowhere, a small white dog, pom-pom tail wagging enthusiastically, came trotting up. The man beamed as if the sun had come out. "There! Where have you been, what have you been doing? Super dog. Super-dooper-whooper-whooper-super dog!"

I said, "Does he bark?"

The small dog was now in the man's arms. I felt almost like an intruder. But he must have heard my question, for he in turn asked the dog: "Do you bark? Do you barky-warky-barky-warky-warky? No, no barking! Useless as a guard dog. Friendly with everyone."

"How about moulting?" I asked.

"Do you moult? No you don't moult; we know you don't moulty-wolty."

"How about putting his paws on the kitchen table and panting?"

Once again, the dog was consulted. "Do you do that? No. You don't do that, do you? No No No!" He attached the lead and put the dog down. "Now, Daddy's getting tired, let's go home."

And they went off, the little dog trotting cheerfully along.

I showed pictures of bichon frise dogs to Lizzy.

She said: "Oh. They look alright."

I said: "And I have it on good authority they don't put their paws on the kitchen table and pant. Or bark. Or moult."

"Really?"

"Absolutely. Go for it?"

Lizzy grinned. "Yeah. Let's go for it."

I showed the kids. The girls said "Awww... cute!" while Josh said, "looks fun."

The nearest breeder with bichon pups ready to go was in Guildford, so Lizzy and I drove up.

It was a small house with a ding-dong doorbell.

From inside came the scabble of small, excited animals. Peering through the frosted glass we could see an exuberant tumble of white fluffy shapes, black noses and scratching paws. A human figure loomed into view and played dog football to clear the door.

She was extremely pleasant and very tired. Breeding dogs, she told us, is no picnic. We sat on her chewed sofa with the puppies chasing each other around her living room, out into the garden through dog flap A and back again into the kitchen via dog flap B.

Effectively, the whole of the ground floor had been turned into dog central. She saw me looking at a small truckle bed, with duvet and pillows. "I'm often down here overnight," she said, "it stops them barking and means my husband can get off." She gazed vacantly at nothing and needlessly added: "I sometimes sleep down here anyway."

I felt a warm feeling along the outside of my leg. One of the puppies had clambered up and was nestling happily between Lizzy and myself. Automatically, I reached down and scratched him between the ears, under his chin and along his back. Lizzy pushed her fingers through his woolly fur. He sighed in satisfaction and snuggled some more.

So, man and woman meet dog. When I tell people about it, they inevitably say 'ahhh.. You didn't choose your dog: he chose you.'

We asked if the puppy was available: the breeder said yes, I counted out a deposit and we arranged to return in a couple of weeks to collect.

Back home, I read the rest of 'first dog' by the dad of the outdoorsy TV chap and bought a crate, a lead, some treats, dog food, a puppy coat and a blanket decorated with little bones. Hannah bought a dog toy that squeaked and - not to be outdone - Beth obtained a dog toy that barked. Josh found a large chewable plastic bone.

I overheard Lizzy saying to the cat: "Now, listen: I'm not expecting you to make pals with the puppy immediately, but he'll be scared and nervous, so best if you stay out of his way."

The cat licked her lips and yawned, showing white, sharp teeth.

We didn't tell the tortoise because – as Lizzy pointed out – hibernating tortoises don't give a toss.

I broached the subject of a name just as we finished the evening meal. Josh said he didn't care and vanished into his room. Beth said she didn't care either but stayed to veto everything. Hannah said she thought we were getting a female, so all the names she liked were – duh! - wrong.

Eventually Lizzy said "it'll be Dad's dog, so he should name it."

I said: "well, how about: 'Pickle'?" There was a disgusted silence. Then Beth dashed halfway up the stairs and yelled: "Josh! Dad wants to call it Pickle!"

And Josh yelled back: "Noooooooooooo!!!!"

Then Lizzy said: "Let's name him after my dad: George."

Beth said: "George?" as if experimenting with the sound, then nodded. "Um. Yeah. OK."

Hannah said: "Yeah, I like that. George, yeah."

Beth shouted up the stairs: "What about George?"

And Josh's reply was "George good."

They looked at me.

For a mad moment, I thought to insist on 'Pickle' or – to really stir things - 'Branston' but then sanity prevailed and I nodded my head. "George it is."

And so it was settled.

'First Dog' said many puppies vomit profusely first time they travel by car. So Lizzy sat - draped in an old plastic groundsheet – in the back. I wrapped George – a little, white, unresisting fluffy bundle - in the dog blanket decorated with bones and put him on her lap.

Immediately, George fell asleep and didn't stir until we got home.

Following 'First Dog' I tried to get him used to the crate, but he looked so utterly abject and miserable I couldn't bear it and after 20 minutes took him out. He never went back in.

Hannah's squeaky dog toy was ignored, as was Josh's plastic bone. Beth's toy (much to her delight) was adopted: over the years it was dragged around, disembowelled and its voice box chewed into silence. I finally managed to put it out of its smelly misery 9 years later, after George had ignored it for a month, and I had hidden it for another two.

And, to wrap this up: George has been with us now for over a decade and I have often thought that if he were human, he'd be a lethargic hippy, slumped in a deck chair, having a spliff and watching a tranquil sunset. Bichons are classed as low energy dogs and George must be at the bottom end of that spectrum. When out for a walk (often dragged reluctantly from a snooze) and another dog comes bouncing enthusiastically up to do the sniff the bits thing, George will – as often as not – just stand there, indifferently observing nothing much. Occasionally he might return the sniff, but usually not.

Like all dogs, he's a unique character: but we all love him to bits. As one does.

People believe anything.

What: I become even more of a cynic.

Where: Turkey

My age: 52

Lizzy was always keener on travel and holidays than me. I liked the idea but not the execution. I found the hassle of getting there always outweighed actually being there. Sun, sea and unfamiliar food was not adequate compensation for queueing in your socks for an hour or so at a soulless airport.

But, come the turn of the year, Lizzy would agitate for us to 'sort' the summer holidays and – eventually - the summer holidays would be sorted. But one year, to surprise her, I was cunningly ready with a proposal.

"Let's go," I said, "for a dingy sailing family holiday in Turkey." I pulled out a brochure full of happy faces, bronzed limbs, salt-spray and the prices in small print. "Look at this."

Lizzy frowned. "Sailing?"

"My dad was in the navy," I said, "and we used to go camping at Hayling Island. I have fond memories of messing about on a small boat called the Water Rat. I can sail a bit. And there's wind-surfing and a kid's club." Hannah was then about ten and the twins five.

She flicked through the bright, encouraging pages. "Umm.... Let's put it to the troops."

The troops were up for it, so the following summer, off we flew. In the early morning we were traipsing through the rain at Gatwick. By 4 in the afternoon Lizzy was having tea and cake watching the kids in the pool while I – resplendent in flip-flops, T-shirt, shorts, sunhat and factor 15 - was exploring.

On the beach I found an array of sailboats of various levels of expertise and speed, with tiny kid's boats at one end and at the other – like cherries on top of the cake – a pair of catamarans: the fast, fearsome looking Hobie Cats.

The next day I insisted we all tried sailing, which was partly successful. Lizzy gravitated to windsurfing while the kids had a half-hearted bash before returning to the pool. But I got on rather well, steering a laser around without even capsizing once. The sky was blue and the sun warm; the Aegean sparkled enticingly and in the distance were mountains.

And perhaps for the first time since becoming an adult, I thought *'Umm ... maybe holidays are OK.'*

We became pally with a middle-aged Irish couple. She (let's call her Fiona) had come for the sailing and he for a quiet time reading. We spent a long somewhat boozy evening with them, during which Fiona and I decided we would enter the Hobie Cat challenge, an event in the weekly regatta. This was run by the holiday company for their clients and billed as a fun, non-serious event with prizes ranging from ice-cream to T-shirts. Henley it was not.

Fiona had sailed catamarans, but I had never even been on one: so – next day - I attended a short, two-hour course called 'A Hobie Cat introduction.'

There were about six of us and a young, talkative instructor. We assembled around an old, beached Hobie Cat with a damaged hull. We were told that, to sail a dingy, all you needed to do was – ha ha - to 'keep the flappy bit upright.' But Hobies were more sophisticated. He demonstrated how to tack. It looked immensely complicated: there is an extremely long pole attached to a strut attached to the rudders. The pole is long, he explained, to let you steer when you're out on the trapeze, but a bit of a bugger in light winds.

He demonstrated twice, smoothly shifting the pole from shoulder to shoulder and changing position. He then asked 'OK: who wants to give it a go?'

A large, instantly dislikeable middle-aged man with a fake tan, paunch, swimming trunks five sizes too small and – as if that wasn't enough – a ponytail! Stepped forward.

He had obviously sailed before: he probably had a Hobie Cat in his third garage. His actions were smooth and well-coordinated. He did it sitting then pretended to be out on a trapeze and did it again. We all hated him. Once his superiority had been demonstrated he sauntered off towards the bar.

The instructor said "OK, who's next?" and the rest of us had a go.

We all – one way or another – sort of got it. Except me. I am many things, but smooth and well-coordinated I am not. I fell off twice, banged my head once and somehow painfully trod on my own foot.

Feeling humiliated, I stepped off and limped over to the others. Trying to make light of my horribly inept performance, I said: "Ha! You wouldn't think: a few years ago I sailed in the Olympics, would you! Ha-ha!"

No-one said anything and I promptly forgot it.

I told Fiona of my clumsy inability to steer and she immediately said she'd do it and - if I could keep out of the way - I could navigate. I knew what that meant: I was now nothing more than ballast. But I nodded and said OK.

That was on the Thursday. The regatta was on the Saturday.

On Friday there was no wind and no sailing, but one of the slightly more extraordinary events of my life happened. It caused a radical shift in my regard for my fellow human beings. I became more cynical and less inclined to think most people weren't stupid.

I was standing on the beach, admiring the sand between my toes and wondering how long before tea and cake appeared when a small bald man – a complete stranger - stopped next to me.

He spoke out of the side of his mouth, as if we were planning to escape a chain gang. "I hear," he said "that you've competed in the Olympics."

My mouth dropped open. "What?"

"It's OK. I won't tell anyone." He tapped his nose and strode off.

Astonished and bewildered, I watched him go. Even his retreating back looked smugly conspiratorial. It seemed completely dumb: how could anyone have possibly thought I was an expert sailor? They had watched me making a total Horlicks of a simple manoeuvre on a stationary boat, then heard me make a humorous/sarcastic comment, and yet someone had chosen to believe the words I said rather than how they were said or the context in which they were uttered.

And I understood: many people were so dumb or careless of thought they'd believe any old crap, despite the evidence of their own eyes or the promptings of logic or reason. Many years later, I realised it explained the insanity of Brexit and the disgraceful support of Donald Trump. But back then, this future we are now in was unimaginable.

At the time, I merely felt the whole human race had been diminished, and this upset me. So I told Lizzy, expecting condolence and comfort. But all she did was sigh. "Jimbob," she said: "I've told you before. You should steer clear of comments you think are witty. You're not very good at them. Or jokes, while I'm at it."

"Oh, thanks."

"You're welcome."

Fiona didn't share my misgivings. "Brilliant! That'll scare them!"

"Don't you think it odd they believed it?"

She grinned. "My husband's a barrister. Nothing much surprises me."

The regatta was held the following day. The Hobie Cat challenge was the last event and had generated an audience of 3 (including Lizzy and Hannah) standing with us on a diving platform out in the bay. The wind was light and hard to read, with an occasional half-hearted gust from unexpected directions.

There were two Hobies and four teams, so there would be two heats with the winners going through to the final.

Needless to say, the ponytailed bastard was there, along with a very small woman made entirely of blotchy leather, who screeched at him from time to time. Undoubtedly his wife, poor sod.

Fiona and I were in the first race, against a genial chap and his even more genial son.

Off we went and our opponents cocked up the start, going over the line too early, laughing heartily and having to circle round to begin again. And by the time they had done that, we were too far ahead to be caught and duly won. So, we would be in the final. Hurrah!

We swapped round for the second heat. The Ponytailed one and his wife hardly said a word as they settled down and cast off. It soon became obvious they really were the business: co-ordinated and tight, switching from side to side with practiced ease. With an increasing sense of gloom, I watched them zig-zagging about. The hooter hooted, indicating there was exactly a minute left before the start line could be crossed and the race begun.

Either by accident or design, they passed near the diving platform and I saw the leather-skinned one glance down at her hand. She said '30 seconds.'

Fiona muttered: "Shit: she's got a stop watch!"

I knew what this meant: they could time to the second when to cross the start line. But I had a solution. "Don't worry," I said brightly: "I'll count elephants!"

Fiona sighed. "Oh …. yeah, OK, why not."

The story of the second semi-final is soon told. Team Ponytail (half horrible human, half leather homunculus), by dint of stopwatch timing, expert sailing and a sudden favourable gust of wind, won comfortably.

Smiling smugly, they stayed on their Hobie, waiting for Fiona and I to sail out for the grand finale.

By now the pool of non-excited spectators had decreased by one, leaving only Lizzy and Hannah. As we moved off, I waved and – after eventually catching their attention - called: "you might at least cheer!" A couple of lukewarm 'hurrahs' echoed back. I waved some more.

Fiona said: "Did you hear the gun? Have you started counting?"

"What?"

"The hooter! One Minute! Oh God: start at ten!"

"Ah!" I began ticking away the seconds under my breath. '11 elephants, 12 elephants, 13 elephants, 14 elephants -'

"Ready about!" I crouched down and the boom swept slowly over my head, but by this time the count had become automatic, and I went steadily on '15 elephants, 16 elephants ..'

Team Ponytail passed us going in the other direction. I heard her say "40 seconds."

I was taken aback. 40 seconds! Was she counting up or counting down? Probably down. Must be down. But by then I'd lost my place.

Fiona, her attention determinedly on the other boat, the sea, the wind and the start line said: "How long now?"

I took a stab "35 seconds left!" I began my internal count again '34 elephants, 33 elephants, 32 elephants -"

Why had I switched to a count down, rather than up? I gave a mental shrug and said: "30 seconds!"

We were inching towards the start, an imaginary line between the diving platform and a buoy.

Our opponents were a little way off, dawdling around like a panther ready to strike.

"20 seconds!"

"Ready about!" We switched tack. The other cat suddenly hauled itself round: its sail filled and a small wake appeared astern.

"They're going for it!" My whisper could have been heard in Timbuktu.

"Were you sure about 20 seconds?"

"Yes! No! Sorry!"

"Gybe ho!"

"What?" But the boom was already crunching towards me. I sprawled down and we were suddenly headed for the start. An unwelcome breath of wind sped us forward: too fast! Fiona let out some rope, the wind spilled from our sail, the cat slowed, the chap on the platform, stopwatch in hand, lifted the hooter, and team Ponytail swept past us.

"Shit!" Fiona hauled the rope back and our sail slowly filled, but we were too late: the hooter hooted and less than half a second later, they were sliding over the start line ahead of us.

There was little else to do but to follow them, like a prisoner being led to a firing squad. The wind was still light and we progressed slowly towards the first buoy. I shielded my eyes, staring intently at the boat ahead, willing for one of them to fall overboard, or the sail to tear in two, or a rudder to break: anything to slow them down.

They reached the first buoy, tacked expertly and headed for the next.

A second or so later, and it was our turn.

Fiona opened her mouth: "Ready ab-"

I hissed: "No!" and put up my hand to prevent the boom moving. "Keep going!" I turned and lowered my voice. "I saw a ripple. Wind."

Fiona frowned: she had seen nothing. And looking again, I also saw nothing. But in those few seconds, we had been committed: the distance between us and team Ponytail had stretched to an unbridgeable 20 or so yards.

So we kept going. And – like a miracle – after 8 endless seconds, our Hobie trembled and I felt a splash of salt-spray on the side of my face.

Fiona – abruptly energised - shouted "Ready about!"

We whipped round, our sail cracking as it filled and instead of moving along quietly and sombrely, our cat – our wonderful, wonderful Hobie Cat – dipped for a moment before – joyously – heeling over and springing forward.

Rapidly, Fiona shifted, sitting fully on one of the hulls, counteracting the wind: her hair was blowing every which way and she had a grin wider than a bus. "Over here!"

I crawled over and sat alongside her, and for perhaps a minute and a half, we sailed, skimming over the waves, leaving a widening track of foam. It was as if we had become a picture in a Hobie Cat brochure.

OK, so the wind wasn't that strong, so we didn't get up on one hull (thank God) or require the trapeze (double thank God), but we overtook those Ponytail bastards as if they were standing still. And when the wind slackened, we sliced round, dismissively crossed well ahead of them and steered straight for the finish.

Obediently, they fell in behind us: there was nothing else for them to do.

As we went over the line, Hannah and Lizzy gave a cheer and a clap. Fiona and I stepped up onto the diving platform feeling like conquerors of the world. Team Ponytail didn't stop: they just kept on, reached the beach and dragged their sorry arses towards the bar. Even from where we were, you could hear her screeching at him.

That evening Fiona and I were each given a T-shirt: a bit of marketing tat, with 'regatta winner' emblazoned on the back. Tat or no, it was well made: after more than twenty years I have still mine and on cold nights wear it in bed.

And whenever I do, I am reminded of that 90 or so seconds of exhilaration which won us the Hobie Cat challenge.

And – as a sad and rather depressing coda – I often also recall how I became even more of a cynic regarding truth and the power of lies.

Buying my current car

What: I actually manage to get a good used car deal.

Where: Southampton.

My age: 72

I am writing this in January 2021. We are in the strange times of yet another COVID 19 lockdown: gatherings banned, always social distancing and mandatory mask wearing to buy an orange.

But I am nearing the end of this narrative: when it is finished, I will put it away for a few weeks while I sort out some photographs. Of my immediate family: Lizzy, Hannah, Josh, Beth; of those I grew up with: Mum and Dad, Peter, Judith, Jane; and those I now live with: Hannah, Jonny, Jude and Evie.

A catalogue of the most important people I love, have loved and still love.

And of course, even as I write this, I am aware it is a displacement activity.

For I have been avoiding writing about Lizzy. Of why she has vanished from these pages. At the end of this month, she will have been gone for three impossible years. Maybe it is too early. Or perhaps too late: but to finish this book, it is imperative I include her and why she is no longer with us. So, on this page, with these words, I begin the process, allowing me to edge towards a chapter – the final chapter I will write, although not the final chapter in this book – entitled 'Goodbye Lizzy.'

But that will come later. For I am now shuffling off into yet another displacement activity: writing about how I bought my current car. In a way it is a companion piece to '**My first car.**'

After leaving college I became in turn a teacher, a salesman, a writer, a computer consultant and finally a retiree. My cars went from being old bangers with rust and quirks to – as my pockets deepened – boringly reliable second-hand vehicles of various sizes.

But whenever I bought another car, often from dealerships in part-exchange, I had the feeling that – if my bargaining skills were superior – I could have made a better deal. Regularly I would trade in a car and – a week later – see it advertised at far more than I got for it. OK, so they have overheads and need to make a profit, but even so I always felt I had been screwed.

And then I saw 'Fargo' (the best Cohen Brothers film by far). There is a scene early on where a car salesman is haggling with a customer. The salesman says he'll have to check with his boss. He goes into an adjacent office and you see him through the window talking to another man.

I realised this had often happened to me, when buying a car. So I sat up and took notice. In the film, the boss is watching a game on a small portable TV. He and the salesman discuss the match for a few seconds. There is no mention of cars or prices.

Then the salesman emerges and – using 'what the boss said' as an indisputable authority - concludes the deal pretty much along the lines he wanted.

It became clear: 'seeing the boss' or 'let me speak to the manager' is all bogus. It's just a way of introducing a remote, omnipotent, Godlike figure into the mix, against which the salesman has little leeway and is revealed as no more than a pawn in the grip of forces greater than himself. You start thinking he would love to give you what you want, but it's impossible, as he can't argue with God. Worse, you want to help him. So you nod your head and say 'OK.'

Never again, I told myself, would I fall for this trick. I would be forceful. I would stick to my guns. If necessary, I'd walk away.

But the next time I bought a car (about a year later) I couldn't face the confrontation of haggling and pretended to myself I had forgotten it all. So when the salesman returned after the 'conference' with his manager, I nodded my head and said OK.

And even as we shook hands, I thought: *'I've been done.'*

But now, let us move on to my current car. I have had it for about 3 years. It is parked outside. I can see it through my front window. A 2014 Toyota Yaris hybrid: red, dented, scratched: but a good little runner. It's all I require.

And here's the thing: I am convinced I got a good deal! From a car dealership!

To take a quick step back for a moment: a blow-by-blow account of used car negotiations is somewhat niche in terms of readership, so skip to the next chapter if it doesn't appeal. After all, reading a book shouldn't be a boring trudge through uninteresting stuff. Call me a barbarian, but I've skipped acres of the classics (Jane Austin's non bodice ripper '*Pride & Prejudice*' springs to mind, not to mention 60% of all Dickens and 70% of Shakespeare) so you're welcome to do the same: after all, it's not as if anyone else knows (or indeed cares).

After going through several cars (4 in 3 years, if I remember correctly) I decided yet more change was in order. I'd had a Yaris before and liked it, so decided on another: and for purposes of economy, this time it would be a hybrid.

To be honest, I can't now remember the actual sums involved, but the way the haggling went is correct.

I did my usual research on how much my current car was worth to the trade, (£4,500) how much cash I had (£3,000) and the prices of various local second-hand Yaris hybrids.

There were a couple that appeared likely: one for £8,000 and another, slightly older and higher mileage, for a thousand quid less. I arranged to see them both on successive days. As it so happened, the more expensive one was first.

The salesman was young(ish) and sharp-suited. We left a mechanic inspecting my old car and clambered into the Yaris for a test drive. He removed the 'for sale' notice, which had two figures: £9,000 (crossed out) and £8,000 (current price). He said nothing, but the implication was clear: there had already been a sharp reduction in price.

The test drive was fine, so he got me some machine coffee and we settled down across his desk.

I said I wished to buy. He said "great!"

And then I said: "But I won't be buying today, as there's another Yaris I'm booked in to see tomorrow."

Immediately, he asked where and how much. I pulled out my phone and showed him. He turned to his keyboard and after a few clicks I saw a little downturn at the corner of his mouth.

I realised he'd been hoping I was bluffing.

"So," he said: "what can I do to stop you going to see this other car?"

Emboldened, I replied: "My car and £3,000 for your Yaris."

He permitted himself a smile. "No chance!" He nodded towards his screen. "Your car has a value of £3,500. So it should be your car and £4,500. But I'm willing to do a deal. Your car and £4,250. Considering it's already been reduced, I think that's absolutely fair."

I sighed, uncertain of what to do. It certainly sounded good, but ….. my voice came out tired and rather resigned "Can't you do any better?"

He stood. "I'll check with my manager, but I don't think there's much movement." He walked off.

Somehow, I'd forgotten, but now, with startling clarity, I remembered 'Fargo.' I half stood and gazed with new eyes at my surroundings. This large, shiny and super-clean showroom, with polished cars and calming music, was all irrelevant. The salesman's desk: intimidatingly free of clutter and resolutely business-like, didn't matter. Even his chair, subtlety higher than mine, could be disregarded.

It was just a stage on which they expected to drag me into their pantomime.

Subconsciously or not, I felt my back straighten.

He returned. "You don't need finance?" I nodded. "That makes it simpler. He'll knock another 50 quid off. Your car and £4,200."

I frowned and asked: "Why does finance make a difference?"

"It makes it quicker."

I blinked at him. "But it's still a bank transfer. Surely it doesn't make any difference to you how I get it?"

He considered, then smiled. "Thinking about it, you're right. Must be a hangover from the old days, when cash was king." He leant back. "Anyway, your car and 4 2 is the best we can do."

"I still think my car and 3."

He puffed out a long breath and shook his head "I'm sure that can't happen, but … I'll see." He walked off again.

I pretended to look at my phone, as though important messages were pinging into existence. He returned. "You're in luck. He says your car and 3 8. And that's it."

I sighed. "Pity." I stood. "I'll let you know tomorrow, after I've seen this other one. Sorry if I've wasted your time." I made to go.

"What offer would you take?"

"I've told you: my car and 3k."

He looked at the ceiling and let out yet another long breath. "I'll see what I can do." He trundled off once more. My coffee was now cold, but I had a sip anyway. Eventually, he was back again. He shook his head disbelievingly. "You are very very much in luck. He's worked the figures again and can just about drop down to £3,385." He was obviously seeking to intimidate me by departing from round numbers.

I stood again and this time held out my hand. "Pity. Well, good bye."

He was astonished. "You're saying no? You're rejecting it?"

"Sorry. It's my car and 3k, or that's it."

This time he didn't even bother with a long, disparaging and hope depressing cheek puffing. "OK" he said. "Wait there."

Off he went. This time he was gone maybe ten minutes. I imagined him and his 'boss' (unless he was entirely fictional) using their fingers to part Venetian blinds to look at me. I tried to make the back of my neck formidable and resolute.

He returned. "Your car and 3k it is."

And we shook hands. The deal had been done.

Now I'm not sure what lessons can be learnt from this. After all, it just might have been they needed desperately to sell a car – any car – to meet some target. Or there was much more leeway than they made out. Or they even decided to take pity on an old codger like me. Or (quite likely) something else entirely.

Having another car to see added to the urgency and definitely helped, but the research on prices was key. The bottom line was – if I was right and the correct trade-in price for my old car was £4,500 and not - as the salesman claimed - £3,500, then *'my car and 3k'* was only asking for a reduction of 500 quid. So, very probably not a stonkingly brilliant deal after all.

But as I walked away from the showroom, the salesman and his (presumed but unseen) boss, I didn't care. For once I felt I had beaten the system. And it made me feel heroic.

But a week later I didn't dare check their website to see what they were now asking for my old car. Why ask for trouble?

Relish the small triumphs and let the big ones take care of themselves.

Goodbye Lizzy

What: My beautiful wife Lizzy dies.

Where: Southampton.

My age: 72

When writing, all you have are words.

You arrange them and you pummel them and you force them into sentences but – in the end – they are but words, tied to the noises a human mouth can make. Every written word, in any language, has been - or will have been - spoken by someone. Even 'dead' or 'forgotten' words were live once.

Too often in this book, I have written about death. Mum and Dad, Peter, Judith, Jane: everyone I grew up with. And to describe to you what happened, all I have are words.

At college, where I studied mathematics, there was an attempt to broaden our horizons with a weekly 'liberal studies' seminar. An enthusiastic chap with curly hair would come in and say things like 'why advertise?' or 'is anarchy the highest form of society?'

Once, he said: 'complete the following: 'the quality of mercy is not ......' what?' There was a chorus of 'strained,' said in the bored tones of those that had been force-fed Shakespeare in the sixth form.

He smiled at the reaction before taking us through the first four lines:

The quality of mercy is not strain'd,
It droppeth as the gentle rain from heaven
Upon the place beneath: it is twice blest;
It blesseth him that gives and him that takes

He stopped and grinned. "What's that mean? What's he telling us?" then – crucially - "Can you do better? G'on - I dare you to exceed our greatest dramatist!"

And - after a lively debate - we decided Shakespeare – in this instance - couldn't be bettered.

The point is, even Shakespeare only had words. True, he could use them with an admirable, poetic economy, but usually he just battered the audience with a tsunami of boring guff.

I am, in writing about loss, aware of giants both past and present, for we all use and have used the same inadequate tool: namely, words.

But, once again, I am prevaricating. I am stalking the subject of Lizzy dying as a tiger might circle a prey it does not wish to catch. I have just altered the previous sentence, changing the euphemism of 'Lizzy passing' to the bluntness of 'Lizzy dying.' To continue the metaphor: the tiger has taken a step closer.

And now – finally – it springs.

A week to the day before she died, Lizzy managed to get to the bathroom. She had been sleeping in our dining room, in a comfortable bed, without my snoring. She was fragile, and stairs were difficult. But she was up there anyway, trying to turn on the taps, her pitifully thin bare legs sticking out beneath her inside-out T-shirt.

I did the taps, and found some bath oil. The radiator was working well and the steam hung like mist. I helped her in. The warm water came up to her hips. I eased the T-shirt over her head and shoulders. She drew her knees up under her chin and wrapped her arms round her legs.

Gently, gently, I soaped her back, the tired, grey skin, the protrusion of vertebrae down her spine, the meagre flatness of her shoulder blades, the surplus folds above her waist. She was 63 years old and her body had shrunk, shedding fat and muscle faster than the skin could tighten.

"Oh, that's nice." She rested her forehead against her knees. "Don't stop." I did her neck, lifting her short, brittle hair out of the way.

It was intimate, quiet, peaceful and warm. A true Diana Moment. To cherish.

Two days later she went into hospital and never returned home.

Sometimes things creep up on you and it is only later you realise their significance.

To take a non-random example: illness. In Nov/Dec, 2016, when she had about fifteen months left, Lizzy's speech patterns began changing. More and more she became less and less connected with the subject under discussion. In short, she started rambling.

But it wasn't fast, or – initially – obvious. At first, she became more outspoken, and seemed to have opinions on everything: but after a few weeks she began adding details which tagged along, one after the other, each one a stepping stone to increasing irrelevance.

Oh God, I have to confess I ignored it. When she went off on one of her meandering, rambling monologues I switched off. I know I was scared at the prospect of dementia and hoping – as I often did – that the problem would go away. Also, Lizzy and I had got so used to each other I think we'd rather stopped listening to what the other said. Our lives had begun to be parallel rather than entwined.

Towards the end of January, she complained of feeling tired and listless. She went to the doctor, who arranged a blood test.

Within a week she was in hospital, attached to a drip. Her sodium levels were dangerously low. She was quite cheerful, pleased that things were happening, that they could fix it.

The hospital shoved fluids into her for a day or so and when she came out the random conversational meanderings had gone. Win Win! Back to normal. For a while.

Lizzy's doctor retired or moved on. A new doctor came in and Lizzy – now feeling tired and listless again – went to see her.

The surgery is not far from our house, and half an hour after she left, I got a phone call from her.

"Jimbob. I need to get to the hospital again. Urgently." Her new doctor had found an overlooked blood test. Sodium levels again.

She was sat in the waiting room, looking pale and drawn. I had to help her into the car. When I could I held her hand as I drove, our fingers interlaced. I saw, on her notes, scrawled across the bottom of the page, a hand-written message: 'Suspected Addison's?'

In a hospital bed once again, wearing a medical gown with ties up the back and propped up against the pillows, she asked me to fetch items from home. Her favourite nighty, toiletries, a charger for her phone: all those small things that make a horizontal, restricted movement existence more comfortable. The nurse probed her arm, unsuccessfully trying to find a vein.

My wife looked up at me. "You'd better go," she said. "This might take some time."

For her blood vessels had always hidden away, as if scared of getting hurt from the needle. When I returned an hour later, with a carrier bag full of goodies, she was all attached. She told me it had taken 3 nurses of increasing experience to finally get it done.

This time she was in hospital for maybe a week or more. She had X-rays and other scans.

I saw her every day, but my times were variable, depending on the size of the queue for the car park. I could have walked, but didn't want to leave George alone, so I would bundle him into the back of the car and he would happily snooze there, while I visited Lizzy.

She did have a constant stream of visitors: pals and friends, people she knew.

One evening she rang. There was an undercurrent to her voice: one I had not heard before, but so slight as to be unidentifiable.

She said: "Jimbob, what time will you be here tomorrow?"

"Oh, usual time, around ten-ish, depending on, y'know."

"Can you make sure you're here at ten? They asked specifically."

"Yeah. Why?"

She took a beat before saying: "I think they might be sending me home, and they need to make sure everything's OK."

"You're coming home tomorrow?"

"I don't know. Might be."

"Oh, that'd be great!"

It is amazing how you believe what you want to believe. I was over seventy and had – I thought - lived in the real world. You'd think I'd be cautious about optimism, about taking a small incident and expanding it into a hope.

Ten o'clock came. Lizzy hadn't slept well, but she had brushed her hair and was looking good. We were chatting about mundane things: the weather; what to have for dinner; the kids; friends who'd visited yesterday; how I'd bought a large bottle of Martini Rosso for her and sod the expense.

Pretty much at ten, a nurse came in, followed by two more. They drew the curtains and a small, unassuming lady entered and calmly sat by the bed. It was probably the body language of the others that gave us pause and made us realise we were in the presence of someone important.

Lizzy took my hand.

The lady introduced herself. She was I think a consultant of some sort: I can't really remember.

Her voice was quiet. She went through the tests they had done, and the scans and X-rays.

There was, she said, a shadow. Her voice remained calm. Her hand moved to her forehead and she placed her forefinger between her eyebrows. "A shadow," she repeated, "just here." The tip of her finger traced a short arc to the right. A curve of no more than two or three inches.

She placed her hand back in her lap and waited.

I knew what we had been told was momentous, but I didn't know – or refused to know - what it meant.

Once, I tried to repair a washing machine I had neglected to unplug. I received a jolt that went through my body, leaving me awake but stunned. It was like that.

I held on to Lizzy's hand, her fingers tense against mine.

She said something to the lady. Who replied. There was a brief conversation between the two. I cannot remember any of it: not because I've forgotten, but because – there, then – nothing made sense.

A shadow? Shadows conceal things. Wolves and ogres lurk in shadows.

The lady – her voice level, perfectly balanced between compassion and a requirement to be professional – said Lizzy could go home, but would have to come back for more tests.

She stood and one of the nurses swept the curtains back and our small space, created and defined for the giving of important, life changing information, unfolded to show other beds, patients, nurses and visitors. A man was laughing; a trolly in the corridor had a squeaky wheel; a woman was being helped into a wheelchair: our lady – the lady with the calm voice and shattering words – was already going out of the door, her cohort of nurses trailing behind.

I said "So, great. You can come home."

"Yes." Lizzy's voice was quiet. She turned to me. "So. Here we are."

"Yes." The woman in the wheelchair was vanishing down the corridor; the man had stopped laughing but the trolly with the squeaky wheel was now in the ward. Newspapers, magazines and chocolate bars were being dispensed. I said "How does this work? Do we just go?"

"Go and ask," was the reply, "at the nurses station."

When Lizzy got home, the shadow came with her, like a silent, dark question mark we didn't mention. I don't think either of us could find the words without acknowledging its existence and thereby making it real. The air became weighty, potent with a misty, hard to discern future. Even in the quiet of the night, with heads snuggled on shoulders and bodies comfortingly touching, we did not talk of it.

It is a regret I carry to this day. For we never did: we never had 'the conversation about cancer.' For ten months we never spoke of it, not directly: instead, her cancer became defined by action and events: the appointments, the pills, the treatment, the infusions, the chemo, the radio, the bleak hospital corridors, the special cancer sanctioned parking permits, the crowded waiting rooms, the white consultation rooms, the desultory conversations: all the paraphernalia of ultimately futile treatments.

At first, right at the beginning, when all we knew was of 'a shadow' we didn't know what to say either to each other or to our children. Hannah was married with a baby and another on the way, Josh had moved out and Beth was in Australia.

One of us rang Hannah. Or – more likely - she rang us. I stroked my forehead and said they have found a shadow. But they weren't sure what it was, that there would be further tests and all we could do was wait.

Hannah went very quiet and asked for more details, but there really weren't any: I'd said it all. Later, I heard Lizzy talking to her, a long, long conversation. But I did not ask about what.

And I talked with Josh. It was in much the same vein as the one with Hannah, only face to face, across the kitchen table. Just him and me: Lizzy was probably watching a cooking program with her friend Hazel in the front room. Soon I would go in and ask if there was anything they needed: a cup of tea, a biscuit.

I said the same things to Josh as I had to Hannah: there was a shadow, just here, but no-one knew what it was, that she would have to go back for more tests soon. And then we should know more.

Josh nodded, asked a couple of questions and left.

I can't now remember if we had a hug or not. I hope we did.

With Beth – on the other side of the world - we decided to wait for more information.

And in a week or so there were more blood tests and Lizzy had to go into hospital again, to be attached once more to bags of liquid drip-feeding what her body had stopped providing.

And they decided to do a biopsy and removed a small piece from far up in her nose. Well, why not.

And they did another scan. As they do.

And we waited.

It felt like an age but was possibly only a few weeks. Maybe less.

And then a brown envelope with a red *NHS* stamped on it came through the post.

We were asked to make an appointment to see an oncologist.

I knew what it meant, but Googled anyway.

'Oncology is a branch of medicine that deals with the prevention, diagnosis, and treatment of cancer. A medical professional who practices oncology is an oncologist.'

So another type of doctor, a specialist. In cancer. Who would tell us what we needed to know, or – to put it more bleakly – would tell us what we didn't want to know. Accordingly, in my mind, 'The Oncologist' assumed a status of almost mythic proportions. At the very least, I told myself, he would have one of those high backed, leather swivel-turn chairs behind an imposing desk of oak.

The reality was different: isn't it always? We were guided to a small, curtained off space, not much more than alcove, with a Formica topped table, a filing cabinet, three chairs and The Oncologist.

He stood, apologised for the temporary office and closed the curtains. His hair was thin and grey. His eyes were kind and his movements precise.

There was a folder on the table. He looked through it. "We are pretty sure," he said, "of the diagnosis: olfactory neuroblastoma. It's very rare." His finger went to his forehead and traced a now familiar curve. Up and over to the right. About 2 inches. "It's in a very difficult place. For an operation, that is."

So Lizzy and I sat there, on our little plastic chairs, hearing – but not always comprehending - words like chemotherapy and radiotherapy, while around us, unseen and mostly unheard, the rest of the world continued.

They decided on chemotherapy. Six sessions at three-week intervals. Regular blood tests between sessions. A daily schedule of pills.

Put crudely, chemotherapy is the process of shoving powerful drugs into your bloodstream in a controlled attempt to kill the cancer before the cancer can kill you. As the blood goes everywhere the drugs go everywhere. I thought of it as an army of good guys surging up to cancer cells, surrounding them and attacking with laser guns, rocket-fired grenades and torpedoes of spectacular impact. It is a comforting image, but ignores the collateral damage of other good guys getting caught in the crossfire and getting destroyed.

We were told the three-week intervals between sessions was to allow the body to recover. The regime of pills sped up the process and the weekly blood tests told them how successful it was.

With Lizzy, the tests revealed this recovery was not going well. The white corpuscle count remained stubbornly low. To give her more time to recover, the gap between her first and second chemo sessions lengthened to four weeks. And between the second and third it increased again, to five.

They never did a fourth. Our new oncologist (our first had by now retired) said carrying on with the chemo might well do more harm than good. I adjusted my metaphor: the chemo army might be zapping the bad guys, but in the process were killing too many of the civilian population. And when that happens, it's best to stop.

They decided to start radiotherapy, as and when it could be arranged.

So, once again, we waited, this time for a slot in the radiotherapy schedule. Before Lizzy became ill, despite losing both sisters and my brother to cancer, I hadn't realised quite how many cancer sufferers there were. In the oncology department, waiting rooms were always packed, treatment areas crowded and appointments seldom on time. There was – and still are - many thousands of people, with cancer, being treated and hoping it would work.

Increasingly, our lives were settling into a pattern dominated by the illness we never directly talked about. We rearranged the furniture and Lizzy moved downstairs, sleeping in what was the dining room. I started watching TV in the games room, sitting in one bamboo chair with my feet on another, while Lizzy sat with Hazel watching property-porn or cooking-porn in the front room.

Hazel lived just round the corner and often, I would walk her home. Five minutes of chatting about the weather, her cat, the children, anything other than Lizzy and her all-encompassing illness.

Gradually, as the energy drained from us, the house became silent and dull.

In the afternoon I would take George to the new forest and we would wander among the trees and along paths. And when driving, I would find myself letting out a screeching shout, a banshee wail of frustration and useless rage. What was the point, what was the sodding point? Nothing had a purpose any more: just going through the motions because it was better than doing nothing. And, at night, in the small hours, my thoughts turned black. I might think ahead, to life beyond cancer. And the truly terrifying thing was, try as I might, in this future world, Lizzy was absent.

It was as if I was scrubbing clean the shelves of my future memory in preparation for another life: the new, sad and dreary existence of a widower.

The first radiotherapy appointment was – oddly – fixed for somewhere called 'the mould room.' I had seen arrows pointing down corridors, but didn't know what it meant.

Radiotherapy, unlike chemo, requires precision: the rays will zap anything they are aimed at. And if – as in Lizzy's case – the cancer cells are near – or even interwoven with – brain cells, you really, really don't want them to miss the target. Not even by a millimetre.

Which meant she had to keep her head absolutely still. And to ensure this, they needed to construct a mask fitting tightly over her face, to be fastened down and held in place. And these masks can be called moulds. Hence the mould room.

When the treatments had finished, Lizzy brought it home. I found it creepy: a translucent golden yellow, pierced by holes for mouth, nostrils and eyes. It also had a small number of crosses drawn in indelible ink: markings so the radiotherapy could be correctly focussed. I imagined my dear, sweet wife pinned into place like a butterfly while monstrous machines (I pictured large bulbous ray guns from old black and white sci-fi movies) were lined up to ensure maximum damage.

It sat for a while in the corner of the dining room, a baleful, blank-eyed presence: after a while I moved it, tucking it away from view. I don't think Lizzy noticed: if she did, she kept quiet.

The radiotherapy sessions happened every weekday for six weeks. Or was it seven? Maybe eight? Memory does not always serve me well on details. It seemed to go on for ever, finishing late in October or early in November. It was just a year since a seemingly fit, healthy Lizzy had begun rambling. It was about three months before she died.

We now knew: surgery was not possible; chemotherapy had been destructive and radiotherapy had yet to prove itself.

So waiting was all we had left. Lizzy kept herself busy: even went away for a few days, touring round the West country with a friend, while I sat at home, plugging away at the novel I'd started as a displacement activity.

Lizzy began complaining about aching in her hips and back. The scans didn't look good and our oncologist prescribed more radiotherapy, 'to nip it in the bud.'

It didn't seem to help.

November turned into December, with Christmas – the most tedious event of the year – looming before us like a miserable tinsel covered turd. We had nothing much scheduled, but then Hannah's plans for a Christmas meal with the in-laws fell through so we had them over, along with Josh, who was coming for afternoon tea anyway.

Lizzy – who had made the invite – revved herself into action. She sent me shopping for a turkey crown and on the day managed to cook all morning to produce the standard Christmas meal of roast turkey with – as they say – all the trimmings.

In the afternoon she went to bed, Hannah put her feet up (she was now over 8 months pregnant) and Jonny, Josh, George and myself took Jude – a very lively 2 year old – to the common to fed the ducks.

In the evening Lizzy and I snacked on remnants and she went back to bed while I tidied up. I went in to check on her before going up. One arm was exposed. I tucked it back under the duvet and kissed her forehead. She didn't wake.

And so, one step at a time, one day at a time, life dribbled on.

Because so many days were now the same, to be endured rather than savoured, the timeline becomes misty. But some dates, in January 2018, are fixed.

Hannah gave birth to our second grandchild, Evie, on Saturday 13th.

They came to visit Sunday 21st. We have a photo of Lizzy with Evie on her lap.

The following Friday (the 26th) Lizzy was very quiet in the morning and refused her pills. In desperation I rang the hospital and they said to bring her in. I did so and a series of nurses, doctors and consultants (including our oncologist) examined her. They gave her morphine. A kind consultant – a specialist in end-of-life care - sat down with me. The prognosis, he said, is not even months. It is weeks. Maybe less. Could be a matter of days. He waited several minutes for me to respond. I discovered it is what I expected. Eventually I asked: "what happens now?"

I am given three options: home; hospital or hospice

I ask if she knows where she is and he says right now she does, but, later – for they will need to increase the morphine - she will not.

I ask – if she comes home – how much help would I get? He says a nurse would be round three of four times a day but overnight all I'll have is an emergency number.

I ask what happens if she stays in hospital. He says they'd find a quiet place.

I ask how far away is the hospice. He says it's in Moorgreen.

I know the area well enough. It's not far, so – with some guilty relief - I chose the hospice. He said that's probably for the best and he'll set things in motion. I was left on my own, so I went back to see Lizzy again, but the curtains were drawn and the nurses were busy. I sat for a while but felt restless and went home.

I rang the children. And – even though the news was expected – the conversations were difficult as we are not skilled in such matters. In lighter times, my conversation with Beth, half the world away and half a day ahead, could be in a comedy script: it was Australia day, so she was at a party. The news made her sit down and she looked in such a state her friend picked up the phone. I did not know this, so continued talking as if she were Beth! Ha ha! But we didn't laugh and I sent her the airfare for a rapid return.

On Saturday (the 27th) Hannah came with Evie and a car load of baby accessories. Josh sat with Evie on his lap while Hannah helped Lizzy to the loo. Her bed was in a quiet corner and we kept the curtains drawn. Her doctor visited, as did her oncologist, wearing a pale blue shirt. Some details just stick in the mind for no reason.

On the Sunday (the 28th) we all visited, but Lizzy was mainly asleep and very drowsy when awake. They had started unrestricted morphine, upping the dose when she was in pain. Palliative care. I rang, texted or otherwise contacted friends and relatives.

One friend said: "Oh dear. Poor Lizzy. I should be able to come by the end of the week."

I replied, "the end of the week might be too late." I let the pause stretch for a few seconds before adding "she goes into a hospice tomorrow."

In the evening someone cooks something and not much is said.

Monday (the 29th). Beth arrives tugging a carrycase with little wheels and an extendible handle. In the morning Lizzy is moved to The Countess Mountbatten Hospice, to the West of Southampton and in the afternoon we all go there. She is in a nice room, on her own. It is peaceful and quiet. She is so gaunt: her cheeks have hollowed out as if her soul is draining away. She is unreachable: a morphine barrier is shielding her from pain, the world, and us.

We are very quiet: there seems to be nowhere to go and nothing to do. Friends visit: some, shocked by the almost miasmic presence of departure, stay for only a few minutes. Others are convinced that somewhere in this resting, eyes closed, unresponsive figure their lovely friend is still present. So they talk, rubbing her hand, recalling times now gone.

And Lizzy lies there, the discretely hidden syringe driver feeding morphine, drop by constant drop, into her bloodstream, keeping her safe. In the evening Beth sits on my lap and I stroke her hair while she weeps.

Tuesday (the 30th) is the last full day of Lizzy's life. We flit like ghosts around the house, while in the hospice, time pauses while my sweet wife, the mother of our children, the heart of the family, is silently ebbing away.

But we do not know there are only hours left. Hannah, driven by the imperatives of small people, family and work, sees her mum once more, then departs, driving back through the evening dusk.

For the second time in my life I receive a call saying a person I love, a person suffering from cancer, has but a few hours left. The first time, it was my sister Judy. They were wrong: she continued, gasping for breath, for another three days. This time it was Lizzy.

I went immediately, to find Jackie and Wendy, old friends both, at her bedside. To my inexpert eye Lizzy seemed to be the same as earlier in the day: gaunt, eyes closed, breathing lightly.

But the doctor had pronounced judgement, so we gathered and we waited, like birds on a cliff.

The quiet hours ticked by. Sometimes we talked in low voices, sometimes not. We found a truckle bed and enough space to put it down. We took it in turns to rest while the world spun and Tuesday the 30th turned into Wednesday the 31st.

I was sleeping for the second time when a hand shook me awake. Jackie. "She's changed," she said. "Her breathing is different."

Lizbob was now breathing with obvious effort, pushing the air out with a groan, drawing it in with a gasping hiccup. Her body was no longer supine and relaxed, but tense, fighting the air as if it were an enemy.

I can't remember if we told the nurse, and if she came in and listened, perhaps checked the pulse. She might even have said it was normal at this stage.

I sat at her bedside, clutching her hand, Jackie to my left, Wendy to my right.

And, after a few minutes, quite simply, my lovely wife, my beautiful best friend, stopped breathing.

And was gone.

It was so simple, so effortless, so hard to comprehend.

One of us told the nurse and the nurse came in and checked, nodded her head and quietly left.

And that was it. I was now a widower; our children were motherless and the wonderful grannie she would have been had vanished.

I kissed her forehead, as I had done so often before, and left.

It was about 3 in the morning. Jackie asked me if I'd be OK. I said yes. I stood by the car for a few minutes, ringing our children. Then I drove home.

The Grand Plan.

What: I decide what to do.

Where: Southampton

My age: 73

My sweet wife Lizzy died on the 31st of January, 2018. There were things to organise, stuff to do. The funeral, insurance, probate, banks, online accounts …. the learning curve was steep, the forms daunting and the people to contact endless.

In the evenings, I would often Google grief. The stages of. How to get over it. Is it ultimately good? How long does it last? What's it *for*? What *function* does it serve? Did Darwin write about it? Is it numbness? Is it OK to feel nothing? Why do I suddenly cry in the fruit and veg aisle of the supermarket?

I learned grief was individual, can takes years and is often never resolved. That there is no sure way to speed this process up, if indeed it is a process.

And it seemed the more I read, the less I knew or understood. Serious matters often have that effect on me: I lack the diligence or intelligence to study and think to the depth required. With grief, I was like a toddler, charging into the shallows of an ocean, getting wet to the knees, deciding it was scary and – chubby little legs leaving footprints in the sand - returning to safety.

But I am sure being unable to understand grief is all part of grieving. Lizzy and I were married for just under 34 years, had 3 babies, moved house 3 times, watched loved ones die and our children grow up. Shared memories of such depth, it seemed impossible to escape. Wait: 'escape' is the wrong word. 'Leave behind'? Even worse. 'Absorb'? That is better. 'Accept'? Maybe better still. My command of language is not precise enough – or even broad enough – to let me understand what has happened and is happening now.

A week or so after the funeral I was walking George on the common. We trudged along our normal route past the fishing lake and through the woods. George – as he always does - visited every other tree to lift his leg, so progress was slow. But I hadn't much else to do and you must let dogs do dog things.

I looked down at my own plodding feet. Left foot, right foot, left foot, right foot, one step at a time. This is, I tell myself, how we got through the last year: Lizzy, Hannah, Josh, Beth and me. One step at a time, one day at a time, one hospital visit at a time: never think ahead: keep it tight, keep it close, keep it in the present.

Now, I told myself as I walked along, now we can look ahead, into the post-Lizzy, hazy, misty future. But for me, that is frightening, so I look down again and resume, one foot in front of the other, one day at a time, while around me the world turns into the spring of 2018. The gathering of the clans to say goodbye to Lizzy is now truly over: the cousins have long departed, Beth has flown back to Oz, Josh has moved out and Hannah has returned to married life with Jonny and two small children.

It's just me, Dawn (the lodger, who was usually either working or out) and George rattling around in our family house. 5 bedrooms, 2 reception, big kitchen, large games room, untidy garden, part double glazing and roughly two thirds underfloor heating.

I have a chat with Hannah. The future – as ever now - hangs in the air. She talks about me moving and living close to them, saying she and Jonny would like that. I look at my sink, at the lonely single bowl waiting to be placed in the large, empty dish-washer and say things like too soon, not ready and yeah, 'course: I'll consider it.

She rings off, I stack the bowl and think: 'in a few more days, there'll be enough in there to switch it on.'

A year ago, we ran it every day.

I meet a dog walking friend, Mary: the most sensible and wise person I know. I ask – as if in passing – how it came to be her Irish dad and mum were now living close. And Mary replies as if she is unaware my question has a personal relevance. But she knows, and I know she knows, that it has.

She says her parents didn't do well after her dad retired. Depression, illness, loneliness. So they moved close and – as a three-generation family – everyone had benefitted, everyone had gained. She used the word enriched and phrases like 'new lease of life' and 'works both ways.'

I put aside the pretence we are only talking of her Mum and Dad. I have a quandary, I say; if I mention to Hannah and Jonny I'd like to move near them, they'd have to say yes, even if they'd like to say no. Like when an elderly aunt no-one likes invites herself over for Christmas.

And Mary asks: "have they said anything?"

And I say "Yes, Hannah has suggested it."

Mary says: "Without you asking?" I nod. And Mary grins. "Um" she says: "sounds good enough to me."

And I remember, not that I forgot: Lizzy for a few years worked for care companies, driving around for a pittance dispensing tea, personal help and affection to those that needed it. She came back tired, with stories of crinkly ancients living on alone in the large, old family home, trapped by memories, clutter, ill health and tiredness, with middle-aged children guiltily, dutifully visiting in the hope of future enrichment.

I find myself looking up house prices in the area and calculating how long I can live on my pension and savings. And – remarkably quickly - the Grand Plan comes into being, as if it had been waiting in the wings, impatient to make an entrance.

And a week or so later, at my insistence, Hannah, Jonny and I met at a pub just off the A27. We sat at a rustic picnic table. The May sunshine was warm and generous. As always, I had George with me and they had brought Evie, now four months old. Jude was at nursery.

I said: "I've been thinking of the future." And stopped. On the table someone had drawn a heart. The curves were thick and black: they must have used a felt-tipped pen. I traced it with my finger.

Evie had given them a bad night, and the future had often been discussed, so Hannah's voice was weary, almost disinterested: "Oh?"

Jonny fiddled with his phone, probably scrolling through Amazon, looking for deals on electronic gizmos.

And I thought of what words I should use. Unusually for me, I hadn't practised what I should say. My Grand Plan now seemed – ridiculously - both simple and complicated.

George suddenly perked up: our order had arrived. Plates of food, knives and forks, napkins but no sauces. Evie woke and Jonny sat her on his lap and fed her with a bottle, Hannah went to find ketchup and I had the Diana Moment.

It was not visual or even aural; certainly, it was rooted in time and place, but only as the backdrop. The Diana Moment itself was an obvious realisation, something I'd always known, but never really considered: that words, serious words, once said, cannot be unsaid. I was standing at the edge of a cliff.

When Hannah returned, I opened my mouth and said: "I have a grand plan. I'm going to sell up. Everything. Turn it all to cash, take what I need for 10 years and give the rest to you and Josh and Beth." I shrugged. "Your inheritance comes early. In terms of timing -" the words were rushing out now, hanging in the air, turning into commitments and solidifying into the past. ".. in terms of timing, I intend selling the Edinburgh flat soon and when I've finished my book, declutter and get the house on the market March or so next year."

I cut up a sausage and started chewing.

Hannah and Jonny looked at me. I gave George a bit of sausage. Evie burped up some milk. Jonny wiped her chin and dabbed at her front.

Hannah said, "where will you live?"

I took a breath and replied, "in a log cabin." I had done my research, chasing an old dream, Googling like mad. A log cabin was the answer: cosy and warm, with a little kitchen, a porch and optional eco-friendly grass roof. Ideal for George and me. Even in suburbia, we could pretend to be in the wilds. I added: "As long as the broadband speed's OK I'll be fine."

They glanced at each other. I went into detail and spoke of how much they could reliably expect. "I know you want to move," I added, "you've probably started looking. So I thought you could get your money when the Edinburgh flat is sold. The tenancy agreement ends in June, so I can set things in motion now. You'll get it by the end of summer, if not earlier. Beth and Josh will get theirs when I sell the house."

Still cradling Evie, Jonny picked up his phone.

Hannah frowned. "A log cabin?"

"Yeah. Proper logs, with those corners where the ends stick out. Criss-cross. I'll show you -" I fiddled with my phone, trying to load Google, but Hannah said:

"Yes, but where, exactly? In a park?"

I looked around, bent and scratched George on top of his head. "I'm hoping," I said, "that you'd get a house with a big enough garden."

There was a pause, then Jonny held out his phone. On it was an estate agent's listing for a four bedroomed house on a large plot. He said "Like this? We haven't been there yet, but it's been on our list for a while."

The garden seemed as big as a football pitch but that was undoubtedly from a strategically placed fisheye lens. "Yes," I said: "like that." I turned to Hannah. "There could be a little covered walkway between us. And I could sit in the sun with a knotted handkerchief on my head. Keeping an eye on the kids."

Hannah grinned. "Yeah. I'd like that. I might join you. Not sure about the handkerchief though."

And Jonny nodded and said "Great."

And so, in about five minutes, in the garden of a pub off the A27, our futures were arranged, neatly packaged like a birthday present.

Maybe grief can be side stepped with plans and purpose, things to do. For as I drove home, for the first time in a long time, I found myself whistling.

PS: to tidy this up, the Grand Plan, with a few ups and downs, worked well. However big houses with big gardens were well beyond budget, so the log cabin became a converted double garage: my Grandpa Annex, where I am typing this now.

Epilogue.

First and foremost, this book is - and always has been - about memory. Many writers and thinkers have spilt oceans of ink on the subject: what it means; how it can be false or true or manipulated; where it resides in the brain and the diseases that affect it and the treatments that can cure it.

But here, I am taking memory as the custodian of the past. My past. It contains everything that has gone into the making of me. Even as I write this, each letter, each word, each sentence tumbles into it. As do the seconds, minutes, hours, days, years. And all the people I have known, the events that have happened, all my wishes, aspirations, fears, hopes, desires. In short, everything that makes me, me.

So without it, I am as nothing. Shorn of the baggage of memory I would be as a baby: naked and innocent.

At college, during one of those long rambling student discussions, someone said "OK, OK, here's one for you: supposing someone invented a forgetting machine -"

To which someone else said "I wish!"

"No, no, listen, listen: you can set the dial to any length of time you like, and It'll eat its way back from now to then. Everything will go, be completely forgotten. If you put it on now, for five weeks, you'd be back to five weeks ago: you wouldn't remember this discussion; you wouldn't even remember turning it on." You'd suddenly wake up, here and now, but with your memory stopping five weeks ago."

A voice was scornful: "sounds crap."

"Yes, but supposing every minute of memory lost gains you an hour at the end of your life." He looked round. "How many minutes would you go for?"

There was a pause while we all absorbed this concept. Then someone said: "Yeah, that'd be good. I'd do it after every shit week. Worth the swap."

"Oh! No: you can't wait, you can't pick your time. You can only do it once and it has to be now, in the next five minutes."

There was another pause before someone – who prided himself on his ability with mental arithmetic - said to get a year extra you'd have to lose 'maybe a week.' This was disputed, so paper and pencils were produced, and figures written down.

But a girl called Jan said: "that's creepy. I wouldn't do it. Sounds like a mini suicide."

Which is exactly what it would be: a mini suicide. I recall this discussion about the 'forgetting machine' to show everyone has thoughts about memory, and what it means. None of my ideas are new, nor are my insights original or profound.

But my Diana Moments are unquestionably unique to me. No one else – not now or ever in history or anywhere in the universe – owns this particular set of moments. The public ones might be shared and many of the others common, but my responses to them, and how they occurred and the shards of other memories associated with them, are unique.

For they define who I am and – to a certain extent – explain why I am who I am.

It is the evening. In my little Grandpa annex, I do the Grandpa thing. I sit in my two-seater, high-backed, comfy cream faux-leather sofa. Snuggled up into my left shoulder is Evie (aged 2). Snuggled up to my right shoulder is Jude (aged 4). George (small dog) has managed to cram himself between the arm of the sofa and Evie. I say "The gang's all here!" and spread a duvet over us, so it is all snuggly-buggly and cosy-wosy.

We read 'Peepo!' and 'The Tiger Who Came To Tea.' The last book, before they go back to mum and dad, and I can close my annex door on the mayhem of bedtime is 'The Paper Dolls.'

It is a simple tale of some 16 pages (I have just counted them) and under 500 words (I have just counted 475, but I could have made a mistake). It touches on many things: love; joy; sadness; nostalgia; fun; loss; imagination …. but ultimately, to me, it is about memory and how it holds what has gone: white mice, fireworks, starfish soap, a kind granny, a butterfly hair slide and lots of lovely things each day and each year including – of course – the Paper Dolls themselves.

And when I read this, my eyes blur and my voice thickens, for I remember my own past, and the things that have gone.

And a couple of pages later the story has finished, sketching a future joyously echoing the past.

The older you get, the more precious the past becomes, the more you realise what has been lost and the more you hope for a future to be cherished.

And that is why I cry at The Paper Dolls.

Photographs: Crinklies and the last ten years.

Circa 1994. Mum and Dad.
This is probably the last picture I have of Dad. He was getting wobbly by then, so mum kept him steady, holding his arm and shoulder.

Circa *2005. Peter in Corfu.*
Taken on his valedictory trip to old haunts. After Corfu they went back to New Zealand. He died the following year.

Circa 2012. Jonny and Hannah. A year before their wedding, kids and all those things that make you tired.

2013. From left: Josh, Hannah, Beth. Messing around in the photo booth at Hannah's wedding.

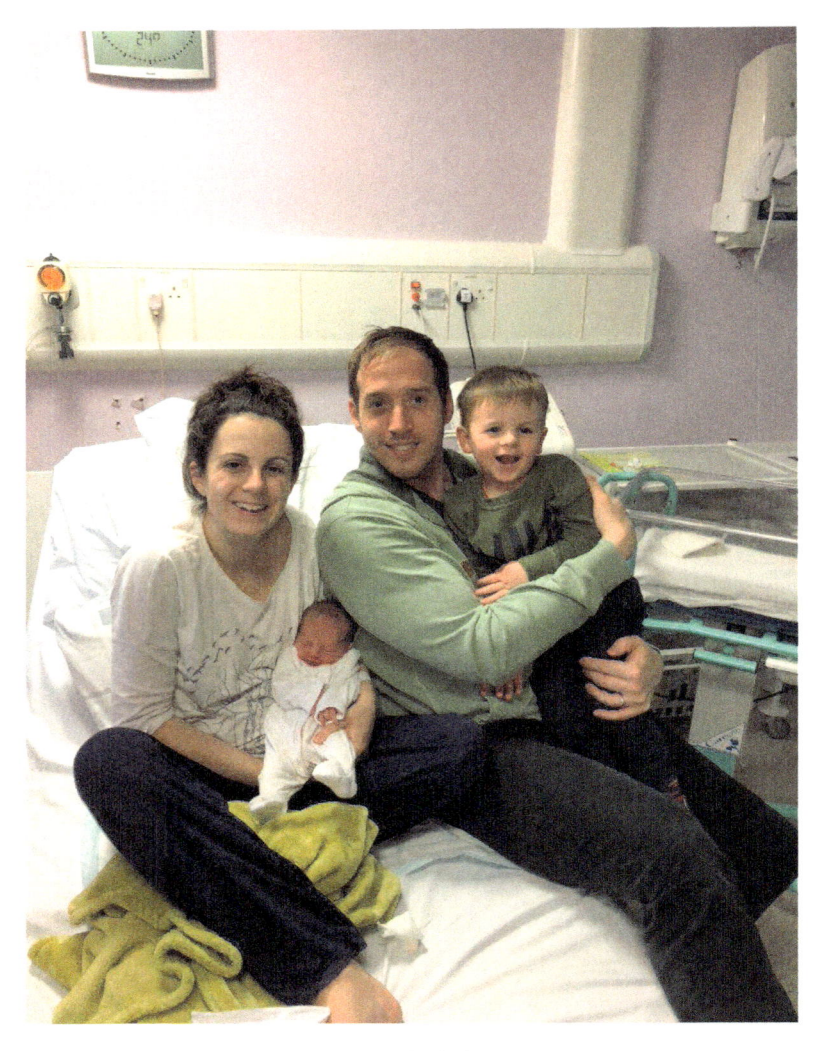

2018. Evie is born.
This is the family I joined just under two years later, as part of 'the grand plan'.

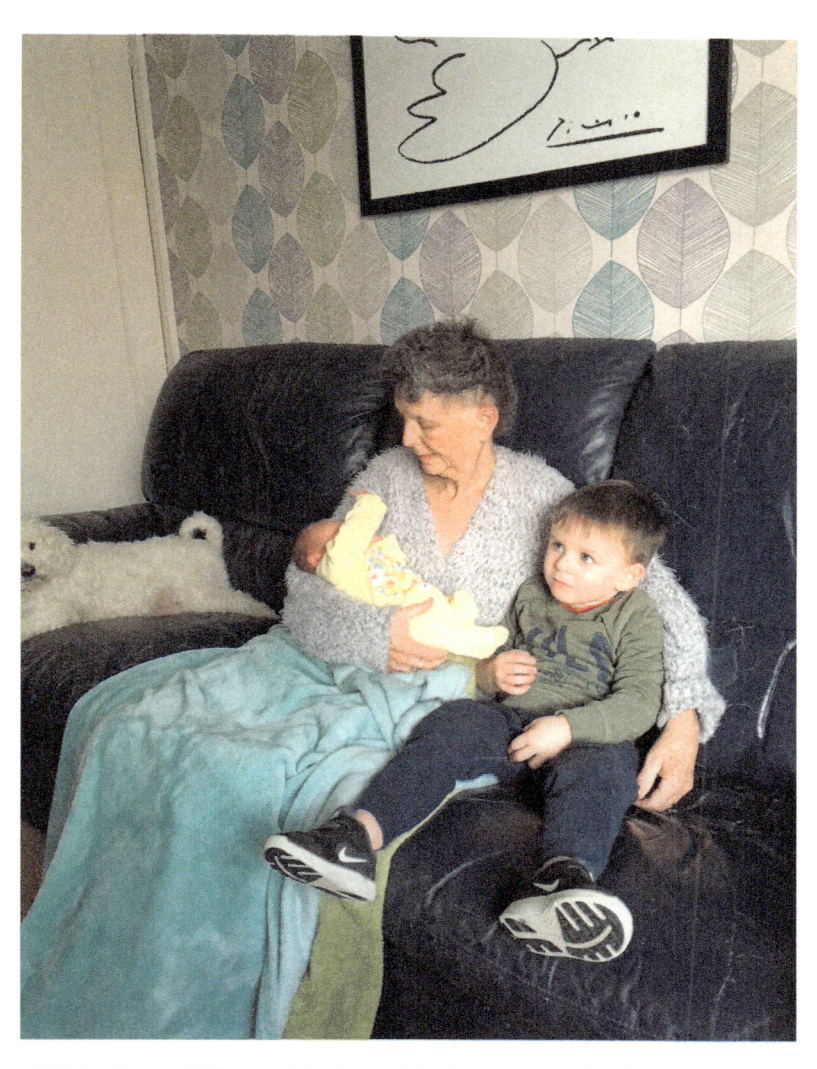

2018. Lizzy, Evie and Jude, with George in the background. Taken 10 days before Lizzy died. I thought long and hard before including this.

2020. Christmas. Evie and George with – in background - Jude bombing around on his bike.
All in matching Christmas knitwear. George has never worn his since.

2021. Jonny, Jude(5), Hannah and Evie(3).
At a park somewhere.

2021. Beth in Oz. She loves it there - particularly the weather. She's now working, studying and living near Bondi Beach.

2021. Josh and Mirka, his partner. They live in Southampton, but would like to move somewhere with better weather, and who can blame them.

2021. Evie and I.

Each of Evie's nails has to be a different colour.
Of course, I made a mess of it.

Afterword.

When to end? Often a problem for any writer and/or teller of stories. But here, it's easy.

I'm finishing at the end. I'm finishing with now.

It is late May, 2021. Most of this month has been rainy, but sun is forecast for tomorrow: hurrah! By my feet George is dozing on his bed. I think I have a headache coming on, but usually – if I look for it – there's always a headache coming on. I am 76 years old and next February I will be 77.

I have finished what I trust will be the final rewrite. Every sentence has been picked over, examined and – usually – changed. Sometimes with the addition of extra words, but – more often – by finding a more precise way of saying the same thing. Whole paragraphs have been erased, footnotes eliminated and at least two of my original 'Diana Moments' have been deleted.

All in search of those twin writing virtues of simplicity and readability.

In total. the whole book has taken me some 20 months. A long time for a short work of around 80 thousand words. I will now spend another month (maybe more) selecting photographs and helping to design a cover.

So, slow going indeed.

But - for me - the older I get, the less the urgency. Why chase rainbows when – every so often – one turns up anyway.

A few days ago, on my morning dog walk, with George amiably zig-zagging from one interesting smell to the next, a small shaft of personal truth came to me:

The more I remember the more I remember.

For these 'Diana Moments' are not isolated and independent from other Diana Moments or from my life as a whole. At first, I thought they were like intense fires: beacons, if you like, populating my internal landscape.

But now I think of them more as an almost random pattern of floating steppingstones in a pond. I step on one, which sends ripples of memory across the placid surface. Another stone wobbles a little, attracting attention. I hop over, causing more ripples, more wobbles. So I follow them, sometimes forward, sometimes back, often sideways.

Until, eventually, I land here, back on the distant shore, writing this epilogue, attempting to wrap it all up.

Probably, when it comes to the blurb on the back of this book, I'll have, in quotes:

'An ordinary life told in an extraordinary manner.'

For the more I have written, poking around in the innards of my remembered life like an old hen lazily looking for worms, the less excited I have become. For - to put things crudely - I have not seized life by the balls. I have drifted along, swimming with the current, making only small waves. Life-changing decisions have been relatively few; in truth I can only think of four: two (giving up teaching and giving up writing) were to escape, while the others (marrying Lizzy and 'the grand plan') were more positive and forward looking.

But - one way or another – all the decisions and switch-points ultimately yielded a positive outcome: me sitting here, typing these words, while my grandchildren play in the garden.

'A positive outcome'? Yes, I think so, albeit one strongly coloured by sorrow and regret of what could have been.

Oh God, it is so tempting to speculate on how chance might have taken a different course. The bullet could have killed me. The car crash could have maimed me. I could so easily have not met Lizzy. A delay of a few months would have made me too old to take the course in programming. Lizzy might not have had cancer. And so forth and so on. These thoughts, careering along alternate pathways are seductive and dazzling but lead nowhere.

For the past is set in stone and cannot be changed. The most you can do is record it in good faith.

Which is what I have attempted to do here.

Stay safe. Stay sane. Thanks for reading.

J.B.

Printed in Great Britain
by Amazon